The Purposes of God

The PURPOSES *of* GOD

Providence as Process-Historical Liberation

G. Michael Zbaraschuk

PICKWICK *Publications* · Eugene, Oregon

THE PURPOSES OF GOD
Providence as Process-Historical Liberation

Copyright © 2015 G. Michael Zbaraschuk. All rights reserved. Except for brief quotations in critical publications or reviews, no part of this book may be reproduced in any manner without prior written permission from the publisher. Write: Permissions, Wipf and Stock Publishers, 199 W. 8th Ave., Suite 3, Eugene, OR 97401.

Pickwick Publications
An imprint of Wipf and Stock Publishers
199 W. 8th Ave., Suite 3
Eugene, OR 97401

www.wipfandstock.com

ISBN: 978-1-60899-740-4

Cataloging-in-Publication data:

Zbaraschuk, G. Michael.

   The purposes of God : providence as process-historical liberation / G. Michael Zbaraschuk.

   x + 184 p. ; 23 cm. Includes bibliographical references.

   ISBN: 978-1-60899-740-4

   1. Theology. 2. Process theology. 3. God—History of doctrines. 4. Barth, Karl, 1886–1968. 5. Bultmann, Rudolf, 1884–1976. 6. Hodgson, Peter Crafts, 1934–. 7. Whitehead, Alfred North, 1861–1947. I. Title.

BT98 Z25 2015

Manufactured in the U.S.A.   06/23/2015

A earlier version of Chapter 3 was published in *The American Journal of Theology and Philosophy* 31 (2010) 33–52, as "Not Radical Enough: William Dean's Pragmatic Problems with God and History." Used with permission.

This book is dedicated to all my theological teachers,
especially Glen Greenwalt and Marjorie Hewitt Suchocki.

Contents

Acknowledgments | ix

1. Why Providence? Introduction, History, Task, Method, Outline | 1
2. Bultmann and Barth: God in Existential Meaning; or God Revealed, God Confessed | 23
3. Historicism: History as Theology, History without God | 55
4. Whitehead: God in the Processes of the World | 77
5. Freedom and Praxis: Peter Hodgson's Fuller Vision of History | 104
6. Freedom for Beauty and the Other: Contexts, Objects, Subjects | 124
7. The Spirit in and through the World | 148

Bibliography | 175
Index | 181

Acknowledgments

THAT THIS WORK IS coming to press is something of a miracle. It could not have happened without help from a variety of sources. First, I must thank my parents, Ivan and Ila Zbaraschuk, for the variety of forms of help they have offered throughout the years. I must also mention two of my undergraduate teachers from Walla Walla College, Ron Jolliffe and Glen Greenwalt. They were mentors, role models, and encouraging voices in my theological education. They also provided a safe place to talk about issues of church, theology, and integrity. I am eternally grateful for their starting me down the path of studying theology. This work is dedicated to Glen, who was the first person who I knew and admired and attempted to emulate as a theologian.

The journey that Glen and Ron started was continued in Claremont. I am grateful to all my theological teachers there, especially the members of my dissertation committee. Jack Verheyden read this and all my work with close attention to detail, and pushed me to improve in a variety of areas. Anselm Kyongsuk Min pointed me towards Hodgson and Hegel, and was generous with his time and advice even after I had finished my time in Southern California. Marjorie Hewitt Suchocki, to whom this work is dedicated along with Glen Greenwalt, inspired me, opened avenues of scholarship and life choices, and never lost faith in me, even when I had lost faith in myself. My life and work would have been immeasurably poorer without her in them. And, finally, I must mention John Cobb's influence on many aspects of my theological journey. His life and work continue creatively transforming my own.

A word in these acknowledgments for friendship: I am a social creature, and one of life's great pleasures is the ability to have good conversations about important things with smart and good people. I am grateful to my colleagues in the theology and philosophy of religion program at

Acknowledgments

The Claremont Graduate University for making our time together not only deep and meaningful, but also fun. Our continuing friendships make time at academic conferences highlights of every calendar year.

A few personal notes: I am grateful to my therapists, Ron Levin and Rebecca Meredith, for hearing me into more effective speech about my own motivations and aspirations. Rebecca especially helped me to acknowledge ambition, ambivalence, and power in my own life. Without her, I would not have gotten this volume to press or be as far down the path towards professional success as I currently am. I am grateful. Also, during the time this manuscript made the transition from dissertation to monograph, I became a father twice over. My two daughters, Ana and Elizabeth, are continuous sources of joy and amazement. I cannot but think that their appearance in my life has been providential. And, last and most important, my wife and partner in all things, Lisa Elaine Zbaraschuk, deserves more acknowledgement and thanks than I can possibly put down in these few lines. She has been with me in good times and bad, and is my primary example of the sheer grace of the divine activity in the world.

1

Why Providence?
Introduction, History, Task, Method, Outline

THE PROBLEM OF PROVIDENCE: GOD *AND* HISTORY?

THE TOPIC OF PROVIDENCE is a difficult one for contemporary people. How can God be said to act in history?[1] In the face of the horrors of just the twentieth century—starting with the Armenian holocaust; through two world wars; the slaughter of the European Jews; genocide and war on a massive scale in Africa; and continuing racial, ethnic, and religious conflicts and widespread ecological destruction throughout the world—how can God be said to be acting in history? What would it mean to say that there is a providential hand in the affairs of the world? That there is a "plan" for history? That God leads the world? In the face of the difficulties listed above, the very idea seems to be non-sensical.

That the *idea* itself is difficult is a contemporary problem. The citation of some of the horrific events of the twentieth century notwithstanding, life was not any easier in the fifth or thirteenth or sixteenth centuries.[2] The

---

1. God's action has been the subject of a great many theological studies in the second half of the twentieth century. Besides Barth and Bultmann, one classic statement is Langdon Gilkey's "Cosmology, Ontology, and the Travail of Biblical Language." See also the two collections of essays: Thomas, ed., *God's Activity in the World*; and Wiles, *God's Action in the World*. Both volumes are more or less inspired by Gilkey's essay.

2. See, for example, Calvin's evocation of the fragility of life in the *Institutes*, 223.

interpretative framework by which the world is understood is different from those times. In earlier frameworks, although there was horror and death and disease, philosophers and theologians still found it credible to believe in the hand of God in history. They found the idea that there was a God, and that God's activity was manifested in and through the historical process, still the best (or only) explanation of the patent facts. Such a situation no longer holds for us today. This is so for primarily two reasons. The first of these is that the idea of God as such has come under increasing difficulty. The second is that history has been increasingly seen as a meaningless struggle, with progress not only impossible, but even the idea of progress *as such* being questioned as a shield and mask for other, less than noble motives of personal or group domination. Certainly it is less and less thought of an evidence of the providential activity of God. Much reflection on the subject has led to concentration on either God *or* history, with few considering both in the same view. Let us briefly examine both the ideas of God and history to see the difficulties in continuing to speak of them in the same breath.

The idea of faith in God is, and has been increasingly, difficult to maintain in contemporary discourse. This is so for several reasons. The first of these is that there is an increasing recognition of the constructed character of the concept of God: is God a "king" because that is the case, or because humans have kings, do we understand God to be the King of kings? And, as social conditions change, the idea of God changes. Witness the change from the idea of God as power to God as love, and the concomitant preeminence of the "problem of evil" in philosophy of religion in the last 200 years.[3]

In addition, the rise of historical criticism as a method of knowing about the nature of the past has led to a loss of belief in the revelatory power of the Christian Scriptures,[4] and a loss of belief in the revelation of God as such. Insofar as the idea of God is based on revelation, it has come under increasing scrutiny as knowledge about the methods and content of the means of revelation has increased. And, finally, modern scientific cosmology has led us more and more to think of the world as its own explanation,

---

3. See, as one example, Charles Taylor in *A Secular Age*, as he discusses the change in the "social imaginary" that has arisen in the modern world.

4. The fundamentalist reaction to historical criticism is precisely that, a *reaction*, and an increasingly untenable one.

with no place in it for God.⁵ Any contemporary doctrine of providence will have to adequately address all of these questions about the doctrine of God in order to be adequate to our contemporary situation.

History, as a category revelatory of meaning, has come under much of the same scrutiny that the idea of God has had. Indeed, to some degree the very idea that history can be revelatory of meaning, that it illustrates a purpose and a plan, is dependent on the ideas about God that have come under so much criticism in the recent past. There is a loss of belief in any kind of social or cosmic teleology (the end of 'salvation history'), and history is seen as merely "one damn thing after another," with no patterns other than those of domination, no meaning other than the striving for existence.

Thus, with both the primary terms of the doctrine of providence coming under increasing scrutiny, and with less and less that commands assent to either of them, the doctrine appears to be in serious trouble. Let us briefly examine several seminal Christian thinkers, to see what their responses were to the problem, and see if they have any resources that can assist us in formulating a contemporary doctrine of providence.

HISTORY OF THE DOCTRINE: AUGUSTINE, AQUINAS, CALVIN

Many Christian thinkers in the past have dealt extensively with the doctrine of providence. They found it credible to believe in the hand of God in history, or that the two were at least integrally related, and found philosophical and theological reasons for doing so. We will examine three of the giants of the Christian past, to see what their understandings can offer us, and how they illustrate the contemporary difficulties of thinking of God and history in the same breath.

Augustine is often cited as having the "first philosophy (or theology) of history," but this is to misunderstand him. In Augustine's great work *The City of God*, he does indeed deal with the working out of God's purposes in history, but his final treatment of the city of God and the city of the world serves to de-emphasize the importance of the earthly city except as a vehicle for the foundation, testing, and flourishing of the heavenly one.⁶ God is seen as bringing into existence the various earthly kingdoms like Persia and Rome, for the purpose of furthering his own will. That we do not

---

5. See, for example Barbour's *Religion and Science*.
6. See Hodgson, *God in History*, 19.

understand how the various actions fit together is not important.[7] What *is* important is that we become part of the reason for the existence of the city of this world—the City of God, the Church.[8] God's plan for history is that the Church, the means of salvation, come into being and that the citizens of this city participate in the eschatological end of history. Although terrible things happen in the "city of this world," and they do indeed happen by the will of God, they are finally not what God's plan is about—it is about the church and its eventual triumph.

The interpretive framework in which this view makes sense is one of Plotinian emanationism combined with an eschatology informed by the biblical narrative. The structure of the world is organized into a hierarchy of value/goodness/existence (all of which are more or less identical), with evil being both a privation of good and a contrast to it, which serves to highlight the difference between the two. The biblical narrative provides the *reason* for the existence of evil in the fall (both of Satan and of humanity), and the assurance of the eventual end in the eschatological consummation promised in the book of Revelation. Although it is not without difficulties, this interpretive framework of Neo-Platonism and eschatological consummation makes it possible to speak of providence more or less coherently.

In many senses, Augustine's position is one that it is possible to continue to hold in the twentieth century. Such a view, that considers the history of the Church the reason for history at all will not be so concerned about the history of the world, and will be less troubled by the seeming difficulties in the realm of history. History as such is not what God's interaction with humanity is about, and thus its seemingly random and horrible activity will not trouble the believer as much. Such a view is most closely replicated in the twentieth century by Barth's view of the history of the covenant with its similar idea of a "history within a history," and its insistence that the relation between God and human beings is disclosed in a special case (the church for Augustine, the history of the covenant for Barth), rather than in history in general.

Such a view, however is not an effective contemporary doctrine of providence. In the first place, the trust in the miraculous history of God as outlined in the Scriptures has been undermined by the advances of historical criticism. In the second, there is a loss of belief that an eschatological

---

7. Augustine, *City of God*, 215–16.

8. In many senses, this is most closely replicated in the twentieth century by Barth's view of the history of the covenant and the idea of a history within a history.

resolution will be occurring, and even if it did, that it could make up for the horrors inflicted on the way.[9] And, in a similar point, the idea of the distinction between the city of God and the city of this world is difficult to maintain. Does God really split the world into two factions, and let one fall by the wayside? How is this the loving God revealed in the Bible? And where exactly is the split between the two cities? The interdependent nature of the world makes that line difficult to draw. And, finally, the idea of emanation is no longer an adequate philosophical account of the world. Thus, even with all its attractions, adopting an Augustinian viewpoint is no longer open to us. His ideas, nevertheless, continue to resonate throughout the remaining reflection on the subject, both historical and contemporary. The ideas of emanation and consummation, for example, also figure prominently in the understanding of providence in the next figure we will consider: Thomas Aquinas.

Aquinas is different from Augustine in that narrative does not figure into his understanding of providence. In Aquinas, the emanation from and return to God is the dominant philosophical ordering pattern of his *Summa Theologica*, and can be said to characterize his general understanding of the providence of God as well. For Aquinas, providence is the ordering of things to an end,[10] what is generally referred to as a final cause. Providence is the way in which God orders things to ends, and the end of all creation is God in God's own self.

In the Neo-Platonic understanding of exitus-reditus, which Aquinas understands as the mechanism of creation, salvation, and consummation, to speak of providence is merely to give a particular understanding to the general way in which God is understood to work in the world. Providence is another name for the process of creation, with a special application to human beings, as befits God's action toward each set of creatures being tailor-made to its particular nature. Clearly, there is no insurmountable difficulty in speaking of providence within this viewpoint. Indeed, once one accepts the initial points of God and emanation-as-creation, then Aquinas' understanding of providence naturally follows.

There is much to be said for a philosophical view that abstracts from the actual history of the place and time and sees God's action in and through all other actions, in the manner of the primary cause. However, Aquinas' vision is problematic for several reasons. The first of these is that,

9. More and more people stand with Dostoyevsky's Ivan Karamazov.
10. Thomas Aquinas, *Summa Theologica*, I, xxii, 1.

as mentioned above in the section on Augustine, the idea of emanation is less and less convincing as an account of the origin and activity of the world. Emanation implies participation, and leads to a form of pantheism. Also, it seems that an account of God's activity in the world should have some reference to the actual history involved. A simple affirmation of that activity, without any examples or means of discrimination, will not do. Let us move on to yet another Augustinian-influenced thinker as we continue to examine the doctrine of providence: John Calvin.

Calvin's version of the providence of God starts in a radically different place than either Aquinas or Augustine. For Calvin, all natural knowledge (including philosophical knowledge) is tainted by original sin and the utter depravity that is the consequence of that sin. The only sure way to knowledge of God is through the revelation of Scripture read under the guidance of the Holy Spirit.[11] And Scripture, under Calvin's reading, teaches that God controls every aspect of every action of everything, animate and inanimate. Speaking of the seeming chaos of events in the world, he holds that "carnal reason ascribes all such happenings . . . to fortune. But anyone who has been taught by Christ's lips that all the hairs of his head are numbered will look farther afield for a cause and will consider that all events are governed by God's secret plan."[12] In order to reconcile the religious experience of salvation and the certainty of election with the seeming chaos of the world, Calvin finds certainty of salvation in Scripture, and certainty of scriptural teaching in the experience of election.

With the strong emphasis on religious experience and scriptural authority and the distrust of "carnal" reason and experience (which would include natural philosophy and theology), it becomes clear that to assert God's control over "every drop of rain"[13] is understandable. Scripture certainly does teach in places that God is in control of the world, and that God orders both the good and the evils that occur. Calvin, distrusting natural reason, could affirm, through the experience of election and the sure word of Scripture, that God controls, and any appearance otherwise was a defect in human understanding, not in God's plan.

Such a view, while certainly philosophically coherent, begs the question of God's interaction altogether. If there is no other way to discern

---

11. See Calvin, *Institutes*, 79, "the Word will not find acceptance in men's hearts before it is sealed by the inward testimony of the Spirit."

12. Ibid., 198.

13. Ibid., 204.

God's involvement than to assert it, no matter what, then questions of sin and salvation become acute. How can we understand what the deviation from the will of God is, and how can it be a fault, or a punishment, if we are not responsible? How can war and peace be the result of the same cause, when their effects are so different? Natural reason cannot be so depraved as Calvin asserts it to be.

CLASSICAL VIEWS PROBLEMATIC

Calvin, no less than Augustine and Aquinas, was confident in his statements that providence was at work in the world. All three thinkers, while experiencing grief, suffering, difficulty, and chaos, still managed to affirm a plan for history and for individuals, and God's control over the process. All had theological and/or philosophical interpretive frameworks that allowed them to hold to God's intimate involvement with and control of the sweep of history. Why, then, if these views are so seemingly profound and understandable, do we as contemporary people continue to have such difficulty unambiguously stating that God acts in history? It seems to me that there are at least three important reasons. First of all, the interpretive framework of the world has changed. The close relation between the ideal and the empirical, which would have been second nature to Augustine and Aquinas, and not repudiated by Calvin, is no longer assumed. Ideals of any sort are difficult to maintain in contemporary discourse.[14] The empirical rules, and its historicisms have no need of the hypothesis of an actual God. The second reason is related to the first—as the interpretive framework of the world around us has moved to the empirical, the "place of religion" has become more and more a part of the human mind, without reference to the outside world. The intuitions of morality and aesthetics and religion, and even the existential emphasis upon choice, are seen as having little to do with the "actual world" where we live most of our lives. Religion has become a private matter, and is in danger of being psychologized away. And, finally, the complex of ideas, which can be categorized as "salvation history," has lost

14. There are many reasons for this. The rise of science through the seventeenth and eighteenth centuries and the development of an historical consciousness in the nineteenth and twentieth are two of the reasons. "Natural science directly challenged teleological explanations of the cosmos, while historical consciousness introduced the critical concepts of change, process, becoming, relativity, as well as challenging references to any sort of transhistorical, supernatural, timeless-spaceless reality, whether conceived as a ground, cause, entity, realm, or telos." Hodgson, *God in History*, 23.

its ability to convince. These attempts to relate the empirical and ideal into a philosophy of history have become casualties of the increasing emphasis upon the empirical and the privatization of the religious. Any kind of social teleology, whether Christian, liberal, Marxist, or scientific, is increasingly seen as self-deception and wishful thinking. The world is more and more seen like "the iron hand of necessity shaking the dice-box of chance."[15] Any appeal to "progress" from one thing to another is seen as sheer delusion or the domination of one discourse of power by another—yet another instance of Foucault's "endlessly repeated play of domination."[16] Thus these historical views of providence, even though exceedingly rich and nuanced and offering much material for reflection, cannot be accepted uncrititcally as contemporary understandings of the way in which God interacts with history. We must turn to other sources, while at the same time not forgetting these historical antecedents, as we seek to formulate a contemporary doctrine of providence.

TASK

Thus, the task of this work is to find a doctrine of providence which can 1) manage to give a coherent account of reality, taking into account both empirical and ideal, and relating the intuitions of religion, morality, and aesthetics to the natural and social worlds; and 2) provide a way out of the meaninglessness into which the end of the traditional idea of salvation history (or any of its secular analogues) places us. This will require an overall interpretive framework, which provides an understanding of the way in which transcendental ideals get translated into the world. It will also entail some examples, along with care to avoid the mistakes of the past, which will do justice to the intuitions of God's action in the historical world. The question "What does the action of God in the world look like?" will therefore hopefully be answered on two levels: the theoretical and the actual. This is not to say that after this essay is written, there will be a calculus by which one can find the degree of action of God in the world (world = 74%, God = 26%). Rather, from a position of faith, this essay will hopefully be suggestive of what the action of God looks like in the ongoing process of the world.

---

15. Nietzsche, *The Dawn of Day*, no. 130.
16. Foucault, "Nietzsche, Genealogy, History," 150–51.

Why Providence?

That the discussion takes place from a position of faith is not to say that it is uncritical, or that it will not be concerned with the actual happenings and history of the world. It merely means that the position taken by the author is one in which the life of faith is considered to be revelatory as to what the providential activity of God means. Such considerations are not necessary for the unbeliever, but the effects of such beliefs are relevant. Indeed, the task itself is shaped by the demands of faith. Without some experience of God's providential action and care, there would be no reason at all to try to outline a more formal understanding of the content of the doctrine. This is not to say that such a formulation will resemble exactly those that come before it in its own tradition. Circumstances change, and thus so will the understandings of the activity of God in history. But the life of faith is an important component of any such reflection.

METHOD

This will be a "revisionist" work. Thus, the idea is not to either a-historically repudiate or naively return to past understandings. Rather, what I will attempt to do is to critically appropriate what is helpful, "good, true, salvific, and liberating" and put away what is "evil, false, destructive, and oppressive"[17] in past doctrines of providence, and then will try to follow the implications of the good and try to construct a new understanding. Both Hegel's concept of sublation and Whitehead's ideas of the initial aim and prehension are suggestive of the appropriate path to follow. In the concept of sublation, ideas are transformed by meeting with concrete manifestations that challenge or instantiate them, and a new synthesis is produced. In the Whiteheadian viewpoint, all the influences of the past are taken into account as the initial aim of God leads one toward a new synthesis. Past actualities (and conceptions are certainly actual) are no longer adequate for present realities, but they are concretely the conditions and limitations out of which the new actualities take shape. Thus as I deal with the various figures, I will try to appropriate what is helpful and integrate it into the new construction, while trying to avoid the pitfalls that make their final formulations ultimately problematic. Theology does not run in contradictions very often. It is often in the emphasis on one profound insight to the exclusion or neglect of others that weaknesses lie. When one system or approach supersedes another it is only as it can adequately appropriate

17. Hodgson, *God in History*, 43.

the profound insights of its predecessor while at the same time presenting some of the neglected insights that it succeeds. So the method will be one of critical re-appropriation, rather than naive repudiation. It will attempt to be true to the deep insights of the views critiqued, while bringing other, less appreciated insights to bear as well. It will attempt to take the widest possible point of view.

At the same time, all possible attempts to avoid any sort of "methodolotry"[18] will be taken. The point of this essay (and all theological discourse) is to get at the truth of the matter. When certain ideas need to be examined, they will be, even if the wider point of view or the systematic exploration of the topic momentarily suffers.[19] The essay will be the truer and stronger for these momentary lapses into methodological irregularity, and thus its ultimate purposes will be served.

OUTLINE

A.1. Rudolf Bultmann: God Encountered in the Existential Moment

This discussion of directions toward a contemporary doctrine of providence starts with two giants of twentieth century thought who exemplify much contemporary thought on the subject: Rudolf Bultmann and Karl Barth. We begin our discussion with an analysis of Bultmann's existential view of the interaction between God and human history. Bultmann, through a powerful synthesis of an existential analysis of the human situation and an almost mystical appreciation and appropriation of the eschatological vision of what he considers to be the earliest layer of the New Testament message, holds that the action of God in history can only be understood as human beings responding to the call of God in the preaching of the Christian church. History, then, as the progress of human events, is not a resource that we can use to find meaning or the action of God in history. God's providential action is not in history, not even in the ongoing revelation of the Christian church, but in the individual responses to the call of God, best exemplified in the radical kerygma of the Christian church. We are searching for meaning, and as we more and more realize that meaning cannot be found in history, we assume a naturalistic historicism is the best way to account for history, rather than any kind of a vision of progress, like

---

18. For a discussion of "methodolotry," see Daly, *Beyond God the Father*, chap. 1.
19. In this respect, I view the work as more constructive than systematic.

Hegel's or Marx's view. We find meaning as we make it, moment by moment, in existential decision.

Such a view has much to commend it to the person searching for a contemporary doctrine of providence. Among other points, Bultmann offers a view that is not subject to the vagaries of history—God calls individual human beings to decision, and does not depend upon historical movements to accomplish the divine purposes. In addition, Bultmann's view also pays close attention to the religious experience of being a Christian.[20] A response to the call of God is a deep and profound point of experience in the Christian life, and such a response brings meaning and affects all levels of the Christian's existence. Nevertheless, it falls short of being an adequate contemporary doctrine of providence.

The reason that Bultmann's existential view falls short of being an adequate contemporary doctrine of providence is that, in its insistence on the response of the believer to the call of God, it neglects what that call might mean, concretely actualized in the world. It offers no concrete doctrine of what God's action in history looks like. Although God's action will of course be expressed differently in different times and places, there is no way to judge that any action done in one manner or another is a response to God's call. Surely one could say *something* about the trajectory of the call of God. There is no way of discriminating between God's call toward opposite results, if two people claim that God calls them toward such activities. Even though specific cases might be difficult to decide, surely there should be trajectories and orientations—something like increasing freedom, for instance. Bultmann offers no such hope, and indeed does not think that God works in such ways. Although any doctrine of providence will have to take into account his contention that the call of God is the life-changing and primary point for any Christian, an adequate contemporary doctrine of providence will also have to give an analysis of history that allows for God's interaction in it, and a means of discerning such action.

A.2. Karl Barth: God Revealed, God Confessed

The importance of the Christian's experience precisely *as a Christian* is also central for the next thinker that we will use as a resource in our discussions

---

20. Or at least to one aspect of being a Christian—one could argue that there are other, equally legitimate forms of Christian piety. There is sacramental, rather than word-oriented, piety, for example.

of the doctrine of providence: Karl Barth. Barth is in some ways similar to Bultmann, but in his discussion of the doctrine of providence he is quite different. This difference can be best summed up by contrasting Bultmann's conscious lack of content in the doctrine with Barth's equally conscious extensive treatment of the subject. Bultmann tries to strip away any of what he views as superfluities to the central issue in Christian faith—the call of and response to God. Barth, on the other hand, tries to expound on the basis of Scripture and Christian experience what a view of God's providential care looks like in the world. In so doing, he holds that understanding being a Christian *is itself* to understand what God's providential care for God's creatures in the world is and looks like. He expounds this view in the Biblical categories of being a Christian under the Universal Lordship of God the Father; a creature of the creator; a member of the covenant between God and human beings. All these concepts are concretely understood in light of the act of God in Jesus Christ and testified to in the Scriptures, It is precisely in the revelation of God, in the "thin line" of the history of salvation, that a Christian understands and experiences the providential activity of God in the world. It is in God's preserving, ruling, and accompanying the creature, and the experience of said preserving, ruling, and accompanying, that the creature discerns and confesses God's providential activity. It is not in the adoption of the correct worldview, but in the experience of being a member of a covenantal community, that the providential activity of God is seen and acknowledged. It is not derived from an analysis of historical happenings, but first revealed in the activity of God in Jesus Christ, and then confessed.

Such a view, again in contradistinction to Bultmann's understanding, is exceedingly rich in content. Barth specifically outlines the divine preserving, accompanying, and ruling, but there is no reason that such conceptions should exhaust the conception of divine providence. And, in keeping with the teachings of the Scriptures, always seen through the lens of the act of God in Jesus Christ, there are actual points at which Barth can point to the activity of God in history, as seen through his particular lens. He holds that the hand of God can be seen in the history of the church, the existence, history, and ongoing activity of the Scriptures, and in the history of the Jews, that is, in their continuing existence as a people and their preservation in the face of so many difficulties. Thus, Barth does not fall into the same difficulties as Bultmann; that is, a lack of attention to any historical content whatsoever.

Why Providence?

Indeed, there is much to appreciate about Barth's viewpoint. His willingness to point to specific areas in which the activity of God can in fact be seen is a welcome change from the existentialism of Bultmann. And, his close and nuanced treatment of what the confession of the act of God in Jesus Christ means in the Christian's life, combined with a vast knowledge and sympathetic portrayal of the various permutations that Christian devotional life has taken (some of his most interesting discussions take place in the footnotes, where he relates his view with the views of theologians through the ages), and the access that such a view has to the traditional language and rhythms of Christian piety, all make Barth's conception of the doctrine of providence one that has much to commend it. In addition, it shares with Bultmann's view the view that, as a confession of faith, it is not necessarily subject to the vagaries of history. If one's faith is not in the historical process, but in the revelation of God's act in Jesus Christ, than no historical activity can ultimately count against such a view.

Nevertheless, even with its positive attributes, Barth's view also falls short of being an adequate contemporary doctrine of providence. This is so because, although he does a masterful job at explicating what a view as revealed in Scripture and the act of God in Jesus Christ would look like, a completely Biblically based view is not adequate to our contemporary age.[21] This is so for several reasons. The first of these is that the Bible, even if one confesses faith in the activity of God in Jesus Christ, does not present the only model of what a Christian life is like, or present the only understanding of a doctrine of providence. This can be shown in several different ways. One is that there are different notions of God's activity in the world presented at different points in the Bible. The viewpoints of the Jahwist and Elohist in the Hebrew Scriptures, with their very different conceptions of what it means to be a creature under the Lordship of God, are a prime example, as are the differing conceptions of God's interaction with history in the Johannine and Pauline.[22] To say that there is a total view of God's interaction with history that is consistent throughout the Scriptures is difficult to maintain.

However, even if it could be demonstrated that the manner and mode of God's interaction was consistently expressed and taught by the

---

21. I understand, of course, that this is a contention, rather than a fact. Its ability to convince will depend upon the later argument in chap. 2.

22. See Bultmann's analysis of these two figures' treatment of eschatology in *The Presence of* Eternity, 38–55.

Scriptures, and even if it was as Barth taught, it would still not be adequate for our contemporary times. This is precisely because the content of such a view is difficult to hold. The idea that God, the father of Jesus Christ, is the King of Israel who is also the king of the world, is difficult in a world where, for example, monarchy has radically changed. If we have no kings in actual life, if we hold as democratically-oriented contemporary people that the relation between kings and subjects should be reconstituted to give more governance to the people, what can God being the king of the world mean?[23] Certainly it is true that God is revealed in Scripture as the King of Israel. But must this notion transcend its time period? In the same vein, in a society where patriarchal relations are being more and more criticized, what can God being the Father mean? These two issues suggest that we cannot universalize biblical metaphors for God. Although in the fundamental point I am in agreement with Barth—that is, a doctrine of providence comes from a confession by a religious person of God's providential care—confining the content of such a view to that outlined by the Bible is problematic. There is a need for a wider point of view. We must also consider the possibility (against Barth's vehement objections) of the revelation of God in nature, and the working out of God's purposes in history outside the history of the covenant, and the revelation of God in other religions. In a sense, this is a re-emphasizing of the universality of God's influence, over against any sort of particularism. To be a Christian does not necessarily mean to be a creature under the Universal Lordship of God the Father—it can also mean living a Christian life in the Spirit-filled world.

B. History without God: Historicism Exemplified in William Dean

After having examined two of the great voices of theological insight into the relation between God and history in the twentieth century, both of whom concentrate upon God, it remains to look more closely at the other side of the equation in a discussion of providence, that is to say, to the question of history. In this part of the discussion, William Dean will be examined as an exemplification of one who tries to take the history of the doctrine

---

23. Indeed, constitutional monarchies such as England's or Spain's, where the king is more or less a traditional and historical figurehead, are so different in type from the type of kingship outlined in the Bible and insisted upon by Barth that very little comparison between them is possible. The relation between the people and the queen or king is totally different.

of God and the interaction of that doctrine with history very seriously. In fact, he allows no "*a priori*, metaphysical, or context-independent truths about God"[24] into the discussion, instead satisfying himself with only the analyses of "sacred conventions" and their effects upon history. He points to the radical empiricism of James and Dewey, and also to their "pragmatic tests for "truth." Such a view will be ambiguous throughout all levels of reality, in philosophy, in the religious tradition, and in everyday reality. Dean, through the use of historical and literary examples, builds a case that the interaction of God and history is only in the *conventions about* "God" with history, rather than any sort of real divine being. He then goes on to consider how he best thinks that the religious critic can affect the progress of history, which is by bringing it into harmony with a greater sense of "the whole."

There is much to appreciate in Dean's characterization of an historicized view of God, and also therefore the interaction between "God" and history. By appealing to the historical record, he places the existence of conventions about God beyond the reach of traditional criticisms against them. Who can deny that the conventions about God have at least as great an effect on history as the U.S. Constitution? In addition, his insistence on paying close attention to the history of the tradition does not allow glossing over unpleasant details in that tradition, but brings them to the fore. And, finally, his orientation toward activity in the world, in the form of his call for activity by religious thinkers in the non-profit third sector of American society, outside the more and more narrow bounds of the university, are all helpful in formulating a contemporary doctrine of providence.

However, it is precisely in his too-close attention to history and his neglect of what it means to be a religious person, a participant in a tradition, that Dean's view of the interaction of God and history ultimately falls short. In his insistence upon the ambiguity of God, he ignores the experience of value that comes from his own tradition of radical empiricism. His analysis of conventions does not address the point of novelty and advance in the lives of the aforementioned traditions. And, finally, his laudable constructive program, orienting the religious thinker toward getting the public to come to a greater appreciation of the character and aims of God, cannot convincingly maintain its insistence on the ambiguity of the divine. Try as he might, Dean still wants to actualize the good. Thus we see that historicism is ultimately too weak in its understanding of God to be a basis for

---

24. Dean, *History Making History*, 142.

an understanding of God's activity in history. However, an insistence upon adequacy to actual history, a concern with the orientation towards value, and an orientation towards action in the world are all contributions that a consideration of historicisms such as Dean's make toward a contemporary doctrine of providence.

C. Whitehead: God in the Processes of the World

At this point in the essay, we will turn to the philosophy of organism of Alfred North Whitehead as an example of a viewpoint that might be able to take into account the strong points of the previously detailed views, while avoiding their weaknesses. Whitehead's understanding of the interaction of God with the world, his understanding of providence, as it were, is a richly textured account woven through and through with the experience of value. It provides for the type of intense and life-changing experience that Barth and Bultmann pay so much attention to in their existential and confessional understandings of providence, while at the same time is more historically realist. It accounts for the ambiguity of historical existence in the same way as Dean, but provides a more coherent and religiously satisfying doctrine of God. It is more effective than any of the previous views as a philosophical basis from which to construct a contemporary doctrine of providence.

The treatment of Whitehead begins with a sketch of his understanding of reality. It is an outline of the relations between two categories of existence—actual entities and eternal objects, their manner and mode of interaction, and the various complexities that arise from that interaction. The discussion is informed by Whitehead's notion of the "Category of the Ultimate," which is an explication of the terms One, Many, and Creativity. Basically it is the statement that things are unique, there is more than one thing, and that both the one and the many are in a continuous mode of becoming, that reality is process, or rather, the process of processes. Actual entities are the things with actual existence. Eternal objects are the pure potentialities for the possibility of the becoming of the actual entities—ideas or ideals or universals. Actual entities interact with one another according to the possibilities inherent in the eternal objects, producing nexus, multiplicities, and contrasts, at times leading to consciousness.

Next we turn to the role and function of God in the preceding account of interactivity that is Whitehead's discussion of reality. God provides the ordering and graded relevance of the eternal objects to a particular actual entity. Thus, its appreciation and actualization of the purposes of God are dependent not only on its actual nature, but also on the feeling of God for its aim. God, put rather crudely and anthropomorphically, sets the valuation of the world by setting each entity in motion as it decides how to constitute itself by giving it a "push" toward certain ideal aims depending on its particular circumstances. God guides the world by aiming it towards certain satisfactions.

The preceding discussion about the role and function of God in Whitehead is very general, applying equally across all forms and types of actualities. God's aims for the cultural world will, of course, be appropriate to the type of actual entities that constitute the cultural world: human beings and social groups. The aim of God for the world (and therefore also individual human beings and social groups) is *intensity*—a "depth of satisfaction as an intermediate step towards the fulfillment of [God's] own being."[25] Intensity hovers between the ideal opposites of permanence and flux, with both being a condition of and reason for the other. These are the generalized aims of God for the world, cultural and otherwise. The *specific* aim that God calls the cultural world towards is what Whitehead calls "Civilization," which is a society exhibiting the "five qualities of Truth, Beauty, Adventure, Art and Peace."[26] Eventually, Adventure and Peace are the aims which the other qualities serve.

Whitehead's vision is more complete than the previously presented ones, in that it is less open to psychologizing explanations, offers a view that is consistent across nature and history, and offers a wider point of view from which to connect the various intuitions towards justice, freedom, and love. It allows us to make more sense of the traditional language of sin and repentance. It provides a way to mention God and history in the same breath, seeing reality as shot through and through with the influence of God, rather than finding God's interaction with the world only in existential decision or the history of the covenant. It provides a doctrine of God that is unambiguously good, while at the same time making sense of the ambiguity of historical existence. It is more religiously satisfying than Dean's, and more realistic than Bultmann's, and has a wider point of view than Barth's. It can appropriate their strengths, while at the same time avoiding their weaknesses.

---

25. Whitehead, *Process and Reality*, 105.
26. Whitehead, *Adventures of Ideas*, 274.

Whitehead's vision is on the whole one that is useful for a contemporary doctrine of providence, but there are points at which it could benefit from possible modifications. One such modification would be attempting to account for an ideal aim towards justice, which has very little discussion in Whitehead's account of civilization. While an orientation towards justice could be accounted for by the aim towards Adventure, I will make the case that it is better accounted for, even within Whitehead's own schema, as an ideal aim within its own right, as a necessary component of Peace. In addition, Whitehead's discussion of freedom in his understanding of Civilization could benefit from more attention. His understanding of the active role that human beings play in the development of that civilization could also benefit from a fuller exposition. We thus turn from Whitehead's understanding of the aims of God for history towards Peter Hodgson's view, with an eye especially on the categories of freedom and praxis.

D. Freedom and Praxis: Peter Hodgson's Fuller Vision of History

One fruitful affinity that Whitehead's formulation of the interaction between God and history is with modes of theorizing inspired by Hegel. The encounter that will be presented in the next chapter is between Whitehead and the Hegelian-influenced theologian Peter Hodgson, in his brilliant treatment of the doctrine of providence *God in History: Shapes of Freedom*. In this chapter, we will first look at Hodgson's basic understanding of God's influence on the world, the trinitarian formulation of God as triune figuration, History as deconfigurative process, and Freedom as transfigurative praxis. Then the relation of his dialectical view of God in history to Whitehead's theory of "civilization" outlined in the preceding chapter will be discussed. Hodgson has an ongoing dialogue in his text with both Whitehead and Whiteheadian-influenced thinkers, most notably John Cobb, and both his specific statements and overarching similarities and differences will be dealt with. Most attention will be paid to their contrasting views of freedom, with Hodgson's view being shown to be more useful to the historical orientation of a contemporary doctrine of providence. After having discussed Hodgson's view of God and its relation to Whitehead, we will then consider that which is particularly helpful in Hodgson's formulation as opposed to Whitehead's: a richer analysis of history as such; a fuller understanding of *human* freedom; and, most compellingly, an insistence on the central role of praxis and the specific shapes that God's presence takes in history. This discussion of what the shapes and forms of God's action with the world in freedom looks like will lead us into a discussion of what "the beginning of the history of freedom" might look like from one perspective, in terms of "freedom for Beauty and the Other," in the following chapter.

E. Freedom for Beauty and the Other: Contexts, Objects, Subjects

Hodgson asserts that the influence of God in history is in the "shapes of freedom" that become incarnate, leading to (hopefully) new shapes and so on in a never-ending, ever-expanding history of freedom in the world. He does not spell out in detail what those shapes are, pointing only to the tantalizing "beginnings of a history of freedom," looking back and forward at the shapes that have occurred, calling for efforts to try to begin to interpret and document the progress of the consciousness of freedom in the world. However, freedom *as such* is a difficult concept. Chapter six is an attempt to contribute to the discussion of the forms and shapes of freedom in history, calling attention to certain objects, contexts, and subjects of freedom. They cannot be considered entirely separately, of course, as they intertwine with and affect one another.

First, we will examine the way in which freedom must be for something or someone, and hold up Gustavo Gutiérrez' insight that freedom is for "the other." We will then also examine the contention that freedom must be for oneself at some level as well, following suggestions from Susan Nelson Dunfee and Toni Morrison. Following this discussion of freedom for the self and the other, we will move into a consideration of the various contexts of freedom—natural, social, and political—and its objects in those contexts—the self, the other, and the poor. Most specifically, Juan Luis Segundo's emphasis on the "Signs of the Times" will be brought out as a concept that unifies the context and object of freedom, and demands the subjective engagement in the building up of that freedom. We will call attention to the subjective nature of freedom, building on Hodgson's insight from Hegel, Marx, and Troeltsch that the point of praxis is the key by which to understand and participate in the action of God in history. Thus the contexts, objects and subjects of freedom for the self and the other will be considered, maintaining throughout the emphasis on the shaping force of God in history.

After the discussion on the contexts, objects, and subjective nature of freedom, we will point the discussion toward a consideration of beauty and its relation to freedom. We will discuss Whitehead's emphasis on art, and argue from Toni Morrison's characterization of the liberative effect of the beauty of the world that natural beauty can be as liberating as "artificial" beauty. The discussion will be recontextualized away from the "high cultural" tone that most discussion of beauty and art take, and move it toward something like an "aesthetic orientation to life" that permeates all socio-economic levels, from the richest to the poorest. Our examples will be theologians Gladys Parentelli and María Pilar Aquino, following their contention that this aesthetic orientation permeates the spiritualities of third world Latin American women.

What remains after considering aim of God for the world in this fashion is to provide a synthesis that incorporates the various important points regarding the action of God in the world, that takes into consideration the contexts, objects, and subjects in and upon which God moves towards the divine purposes in history, and also points us to the future, opening us to the action in the present for the future. In the next and final chapter, we will attend to the theological conception of the Spirit in the World as a way in which to understand God's activity in and through and for history.

F. The Spirit In and Through the World

The final analysis in this contemporary doctrine of providence will be an attempt to weave together the various insights of the disparate thinkers into a convincing, theologically-grounded, adequate account of the divine activity in the world. It will appropriate the important insights of all the thinkers presented in the previous accounts, at the same time being aware of their weaknesses and taking care to avoid them. Such a view will be adequate to the nature of Christian experience, like Barth and Bultmann, yet take care to be adequate to the intricacies of the historical record. In a sense, we will return to Barth's notion that the doctrine of providence is confessed, rather than derived, but change the content of such a view so radically that it will not appear to be the same at all. Instead of the doctrine of providence being understood as that of creaturely existence under the Universal Lordship of God the Father, we will move to an understanding of that of being a Spirit-filled person in a Spirit-filled world.

Such a view will take into account the doctrine of God formulated by Hodgson and Whitehead in chapters four and five, and also the account of the shapes of freedom in chapter six. It will bring the discussion back around from the cultural analysis that occupied that chapter, and return to more purely theological discussion. A doctrine of persons and communities living in a Spirit-filled world is the best way to understand and participate in the providential divine activity in the world.

The doctrine of the Spirit in and through the world that constitutes this contemporary doctrine of providence will have three major foci: the primacy of the Spirit, the Spirit incarnate, and the work of the Spirit. In the first place, discourse in and about and through the spirit is the best way to understand the activity of God in the world, as opposed to discourse about any permutation of the first or second persons of the Trinity, or the Trinity as a whole. This is primarily because it is in and through the Spirit that we experience God. The other types of language are too laced with problems to be primary modes of communication about the Spirit, and Spirit-language is appropriately universal and with enough distance from human modes of being that anthropomorphism, with its concomitant difficulties, is less of a danger.

Such Spirit-oriented discourse, however, cannot be in the traditional, flesh-denying, dualistic, oppressive manner that so much discussion about the Spirit has taken in the past. Any doctrine of Spirit will have to be a doctrine of the Spirit Incarnate, taking into account that whenever and wherever the divine Wind moves, it moves something, and its effects are felt in the flesh. It is precisely in these incarnate forms that we know and feel the action of the Spirit, and "Spirit" which does not incarnate is not the true, but a false Spirit, leading to destruction and death. In such a contention, we follow Peter Hodgson's Hegelian insistence that there is never *Geist* (Spirit) without *Gestalt* (Shape). All activity of the Spirit looks like something in the world. This shape also shapes contexts and objects, and is a spirituality of space, and of time, and of social groups of people. In this, Hodgson's presentation of the paradigmatic shapes of the Christian experience—the *basileia*, the cross, and the resurrection—are also key for our insistence that Spirit be incarnate if it is to be Spirit at all.

And, finally, we will pay attention to the work of the Spirit in the world—its orientation and dynamic movement. In many senses, of course, the incarnation of the Spirit is its work, and its work is incarnation. God is what God does—to make distinctions otherwise casts an overly speculative tone upon this theological enterprise. However, attention needs to be paid more specifically to what this work is. My contention is that the activity of the Spirit is felt most clearly and deeply in the praxis of liberation, in acts of mercy directed towards something like Whitehead's ideal aims, always concretely realized in the world. And this work of the Spirit, this praxis of liberation is one that is, in the words of Marjorie Suchocki, the "abstract technical notion of God, clothed with love, leading to hope."[27] Hope is the last, but of course not the final, word on the subject. The Spirit leads us into the future, and that future is open, and contains within its own comprehension the hope that things can and should and will be different. This vision, shared by Cobb, Daly, Hodgson, Keller, Moltmann, Ruether, and others, of a primal, incarnate, active Spirit, living in people and communities, taking the form of love-in-praxis and issuing in hope, is the action of God in history. This is where, by my judgment of faith, and in virtue of my own partial and fragmentary and at times conflicted life in and of the Spirit, I point to the providential activity of God in the world.

---

27. Suchocki, *Spirit*, 105.

2

Bultmann and Barth

*God in Existential Meaning;
or God Revealed, God Confessed*

THE QUESTION OF THE relation between God and history has, as was argued in the previous chapter, been a central topic for several major theologically-oriented thinkers in the twentieth century. One of the most influential strands in twentieth century theology seeks to place the relation between God and human beings outside the realm of history, and make it an existential or confessional relation that is not subject to either the inexorable processes of nature or the vagaries of history. Such an approach is illustrated, with different emphases and orientations, in the writings of Karl Barth and Rudolf Bultmann on the subject.

Both Barth and Bultmann are acutely aware that we are no longer living in the past, and thus cannot access past interpretations of God and history. Both also hold that the religious life (that is, the individual life lived in relation to some transcendent reality) is paramount, and do a magisterial job in detailing what a religious life would look like—a type of phenomenological spelling out of the life of a religious person. Bultmann holds that God's will cannot be determined by looking at the historical world, and that the relation between God and humanity is related to the salvation of human persons, rather than historical processes. Barth pays more attention to history, but limits his positive statements on the role of God in history to the history of the covenant, outlined in the Bible as understood from the perspective of a believer in Jesus Christ. For all their strengths, however, neither is an adequate foundation on which to build a contemporary doctrine of providence. Bultmann is not adequate because such a doctrine would be virtually content-less, with his radical sundering of the concepts of God and history. And Barth, although his own view is rich in content, is not adequate because he is too limited in what he feels the work of God to be. His confessional and revelational view does not to justice to the range and scope of the contemporary experience of the divine in history to be an adequate base for a contemporary doctrine of providence. Let us turn first to Bultmann, and examine what an existential understanding of the relation between God and history might offer for a contemporary doctrine of providence.

RUDOLF BULTMANN: GOD AS SOURCE OF INDIVIDUAL MEANING

Rudolf Bultmann is one of the most influential figures in twentieth century theological thought. In his combination of radical biblical criticism with Heideggerian existentialism, his influence is felt across the range of scholarly and theological approaches to religion, with most thinkers responding either positively or negatively to his work, even unwittingly. In thinking about the connections of God and history, Bultmann represents almost a pure 'type' that tries to pay close attention to the religious life, the radical call of God, without paying any attention to the consequences or shape of such a life in the ongoing stream of history. A closer examination of several of his writings on the subject will reveal this tendency beyond the shadow of a doubt.

Bultmann is absolutely clear in a variety of works that his idea of the God-human relationship is that God is outside history, calling each individual human being to some sort of "radical decision." History as such has no "meaning," no purpose, but is the ground for finding individual meanings and purposes. God is not a force in history, or the world-spirit, or any such thing. Instead, God is encountered in the meaning-finding activities of individual human beings as they make decisions, regardless of the consequences.

Such an emphasis in Bultmann's thought is clear, almost from the beginning of his work on the subject. As Robert W. Funk points out in his introduction to Bultmann's early volume *Faith and Understanding*, "nothing appeared later...the preparation for which had not already been made during these formative years"[1] [of 1923–33], and that includes his insistence that God's traces are not found within history. Several examples from these early essays will suffice to illustrate Bultmann's indifference to history. In an essay from 1924, Bultmann criticizes the liberal theologies' insistence on the personality-changing influence of Jesus' personality:

> In all these varied formulations [of liberal theology] the 'stumbling block' has been removed from Christianity. All of them totally lack the insight that God is other than the world, he is beyond the world, that that this means the complete abrogation of the whole man [sic], of his whole history. Their common aim is to give faith the kind of basis, which destroys the very essence of faith, because what they seek is a basis here in this world.[2]

Bultmann is clear that human history holds no clue to the presence of God in the world. No act is better or worse in the eyes of God than another: "No act exists which can relate itself directly to God and his [sic] kingdom. All forms of community life, the worst and the most ideal alike, stand equally under the judgment of God."[3] What is such a position saying? Are they the same sort of community life, and if they are not, can one have any basis for judging them except the differences in what they are? Where is the intersection between talk about God and talk about the actual circumstances in which one lives one's life (that is to say, history) if it is not in the quality of the acts themselves? It may be, of course, that God's judgment will be different in different cases. However, Bultmann's position offers no clues about how one is to look for the differing judgments, and what that difference might mean for human beings. If, in an ultimate sense (which is what Bultmann is talking about) there is no distinction that we can discern, how are we then to act?

Bultmann makes his point about history not mattering for Christian faith in another sense—in the theological interpretation of the Bible. In his essay on "The Significance of the Jewish Old Testament Tradition for the Christian West,"[4] Bultmann brings his sharp critic's mind to bear on the question of the relation between the idea of history in the Jewish tradition and the idea of human existence before God. In the sections of the

1. Funk, "Introduction to Bultmann," 10.
2. Bultmann, *Faith and Understanding*, 40.
3. Ibid., 42.
4. In *Essays: Philosophical and Theological*, 262–72.

Bible where history and God's revelation in and through it figure heavily,[5] Bultmann finds an entirely negative significance for the "Christian West" and for Christian faith. God's call is not demonstrated, God's covenant is not outlined, God's actions are not revealed. Even the "rational comprehensibility of the divine action"[6] is excluded from consideration as a means to participate in the divine-human dynamic. Instead, the Jewish Old Testament tradition of history (and its Christian outgrowths), with their orientation to the future and their attempt to see history as a unity and therefore with a discoverable plan, are seen entirely in contrast to the existential response of human beings to the divine transcendence, with the latter representing the correct way to view God/human relations.[7] The Jewish Old Testament tradition takes its classic Lutheran place as "law," having only the power to convict of sin, and not even having the pre-figuring relation to the gospel that comes after it to abrogate it. According to Bultmann, the historical orientation of the Jewish Old Testament tradition has an entirely negative significance for true Christian faith, which consists only of an existential reaction to, and decision about, the call of God.

Another of Bultmann's essays, in which he speaks about "The Meaning of God as Acting,"[8] spells out further his contention that God's action (if it can be spoken of as such) is not understood by looking at history or nature, but is understood only as a response in the personal life of a believer to the call of God, encountered in the proclaimed Word. God's act is understood analogically to the personal acts of human beings,[9] with the paradigmatic example being the conception of God the Father. We do not consider the notion literally, but as a "purely personal relationship." In the same sense, God as creator is not understood that God created the world as we know it, but as "a personal confession that I understand myself to be a creature which owes its existence to God."[10]

Bultmann's position appears ripe for psychologizing explanations. How is such an understanding different from a purely naturalistic view of

---

5. The sections that Karl Barth will draw on in his construction of a doctrine of providence.

6. Bultmann, "Significance of the Jewish Old Testament" 271.

7. Although this might seem anti-Semitic, Bultmann also grounds the view of divine transcendence in other sections of the Jewish Scriptures—in Job, Jeremiah, and certain Psalms.

8. Bultmann, "The Meaning of God as Acting."

9. Ibid., 68–69.

10. Ibid., 69.

the world? Indeed, Bultmann is aware of such difficulties: asking, "If what we have said is correct, does it not follow that God's action is deprived of objective reality, that it is reduced to a purely subjective, psychological experience (*Erlebnis*); that God exists only as an inner event in the soul, whereas faith has real meaning only if God exists outside the believer?"[11] Bultmann goes on to maintain that faith cannot defend itself against the charges of being an illusion, but that this characteristic is its strength, rather than its weakness. He compares it to trust in a friend or the love of family, in that it cannot be "proved" by observation, but only experienced and trusted in an act of personal decision. He points out that there is no relation without risk, and that personal relations are not considered "objectively," but subjectively.

While Bultmann's analogical understanding of the meaning of God as acting has obvious strengths—the ability to have nothing count against it, the attention correctly paid to the subjective realms of experience, among other things—it still falls short of being an adequate understanding of the interaction of God and history. This is most clearly demonstrated in his analogy of the God-human relation with the relation between human persons. Although it is of course true that personal relations are subjective events, it feels strange to speak about them as if they held no relation to the acts that take place in the relationship. In another essay, Bultmann proposes that "one cannot speak meaningfully about love if such speaking is not itself an act of love."[12] Such an assertion is difficult to understand. What about love poetry? What about traditional Christian or philosophical discourse on the nature of love? What about ethics, especially Christian ethics that try to speak about incarnating love in the world? To divorce questions of love and relation from their concrete circumstances is to place them entirely in the subjective world of the person in question, and to make them other than what they are: real love and real relation with other human beings. There are certain acts that are incompatible with love and trusting relation, and it is precisely these acts that constitute an unloving relation. To speak in Bultmann's manner about love, and analogically, about history, feels like a very un-human way to talk about it.

Bultmann consistently holds such views throughout his theological career. In his last major work to deal with the subject of God and history, his seminal Gifford Lectures of 1955, published as *The Presence of Eternity:*

---

11. Ibid., 70.
12. Bultmann, *Faith and Understanding*, 53.

The Purposes of God

History and Eschatology, Bultmann puts forth in clear (and historical) outline his own views and their relation to other views of God and history that have come before. He can thus highlight differences with and problems solved by his own view, and can illustrate why he finds an "existential" view to be the "only possible option"[13] in considering God and history. Bultmann's basic point is that the early Christians, and thus by implication all who respond to the call of God when and where they hear it, are living in an "eschatological moment," where history is ended. History is not meaningful in and of itself, but is only the ground where individual persons find meaning as they respond (or don't) to the call of God.

Bultmann's presentation of the earliest Christian community in its context makes his point quite clear. He situates it in its context of apocalyptic Judaism, with the apocalyptic ideas that time and history have ended, and a new age has begun. "The new people of God has no real history, for it is the community of the end-time, an eschatological phenomenon. How could it have a history now when the world-time is finished and the end is imminent?"[14] Bultmann then points out eschatology in the Christian community became historicized in the thought and writings of Paul and John, and then became neutralized by sacramentalism and the hope of immortality.

In later ages, Bultmann maintains that the eschatological ideals became secularized in the idealism of Kant and Hegel, and became ultimately the progress of the consciousness of freedom, or the cunning of reason in history. This viewpoint is taken up and modified by Marx, also trying to usher in a "new age" ruled by the proletariat. And, finally, there is the idea of progress, which is also a type of secularized eschatology, a hope and belief that the world is getting better.

Eventually, however, relativism and historicism win out, as history is seen more and more as a natural process, with it's own laws of cyclic or selfish origin, that have little or nothing to do with God—we begin to "no longer have need of that hypothesis." For Bultmann, the question then becomes: what meaning can individual human beings have in a meaningless history?

Bultmann then goes on to examine different anthropologies in the relation to history, centering on what he holds as the Jewish and Christian view that the ultimately best way of understanding human beings is through

13. Bultmann, *The Presence of Eternity.*
14. Ibid., 36.

"will."[15] Moving through the Greek, Old Testament, and New Testament views of human being, though idealism and a thoroughly historicized naturalism, he finally comes to the conclusion that "Man [sic] is determined by historical, economic, and social conditions, by his [sic] milieu . . . All this is at bottom nothing but fate, . . . and a genuine self seems not to exist at all."[16] At the same time, Bultmann holds that we are drawn to be "real selves" and to have "true existence."[17]

Moving back to the problem of hermeneutics, Bultmann finds that it is the principle of selection of the historian always has to do with the interests of the historian, thus, meaning in history is personal and individual. The only people who claimed to understand the "universal" goals of history came out of or were influenced by the Jewish and Christian traditions that had eschatology at the center of their understanding of history (Marx, Hegel, the Enlightenment). However, Bultmann now holds that "[t]oday we cannot claim to know the end and goal of history. Therefore the question of meaning in history has become meaningless."[18] The only meaning is the meaning that persons bring to history.

The way out of the meaninglessness of a naturalistic historicism, according to Bultmann, is found in the radical decision of Christian faith. We are free from the "old man" of sin, from ourselves, from our naturalistic worldview, by receiving the freedom of the grace of God. This takes place, again according to Bultmann, in "the preaching of the Christian church [where] the eschatological event will ever again become present and does become present ever and again in faith."[19] This takes place in the preaching (kerygma) that demands a decision. The Christian then becomes a "new person" free for responsible historical living, born of love.

All of Bultmann's thought, his theology of God and history included, is a vigorous combination of the historical demonstration of his viewpoint

---

15. In so doing, he neglects the myriad ways in which human being has been understood in the history of Christian thought (I cannot speak authoritatively on Jewish anthropology, although I suspect that it is as varied as Christian on the subject). Although will has been understood as an important aspect of human being, it has never been the total way of thinking about human life and existence that Bultmann's presentation of the material implies. The will may be the "first among equals" in reflection on the composition of a total human being, but the passions figure in as well, as does reason.

16. Bultmann, *The Presence of Eternity*, 108–9.

17. Ibid., 109.

18. Ibid., 120.

19. Ibid., 151.

combined with an existentialism that drives relentlessly for the individual meaning found in moments of decision. However, one wonders if he is not the prime example of his assertion that the historian brings his criteria with him to the historical project. Did the early Christians really believe that history didn't matter at all? Are all viewpoints that promulgate an idea of universal history offshoots of Christianity? Is it a return to the pure roots of Christianity to adopt an existential viewpoint? I become suspicious at a certain point—it almost feels like an offshoot of the quest for the historical Jesus in the classic sense, but instead becoming a "quest for the genuine, non-historical kerygma leading to existential decision that was and is the true Christian message." It feels motivated by the same sense that if we can get back to the original, the true, the pure Christian message, then everything will be all right. I would question that the "original" Christian message he attempts to isolate and his existential analysis correlate so completely.[20] It feels somewhat forced.

Also, if one is a "new person" free for historical living, surely this unworldly living has a shape? A form? Can we say *nothing* about it? Bultmann himself points to the concrete realities of the situation when he insists that the Christian will make decisions "born of love." Surely these decisions of love have shape, form, actuality, consequences in the world? Is there no difference between Himmler and Bonhoeffer, to use examples contemporary to Bultmann himself? Surely Bultmann would say that one was Christian, the other not; but that begs the question. The way we would know would be in looking at their lives, seeing what they do—seeing their effect on history, one might say. A view such as Bultmann's would seem to indicate that the actual decisions and their effects don't matter, but the decisions leading up to them are the only consideration. Such a view is difficult to maintain, to say the least.

An interesting point that seems to further emphasize the unworldliness and un-tenability of Bultmann's a-historical view of God and history is that he finds the need to defend his existential view against charges of quietism,[21] that is, against the charge that his understanding provides no basis by which to commit to concrete ethical action in the world. Bultmann vigorously defends himself against the charge, but tries to do so without

---

20. See, for example, the location of early Jesus communities in their social and political contexts examined by such scholars as Crossan in *Jesus: A Revolutionary Biography*; and Oakman in *The Political Aims of Jesus*.

21. Ibid., 61, 75.

saying something like there is a moral code that one should live by, or that certain actions should or shouldn't be done. He holds that existential decisions are the only "real" decisions, and such decisions are meaningful regardless of their content. It's a difficult road to travel, and ultimately fails in its ability to convince. It would seem that critics of a "pure" existentialist position like Rosemary Radford Ruether have a point when they insist that a purely existentialist view, without reference to concrete realities, leads to a "status-quo position, since no divine sanction can be given to a preference for different social order from the present one, all social orders being equally sinful."[22] Of course, an orientation to changing the status quo merely for its own sake is not what is needed, but some kind of orientation to making it better. Why, if all forms of social life are equally sinful, should one participate in one rather than another? What theological reason can one give?

Why, one might ask, is he so loath to make comments, predictions, judgments about the actual happenings of history? It seems that it is because Bultmann ultimately does believe that it is only in human consciousness that "meaning" exists at all, and that it is a human question, a question of decision, of motivation, and human existential relation, which is (of course) malleable and contingent on the particular circumstances. Thus, he does appear to be attempting to formulate some kind of general rule about these things. However, without *some* consideration of the actual contexts and realities of history, such a characterization has given up too much to the naturalisms Bultmann thinks he has overcome. If one cannot point to the concrete results of action in the world, how can one tell those who "have the modern worldview" from those who are "living has though they have none"?[23] It surely must be in the way their lives are lived, and in the impact that these lives have upon history.

Thus we have seen that Bultmann's existential understanding of God and history radically divorces the concepts from one another, ultimately making it difficult to see how they relate at all. If one cannot somehow speak about the actualities of history in relation to God, the actualities of history can easily become the only reality there is. That Bultmann feels he has to defend himself against quietism and psychologizing explanations shows that he feels these currents, but his defenses against them ring hollow. Within his framework, he cannot effectively neutralize such charges.

22. Ruether, *Disputed Questions*, 91.
23. See *Jesus Christ and Mythology*, 85.

In the final analysis, it is telling the Bultmann does not, in his vast and varied work, find it necessary to speak of providence at all. He speaks of Jesus' views of providence, but mostly as a historical critic, rather than thinking of it as a theological view worth considering.[24] But as far as finding meaning in God's activity in history, or in the course of history generally, Bultmann consistently and clearly just does not touch the topic at all, except to decry the activity as a foolish endeavor.

While Bultmann is almost the "pure" type of existentialism with relation to questions of God and history, his contemporary Karl Barth holds a different, much more complex and content-rich view. Barth also pays attention to the relation between God and human beings, but rather than trying to frame it within an existential analysis, he attempts to outline a view of providence that is revealed in the Bible and understood as the confession of the creature's faith in the Creator who rules history. Barth will spell out much more fully where and how he sees the divine activity in history. Let us turn to his much richer view to see if a very traditional view of the activity of God in history can be of more use as we attempt to construct a contemporary doctrine of providence.

BARTH:
PROVIDENCE REVEALED; PROVIDENCE CONFESSED

Karl Barth's sustained discourse on the doctrine of providence[25] is one of the most extensive and influential treatments of the subject anywhere in the twentieth century. He analyzes the life of the Christian Under the Universal Lordship of God the Father, spelling out and exploring what it means and looks like to live as a creature, part of the creation of God. In doing so, Barth has many useful insights which continue to inspire one to reflect, and pay attention especially closely to the phenomenon of being a religious person (Barth would say a Christian, rather than a religious person), and what that means in one's life. However, a closer analysis of Barth's doctrine of providence will show that his understanding of the Christian Under the

---

24. See *Jesus and the Word*, 160–72. Bultmann seems to consider the Christian message of radical decision, rather than anything he thinks he can deduce from the New Testament regarding Jesus' views, as normative, if anything. In any case, he views the attempt to extract Jesus' views as misguided, as he finds them buried so deeply under layers of tradition that they are very dubiously known.

25. Karl Barth, *Church Dogmatics*, III/3, 3–288. Also integrally related are the discourses on Nothingness and Angels that follow his treatment of providence.

Universal Lordship of God the Father, while exceedingly rich and suggestive of the existential meaning of the Christian life, ultimately cannot meet our needs for a contemporary understanding of God's interaction with the world. We will see that it is not broad enough, and does not pay enough attention to the total experience of a complete construction of life, to be an adequate contemporary doctrine of providence.

In addition, a purely revelational understanding is not adequate to our present life in the contemporary world. This is so because the concepts that are integral to the meaning and vision of the revelational understanding are increasingly problematic, and through their problematic character illustrate the dialectical and multifaceted synthesis that is how contemporary people see and experience the divine activity.[26] Any doctrine will need to take into account such multi-faceted experience if it is to be an adequate contemporary doctrine of providence. Nevertheless, let us turn to Barth's confessional understanding of providence to see what a confessional and existential view, spelled out by close attention to the content of the Bible, understood especially in the light of a particular understanding of Jesus Christ, looks like.

The Christian Doctrine of Providence

Barth's concept of providence, as in the traditional doctrines we looked at in the first chapter, has to do with the relation between the creature and the creator.[27] Barth states his position succinctly in the proposition at the beginning of his discussion of providence:

> The doctrine of providence deals with the history of created being as such, in the sense that in every respect and in its whole span this proceeds under the fatherly care of God the Creator, whose will is done and is to be seen in His [sic] election of grace, and therefore in the history of the covenant between Himself [sic] and man [sic], and therefore in Jesus Christ.[28]

---

26. See, for example, Charles Taylor's account of the role that social imaginaries play in the ongoing historical construction of Christian belief in *A Secular Age*.

27. Barth places his doctrine of providence under the doctrine of creation, following Calvin and the Protestant dogmaticians, rather than in the doctrine of God, following Aquinas. This is to highlight both the supremacy of God (understood as self-sufficiency) and the creaturely nature of the human being in question.

28. Barth, *Church Dogmatics*, III/3, 3.

The Purposes of God

A proper understanding of providence, according to Barth, has to do with a proper understanding of who and what God is—namely, God the Father who is the creator and Lord of the creature. It also has to do with who and what the creature is—the subject and creature of God the Father who is her or his Creator and Lord. This concept of God as the creator and Lord of the creature is not to be understood in some ontological or philosophical sense:[29] "God is not a manufacturer of products."[30] The idea of creation and Lordship is instead understood in relation to the "history of the covenant" between God and humanity, which is understood in Jesus Christ.

This understanding of providence as a particularly *Christian* doctrine is key for Barth. He states that "the Christian belief in providence is faith in the strict sense of the term, and this means first that it is a hearing and a receiving of the Word of God."[31] The belief in providence is part of the confession of Christian faith, not an analysis of historical or natural happenings.[32] The assertion that God rules all things is not unproblematic for Barth, and he holds that even the sincerity of the confession is not in the Christian's belief in the view as such or belief in any of the implications of such a view, but is in the command by the Word of God to confess it. Barth specifically opposes his understanding of the Christian doctrine of providence as confession and faith to a notion

> which regards the Christian belief in providence as an opinion, postulate or hypothesis concerning God, the world, man, and other things, an attempt at interpretation, exposition and explanation based upon all kinds of impressions and needs, carried through in the form of a systematic construction, and ventured as if it were a pious outlook which has a good deal in its favour [sic] and may be adopted if we ourselves are pious.[33]

---

29. Although it seems that Barth means this too—I think that he collapses religious conviction and confession with ontology (his treatment of the "Word of God" on p. 29, for example). Perhaps he is making the point that the religious life of a believer *is* ontological in the construction of personality or worldview.

30. Barth, *Church Dogmatics*, III/3, 9.

31. Ibid., 15.

32. Barth's citation of the literature of "Christian instruction, edification and not least hymnology of the 17th and 18th centuries" (14) as an example of the confessional nature of the Christian belief in providence is a good example of his approach. Providence is taught and confessed, not derived.

33. Barth, *Church Dogmatics*, III/3, 16.

Barth argues against the idea of a "Christian worldview"—a systematic outlook of interpretation of the world that can be modified or updated—as opposed to some other kind of worldview: "What we have to avoid is the equation of the belief in providence and its confession with a philosophy of history."[34] He holds that if the belief in providence is like a worldview it would be only the interpretation of the human subject, and would thus be "unstable."[35] On the contrary, because the Christian teaching on providence is the confession of the lordship of God over the history of creaturely being as revealed in the Word of God, it is (according to Barth) not subject to change or revision or (implicitly) the assaults of other systems of thought.

What, then, is Barth's understanding of the doctrine of providence? What is the secret and key for understanding the entire Lordship of God over history? It is, not surprisingly, in the self-revelation of God in Jesus Christ that we understand the purposes and work of God in history:

> If faith in providence is Christian faith, and therefore faith in Christ as the Word of God and therefore the self-revelation of God, there is for it no obscurity concerning the nature and will and work of the Lord of history, no ambiguity concerning His [sic] character and purpose, and no doubt as to His [sic] ability to see to His [sic] own glory in this history.[36]

God's self-revelation in Christ is "that His [sic] free grace should be radiant, and take form, and conquer and rule in the creaturely world."[37] It is thus a specifically Christological understanding of providence. It is the

> history of the covenant between God and man [sic]. It is the history in which God establishes His [sic] fellowship with man [sic], and prepares and accomplishes its completion in His [sic] own self-giving to human nature and existence, to conduct it to its manifestation at the expiration of the last time.[38]

This history of the covenant is the "astonishingly thin line in a confusion of apparently much more powerful and conspicuous lines which seem to be independent and mutually contradictory, [that] run quite contrary to

---

34. Ibid., 21.

35. Although it is difficult to see what 'unstable' means in this context. We certainly have ideas, provisional though they may be, about the functioning of nature and human societies, that seem to be functional. What does "stability" consist of?

36. Barth, *Church Dogmatics*, III/3, 34.

37. Ibid.

38. Ibid., 36.

the one narrow line of the history of the covenant."[39] However, all the other lines are, by virtue of the experience of grace that the Christian has, held to be ordered by and oriented to the same source, and all ultimately run in its direction—that is, from and to God.[40] It means to understand the rest of the world-occurrence in terms of the history of the covenant between God and human beings, revealed in Jesus Christ.

Barth's doctrine of providence means that all of human history is understood in terms of the history of the covenant, rather than including that special history within a general understanding of history. "The doctrine of providence must not level down the special history of the covenant, grace, and salvation; it must not reduce it to the common denominator of a doctrine of general world-occurrence."[41] It has to do with the history of human beings precisely as creatures of the creator, rather than in their other roles as women and men in political systems, or in familial units, or as mammals striving to thrive and reproduce on this planet. All these other ways of being and existing are evaluated in light of what it means to be a creature of the creator, part of the history of the covenant, revealed in and through the Word of God. God is revealed as the Lord of history, and all other historical aspects are to be interpreted in light of that Lordship.

Barth takes this idea of the Lordship over history seriously, but not naively. He is not blind to the seeming difficulties in such a view. He maintains that the Christian will believe in the revelation of God's Lordship

> even at points where . . . to all appearances we have to do only with creaturely occurrence, where the orders and contingencies of nature, the works of caprice and the cleverness or folly, the goodness or badness of men seem to be the only reality.[42]

The Christian will maintain that "Nevertheless, God Himself [sic] is He [sic] who is freely and graciously and mightily present and active at these points too."[43] Barth acknowledges that "this Nevertheless is the problem of the belief in providence,"[44] but holds that this is the way it must be because

---

39. Ibid.

40. A striking similarity with Augustine and Aquinas in their Neo-Platonic *exitus-reditus* schema, and indeed with much of the tradition.

41. Barth, *Church Dogmatics*, III/3, 37.

42. Ibid., 44.

43. Ibid.

44. Ibid.

of the limited capacities of the creature and the character of the relation between the creature and the Creator.

Is there then in Barth's understanding of providence a concrete role that the creature plays in the working out of God's ways in the world? Barth is leery of stating so unequivocally, but sees that there must be some sense in which the creature fulfills God's purposes. He takes a metaphorical approach, hinting at what the role of the creature in the divine purposes might be. His metaphors for this process are mostly taken from the Scriptures, and include the creature as a servant of the Lord, as an instrument for accomplishing the divine purpose, as a player in the theater of the divine drama, and as a mirror and likeness of the divine (but with a mirror's inherently distorting properties, to reinforce the distance between the creature and the creator). All these metaphors, and the manner with which they are dealt, emphasize the primary role of the Creator and the dependent nature of the creature in the process. The creature can "only receive, and receive grace for grace, and receive of his fulness [sic]."[45] There is no "independent co-operation of creation in the establishment, direction, and fulfillment of the history of the covenant of grace, [or] a participation of creation in the procuring, attainment of mediation of the love of God which comes to it in this covenant."[46] Providential action is on the side of God, and the confession of providence from the believer comes from the life of faith.

This realization that God is source and worker in the doctrine of providence will lead to four important deductions for Barth. The first of these is that creatures are not co-redeemers any more than they are co-creators. They do not form the history of the covenant, but are receivers of the love of God. Any co-operation that creaturely being has in the fulfillment of the covenant is itself arising out of the free love and grace of God. Thus its roles of servant, mirror, etc., are themselves the work of God in assigning it such a role.

The second is that "creaturely occurrence is the external basis of the history of the covenant."[47] What this means is that while we affirm that historical existence is the site and context of the history of the covenant, and as such is under the rule of God as well, we affirm such understandings only from and in light of participation in the context of our own "divine

---

45. Ibid., 53.
46. Ibid.
47. Ibid., 54.

election of grace revealed in Jesus Christ."[48] Fundamentally, this means that "we walk by faith, and not by sight."[49] This signifies that we cannot take the means and methods of historical or natural analysis and apply them either to the history of the covenant, or our interpretation of world-occurrence generally that is the basis for the history of the covenant. Such a move would be illegitimate: "The freedom of the divine providence by which all things are upheld and sustained and meaningful and right can only be known in the freedom of faith."[50] History is understood from the perspective of a creature of God, not as an independent happening.

This also means, according to Barth, that the revelation of God *in* the Word of God can only be understood *from* the word of God, which is the Bible, properly understood and interpreted. Even systems and theories that take as their material the work of God in Jesus are illegitimate ways in which to understand the working of God in history. This is so, according to Barth, because if do not have this continuous anchor point, another aspect of world-occurrence will be seen as paramount, and the methods of its evaluation will continually be in doubt, and therefore also unsure. It must always be considered from within outwards, and not the other way around.

And, finally, this means that for Barth there cannot be a "closed and static Christian system."[51] There is only the confession of individuals or small groups of individuals about their reception of the free gracious activity of God. Barth holds that no such system can be constructed because such construction would close off the Christian to the activity and grace of God in times to come. By paying attention to what they would expect under the system, the constructor of the system might miss the action of God.[52] This is not, according to Barth, to say that God is changeable or changing in an ultimate sense—God always acts in and through grace and love. But the form may change: "What God has done to-day [sic], and revealed to man [sic] as His [sic] action, He [sic] will do again tomorrow, but perhaps He [sic] will do it quite differently, and reveal it to man [sic] in a very different form."[53] Christians will, of course, form a "partial world-view

---

48. Ibid.
49. Ibid.
50. Ibid.
51. Ibid., 55.
52. This is something like committing the sin of idolatry.
53. Barth, *Church Dogmatics*, III/3, 56.

which is provisional and modest,"[54] but they will not believe in it. Only God deserves belief, and all other aspects of world-occurrence will be open to new insights based in the divine self-revelation.

Thus we have seen that in Barth's conception of the doctrine of providence, he is deeply concerned that it be a Christian doctrine, always constrained and informed by the self-revelation of God in Jesus Christ. He is not content to leave it as a mere stance, but is also concerned to fill the doctrine with content as well. He engages in a multiform effort to "unfold and clarify what takes place when God accomplishes what we define as His [sic] providential ordering and therefore His [sic] fatherly lordship over the creature."[55] Following the previous tradition of dogmatics, Barth then lays out in more detail the content of the doctrine of divine providence, holding that "God fulfils His [sic] fatherly lordship over His [sic] creature by preserving, accompanying and ruling the whole course of its earthly existence."[56] And this is always in and through the revelation of the gracious act of divine mercy in Jesus Christ. Let us look more closely at his spelling out of the first of these characteristics of the Fatherly Lordship of God: the divine preserving.

The Divine Preserving

Barth understands the divine preserving of the creature basically to be the preservation of the context of the creature and the preservation of the creature in its creatureliness. The preservation of the context of the creature has to do both with the creation of a reality outside of God and the maintenance of that reality, both in its actuality and in a temporal sequence.[57] Barth understands the mode of the divine providence as the continuing faithfulness of God to the divine election of the creature, which is the basis of the relation between the creature and the creator.[58] But why would the creature need preservation in its context if it is created for it and to be within it? Barth holds that there are two reasons for this preservation. The first is that it is the nature of creatureliness to be preserved. The creature is dependent upon the grace of the God for existence, meaning, and salva-

54. Ibid., 57.
55. Ibid., 58.
56. Ibid.
57. Ibid., 61.
58. Ibid., 70.

tion. It is the condition of creaturehood. The second reason is prior to the first, and it is that the creature was created out of Nothingness, which is the result of the "No" of God as the creature and creation are the result of the "Yes" of the eternal election of God. This nothingness, the "unelect of God," menaces the creation, the "elect," by reason of its state of being unelected.[59] In the election of the creature lies the roots of the need for preservation in the face of the chaos and nothingness of the unelect. The creature understands that it is elect (rather than unelect) because it has the experience of the Word of God: "that creative Word means Jesus Christ and therefore covenant and grace and mercy and goodness."[60] The divine preservation is the way in which a believer understands God to preserve its existence from the standpoint of faith in her or his election by the free grace of God to enter into the covenant of grace.

The Divine Accompanying

The second aspect of Barth's unfolding and clarifying what happens in the workings of providence is the divine accompanying. The divine accompanying, according to Barth, has many facets. God is understood as accompanying the creature in that God does not "preserve it merely to abandon it to its own activity once He has set it in motion."[61] That God accompanies the creature also means that God "affirms and approves and recognizes and respects the autonomous actuality and therefore the autonomous activity of the creature as such."[62] And, of course, that God accompanies the creature does not mean that God goes with it as just any kind of companion, but as its creator and Lord.[63] This means that Barth holds that the divine accompanying is different from an understanding of "law"—natural or otherwise.[64] It is also different from either material causes or formal ones (as norms)—Barth maintains that the God who is revealed as the Father of Jesus Christ is not the world-soul. In addition to the above delimitations, Barth also denies that the divine activity accompanies that of the creature. In contrast to this older view, he maintains that there is "one indivisible op-

59. Ibid., 76–77.
60. Ibid., 84.
61. Ibid., 91.
62. Ibid., 92.
63. Ibid., 93.
64. Ibid., 126.

eration" of creator and creatures which is revealed in Scripture.[65] The divine activity is simple and united, but also manifold rather than uniform, monotonous, or undifferentiated.[66] Barth understands the operation of God in the divine accompanying to be a "fatherly operation"—God is not only Lord and Master, but also "our Father in Jesus Christ, the eternal Father of all His creatures."[67] The divine accompanying is the activity of a God that is not impersonal, not some kind of principle, but is in fact the continuing care of a Father and creator for his children and the work of his hands.

The Divine Ruling

The concept of the divine ruling holds a special place in Barth's understanding of the divine providence. He maintains that it "is decisive for the whole doctrine."[68] This is where the examples become concrete in Barth's understanding of providence—the "how" of the interaction between God and the world. Barth maintains that the rule of God means first of all that God alone rules—as a father, with a "meaning and purpose, plan and intention."[69] This does not mean that the believer can make deductions from God's transcendence to various aspects of world occurrence.[70] But is does mean that God controls creaturely activity, both in the divine preservation (as detailed above) and in the end or goal toward which the creature is oriented. "Both in general and in particular God Himself [sic] fixes for the creature its goals . . . ."[71] The common goal of creation is God in God's own Self.[72] The particular goals are varied, but they are directed to and swallowed up in the common, all-encompassing goal of God's own Self.

How it is that Barth comes to this conviction? It is, not surprisingly, in and through the revelation of the Scriptures that comes to the community by the power of the Spirit. It is only as the community "sets in [the relationship of reality to idea] its confession of the Father, the Almighty, the Creator of heaven and Earth . . . that the thinking and perceiving and confessing

---

65. Ibid., 131–33.
66. Ibid., 137.
67. Ibid., 154.
68. Ibid.
69. Ibid.
70. Ibid., 162.
71. Ibid., 167.
72. Ibid. Again, similar to Aquinas and the tradition.

become an activity filled with real meaning."[73] This is not a philosophical God, which Barth holds even if it did exist would not do justice to this concept of providence. This Biblical God is the King of Israel who is also the King of the World who rules all things.[74] This is not an intellectual understanding, but a relational and confessional one. Barth asserts that this confessional experience of the divine ruling escapes the conundrums of a philosophical God:

> Belief or unbelief in the divine world-governance, whether we do or do not apprehend and confess it, it no longer a matter of the right or wrong development of the idea, but of the right or wrong relationship to this reality to which the idea has reference.[75]

This confessional understanding of the rule of God is at the heart of Barth's exposition of the history of salvation or history of the covenant between creature and Creator as the key to understanding the divine providence.

In his development of the idea of the history of salvation, Barth goes through the Biblical material trying to illustrate the character of the "I am" in the Hebrew Scriptures and the Christian New Testament. He holds that

> the rule of God as opposed to the control and outworking of a natural or spiritual cosmic principle is characterized by the fact that it is here in the particular events of the Old and New Testaments, in the 'I am' spoken and actualised [sic] by the king of Israel, in the covenant of free grace instituted and executed, promised and fulfilled by Him, that it has the centre [sic] which controls and is normative for every thing else.[76]

This history of the covenant is related to the events of the history of the world as their center and key.[77] In this understanding of God's rule there is no conceptual solution to the difficulties of life, but Barth holds that there is "something far greater and better, the fact of a relationship between the Creator and His [sic] creatures . . . ."[78] This leads beyond the seemingly insurmountable difficulties of a philosophical or historical consideration of the divine rule to an existential participation in the dynamic of salvation. "The

---

73. Ibid., 176.
74. Ibid., 176–77.
75. Ibid., 177.
76. Ibid., 183.
77. Ibid., 186.
78. Ibid., 189.

idea of divine world-governance is no longer a theoretical and speculative idea. It is a practical ('existential') idea."[79] All history is understood from the perspective of one who is a participant in the history of the covenant of free grace between the Lord of the World and "his" beloved creatures.

This view of salvation history as the center and key to understanding the divine ruling leads Barth to pay special attention to four extra-biblical areas of world history. He maintains that, seen through the eyes of faith, they are "certain constant elements" which point to the divine world rule, standing "in a special relationship to the history of the covenant and salvation."[80] These four areas are: the history of the Scriptures; the history of the church; the history of the Jews; and the limitation of human life. Barth sees these as "standing permanent, objective reminders that the penetration [of God] did occur at that point,"[81] and that it might again. Thus we see that the divine ruling is a conviction the believer comes to within a community of faith, and is something that she or he confesses rather than is argued into. The Christian becomes convinced that God preserves and accompanies her or him in their journey of life, and that God rules the cosmos in which she or he finds herself or himself. The believer comes to confess this as she or he comes to believe, through the Word of God, that the King of Israel mentioned in the Bible is also the King of the World, and is the Creator and Father of everything that is.

The Christian Under the Universal Lordship of God the Father

In this final section of his doctrine of providence, "The Christian Under the Universal Lordship of God the Father," Barth addresses what the life of the Christian as such will be. It is basically a theological anthropology. First, the subject who affirms the doctrine of providence is a "living member of the Christian community, the Christian."[82] The Christian is not her or his own lord—s/he cannot be that, and yet s/he is not anxious.[83] The believer has a choice to either affirm or deny her or his creaturely status—although, from the perspective of a Christian, this of course does not change that status. There is no occasion for self-glorification in the Christian life. The Chris-

79. Ibid., 194.
80. Ibid., 199.
81. Ibid., 200.
82. Ibid., 239.
83. Ibid., 240.

tian sees Jesus Christ in humiliation and exultation, and sees that she or he belongs to Jesus Christ and is at his disposal. This view of oneself is not more honest that not admitting it—the Christian is "simply made real by what he [sic] sees."[84] There are three things which Barth sees the Christian attitude being made up of: faith, obedience, and prayer. Barth understands faith to be "the receiving of the word of God as such."[85] He understands obedience to be "the doing of the Word of God as such."[86] And, prayer is the "simple and basic form of the first two forms of Christian attitude, faith and obedience."[87] Prayer is not centered primarily on praise, worship, or penitence and confession. For Barth, prayer is primarily in the asking, and in the feeling that one can ask, and hope to receive. "Petition [is] the constitutive element in what takes place in prayer."[88] Thus we see prayer as the element in which faith and obedience take their forms in the Christian life, which is living under the providential direction of the Lordship of God the Father.

Helpful Emphases

There is much to be said in favor of a doctrine that takes the action of God out of the vagaries of historical happenings. No matter what happens in history—World War I, World War II, the Holocaust (all of which Barth lived in and through)—God's Lordship can still be maintained. Nothing can touch such an understanding. Another aspect that weighs (emotionally, at least) in favor of Barth's characterization is that it touches and draws from the rhythms and language of traditional Christian piety. Although he steadfastly maintains that his is not a "pious worldview," his use of traditional language and pastoral cadences can have an effect in the listener of reiterating the point that no matter what happens, God is in control. Such continuity with the tradition can be a great good. It allows one to access the resources of the Christian tradition with a minimum of "translation" into the idiom of today, providing a bridge between the past and the future. And, finally, Barth's understanding tries to do justice to the reality of the spiritual life, where one feels so connected to and dependent on the source

---

84. Ibid., 242.
85. Ibid., 246.
86. Ibid., 253.
87. Ibid., 265.
88. Ibid., 267.

of one's being that any question of the experience seems totally false, even irreverent and blasphemous.[89] All these are reasons (with varying degrees of persuasiveness) to maintain a doctrine of providence that is close to Barth's—one based on a confession of the revealed word in Scripture, rather than any sort of wider analysis—historical, philosophical, sociological, or otherwise—with an attempt to discern the activity of God revealed there.

At the same time, such a view cannot, in the final analysis, be adequate for a contemporary doctrine of providence. Precise attention to the content of the revelation of the Scriptures, and its disjunction with other aspects of contemporary life, will show that Barth's view, while rich and multiform in its analysis, cannot ultimately be adopted whole cloth. That the experience of God's providence is a confession of faith is a given. Such a view could not be held by an atheist, or a Buddhist, or a skeptic. However, it is not constrained to the content of the Scriptural view. Let us examine Barth's views in more detail in order to see in what ways they fall short, and in what directions they can point us as we search for an adequate contemporary doctrine of providence.

Problems with Content . . .

There are several points at which the concrete content of Barth's view of providence are very hard for the contemporary person (such as myself) to absorb and existentially affirm. This takes place primarily at the level of his patriarchal and royalist metaphors, summed up in the phrase that Barth uses in his inimitable manner to sum up the creature/Creator relation: "The Christian Under the Universal Lordship of God the Father." Such a characterization of the ultimate relation between the Christian and God is one that many people find unable to affirm in any sort of good faith. Let us briefly turn to questions of Fatherhood and Kingship, and see why these are difficult to affirm, and also examine what such difficulties can tell us about our problems with a view based solely on the confession of any sort of revelation.

---

89. There are, Barth's protests notwithstanding, echoes of Schleiermacher in his attitude toward the religious experience of being a Christian under the universal Lordship of God the Father. Barth would, of course, say that the difference in characterization between absolute dependence as such and Christian life makes all the difference in the world. I am not so sure . . .

First, let us turn to the question of kingship. Barth is convincing in his outlining of the history of the covenant between God and human beings takes place, in the revelation of the Bible, in a relation of a creature to the creator, in a relation of a subject to a Lord. This is the way in which the Scriptures, in general, outline the relation between God and the people with whom he has a special relationship. However, in this contemporary context, the language of kingship has become and remains problematic. The institution of monarchy is an unjust one, and has been dying out for at least 200 years. The European constitutional monarchies are not the kind of monarchies of the Bible, and the kind of hierarchical, absolutist regimes that they were tend to get called "dictatorships" and are the subject of numerous popular insurrections. The idea that one person owns an entire area of the world, with rights to all its people and places and anything that comes from them, has been effectively called into question by the political events of the last 200 or so years.[90] The question is, at its roots, similar to the question of slavery. If the relation of persons owning one another is unjust, so is the relation of one person having the absolute rights to the life and livelihood of another. Such relations are, on their face, unjust, and no longer tolerated by the majority of the world's population. Such a situation makes it increasingly difficult to speak of the relation of kingship as the way in which to understand the relation between God and human beings.

Barth, of course, will point out that the Kingship of God over the Christian is not of this kind, but he argues against the logic of the revelation that he tries at other times to hold close. The fact of the matter is that in the Bible, monarchy is assumed to be a correct relation between God and human beings. God is the monarch to be obeyed, over against all other (merely) human monarchs. If it is a question of which king is to be obeyed, the question of the correct monarch to owe one's allegiance to, then monarchy itself is not called into question, but is assumed to be *in the ultimate sense*, (that is, in the relation between God and human beings), the correct way of relation between beings of different powers.[91] Barth, of course, says that the difference between submission to God and submission to earthly powers is different, and that all human beings are equal in their dependence upon the grace of God, and in their subject status—God alone

---

90. For example, the famous quote by King James of Great Britain in 1603—"I am the husband and the whole island is my lawful wife"—such an attitude, with its overtones of sexual and legal proprietorship is unacceptable today.

91. Charles Taylor makes this point powerfully, albeit in a slightly different way, in *A Secular Age*.

rules. This is a possible interpretation, if it were not for two things. First, the habit of submission is not easy to break, once instilled. Barth's continual insistence upon the complete and total divine rule runs counter to creaturely freedom, his own protests notwithstanding. Those insisting on the divine right of kings understood this. And, second, the tradition and teachings of the church have most often come down on the side of submission to earthly authorities as well: from Paul, through Augustine and Aquinas, to Luther's "two swords" doctrine, to Kant's notion of duty as the primary virtue, submission to God and King (or other authority) are often spoken of in the same breath.[92]

Barth himself seems to be speaking out of both sides of his mouth as he holds that God "directs [all creatures] to one goal and subordinates them all to His [sic] own operation" while in the next sentence proclaiming that God "does not suppress them in their distinctiveness over against His [sic] own operation."[93] Of course, he holds that it is precisely in God's activity that creatures have their own creaturely dignity. But he does seem to be arguing against such a characterization in his attempt to remain faithful to the language of the Bible. His examples of the creature as a servant and an instrument are concrete realizations of this difficulty. The "service" that the creature renders is a "pure service in which the servant can have in view no purpose or advantage of his own,"[94] and an instrument has no effect on the purposes of its wielder. Both of these examples reinforce the notion that hierarchical power relations are well and good, and indeed are instantiated in the ultimate nature of things. Such a view is a close and careful exposition of the revelation of God in the Bible.

In much the same fashion, the continual insistence upon the Fatherhood of God, and that Father's control over his children, is unacceptable for a contemporary understanding of providence. Many of the reasons for the unacceptability of divine parent-language are explored in greater detail in chapter seven, but a quick sketch of the difficulties will suffice to make much the same point as the problems with divine king language. Insofar as this Father is understood as ruling over or controlling the fortunes and trajectories of his children's lives, such a characterization is not useful in

---

92. All the attempts to show resistance to earthly authorities in the tradition notwithstanding, much of the received tradition—perhaps that which has come down to us—has been on the side of the established order.

93. Barth, *Church Dogmatics*, III/3, 188.

94. Ibid., 46.

a culture that sees such control as hampering genuine human fulfillment. Again, Barth can make the same caveat that the nature of the divine accompanying, preserving, and ruling that characterizes the Fatherly relation is so different from anything human that it implies a qualitative difference. The point against such a contention is the same as against kingship—if this is so, then why use the metaphors at all, and why do we have to argue against the plain meaning of the tradition that Barth tries to gain his content from? If, in so arguing that kings and fathers who rule, constraining the orientations and activities of their subjects and children, do so in such a different manner from the normal understanding of the words that they are not commensurate, then the attempt to save the tradition becomes less and less convincing. If, on the other hand, the relation of the tradition is affirmed, even in the face of the seeming difficulties, then the question of why a seemingly unjust relation should be affirmed as ultimately correct rears its ugly head. These problems with the content of Barth's doctrine of providence based on confession of the revelation of God in the Bible leads us to some reflections on the method that led to such a characterization.

. . . Leading to Problems with Method: Adequacy, Worldviews, and the "Nevertheless"

Keeping in mind our discussion of the problems in the characterization of the divine-human relation as one of king-subject or father-child, the question remains as to what gives the reason why one feels that such a characterization is inadequate. If the relation between a king and a subject is in its nature unjust, what gives this information and conviction? It must be something from outside the tradition, because the tradition teaches that such a relation is in fact just. Thus, an account of the divine providence, God's hand in history will, if it is to be adequate, must take the question of the critique of the tradition into account as well, and have some more formal and generalized way of accounting all the intuitions of love, joy, freedom, and communion that are part and parcel of the felt and confessed experience of God's providential care. A contemporary doctrine of providence must have a wider point of view then merely that of the tradition.

Essentially, the question is one of paying attention to the current activity of God, and not making the past activity normative for the present and future. It is a question of attending to the activity of God in history, and realizing that the past understandings may not be adequate to present

Bultmann and Barth

situations. Barth, of course, does point in this direction by saying the God will not do the same thing tomorrow as today. However, his insistence that the account of the activity of God in history follow the general outlines presented in the Bible leave very little room for truly radical critique. If one is to say that God is not a Father at all, and that this way of understanding God as parent contributes to spiritual and political infantilism, Barth would call such a characterization illegitimate, on the basis of its being contrary to the revelation of God in the Bible. Such a view constrains one's view of the activity of God and is not properly universal. A method that holds that the confession of the revealed information about God and the world from the Bible is not adequate as it does not take into account the totality of experience.

In addition to the questions of the suitability of understanding God as King and God as Father, and the implications of such views for the proper method for coming to an understanding of God's activity in the world, there are other questions of method as well. One of the most important of these is Barth's insistence that there can be nothing like a "Christian worldview," that the attempt to formulate such a view lead to denying the faith of Christianity.[95] Why is such a view necessary? Why does the making of system preclude (*necessarily*, according to Barth), on-going participation in the Christian faith? Perhaps the adoption of a systematic element can lead to a greater insight. It is certainly possible that people will come to worship their own systems (which is what Barth is concerned with), or try to substitute correct thinking for a right relationship with the divine—something like a "gnostic" type of spirituality. Such a result is *possible*—but it is not *necessary*. Why isn't it possible to have a worldview that that includes God? Barth says such a view is necessarily impossible because in making up such a system we give ultimate allegiance to the system rather than God. I don't see that this follows if we truly remember that the worldview is provisional. Barth, of course, has no problem with "provisional worldviews" but prefers them to be naturalistic, rather than theistic or "Christian." Such views are getting close for his comfort to identifying God with a particular view. But, what if one took seriously that notion that all knowledge is provisional, and that we must continually be open to the leading of God, *and* that God was involved in such and such a fashion (to the best of our provisional knowledge) in the coming to be and passing away of the larger project of history or world-occurrence or something like that? Why does a dialogi-

---

95. Ibid., 55–57.

cal, relational view that considers all aspects of culture and history to be potentially revelatory of God have to be idolatry? Why cannot we perceive God and God's action outside and independent of revelation? And why does revelation have to hold the key to the other aspects?

In an sense, I am arguing for the view that while confession of the providential activity of God is the *sine qua non* for a doctrine of providence, such confession does not have to conform to Barth's view of revelation. Christianity is wider than his view, and one can easily have different understandings than Barth's of the nature and activity of Jesus, and what it means for an understanding of history, and still be within the Christian tradition. Indeed, other constructions which take wider points of view are more adequate to the notion that God is potentially revealed in all aspects of creation and culture, and can therefore dialogue with the tradition as well.

In fact adopting a view such as Barth's also implies a system, albeit one that comes from the revelation of the Scriptures, rather than something from a philosophical source. But can't a system such as Barth's also have ill effects? Can't the confession of faith in Jesus Christ also become empty words, in which the intellectual understanding of such a view substitutes for the freeing relation?

One more point regarding the difficulty of Barth's confessional and revelational method that will continue to have resonance as we discuss the relation between God and history is the question of the relation between how one understands world-occurrence generally and the so-called "special" revelation of God in the history of the covenant. It is not possible to have a strictly revelational view without reference to and dialogue with actual world occurrence. Barth admits something like this as he points to creation as the external basis of the covenant. God's providential activity takes place somewhere. This point would be that the ideas about how the site where the divine activity takes place *matter* as one constructs a doctrine. If one has a worldview something like Spengler's view of the decline of the west, then the responses to the providential activity of God will take a different form than if one has an Hegelian view of the progress of the World-Spirit. The view of God's activity and the view of its context condition one another. The providence of God and the worldview in which they take place form a dialectical relation: they cannot be as separate as Barth would like them to be.

Barth, of course, would like to say that there is an absolute distinction between the history of world-occurrence and the history of the covenant. He holds that world-occurrence as such does not speak unequivocally. A point that needs to be made is that the history of the covenant does not speak unequivocally either, and why therefore is a distinction made? There is no categorical reason why insights from other areas, such as ideals from outside the Christian tradition, should not form a dialectical ongoing process by which we try to discern the hand of God in the providential activity of the world. Perhaps the point can be made by saying that we are not only creatures under the universal Lordship of God the Father, but also human beings in a variety of social circumstances, which are dialectically related. Concepts from the natural world, from religious and moral experience, do make a difference—they cannot be sundered from a consideration of God's activity in the world, and they affect one's understanding of that activity.

Barth, of course, does not think that world-occurrence as such does not reveal God, nor does he in fact hold that the history of the covenant is entirely without difficulty—just that the revelation of God's activity in the Scriptures, understood in and through the key of God's activity in Jesus Christ, is the normative understanding, and is to be confessed "Nevertheless" even when such a view seems equivocal with regard to some other understanding. It is the revelation of God in Jesus Christ and therefore in the Scriptures that, even though at times seemingly difficult, is to be affirmed by those who are Christians and who confess a *Christian* doctrine of providence.

Why is such a strong confession of God's providential activity at difficult points necessary? Why must we hold that God works "Nevertheless," even when "the orders and contingencies of nature, the works of caprice and the cleverness or folly, the goodness or badness of men seem to be the only reality"?[96] Why cannot we hold that at times, the aims of God get thwarted, and that the world is at times a tragic place? Why must we conceive of God's activity being "freely and graciously and mightily present and active at these points too"?[97] If one cannot see something of God's activity, then why should we confess it? Or, rather, (and this is the key point of the matter) why can we not say that God's activity is not the only activity in the world, and that the activity of other forces is not entirely controlled, and that sometimes things simply go awry? Such an understanding would

96. Ibid., 44.
97. Ibid.

be consistent, clear, and still do justice to a confessional worldview. In fact, it might be said to do more justice to a Biblical worldview that sees human beings as actors on the historical stage as well, with real actions and effects, than Barth's more monist view of God's overruling, or his concern to preserve the honor and glory of God as redeemer, without allowing any creaturely participation in the process at all.

Indeed, some kind of view that has more creaturely activity in the working out of God's providence will be necessary to have an adequate contemporary doctrine of providence. It is not an affront to God's dignity or an attempt to take the divine prerogative to point out that human beings have real work to do in the divine plan and activity, and that it takes place as a result of their cooperation with the divine aims. Barth's protestations notwithstanding, an adequate contemporary doctrine of providence will have work for the creatures to do beyond being the servant only doing the master's bidding, or the instrument that only moves when pushed by its user. It is, primarily, a question of being adequate to contemporary experience of the nature of being human, the nature of the divine call, and the nature of the two and their interaction. A contemporary doctrine of providence will have to take all aspects of the dialectical, processive qualities of existence in general into account if it is to be adequate to the experience of God's providential activity.

DIRECTIONS FOR FURTHER REFLECTION

Thus we see that while there are important foundations for building a contemporary doctrine of providence to be found in Barth and Bultmann's reflection on the subject of God and history, we can adopt neither whole cloth if we wish to be adequate both to the nature of the discussion and to contemporary experience and reflection on the subject. There are, however, many important emphases to be taken from both thinkers.

From Bultmann (as with other existentialists), the primacy of the call of and response to God being determinative of Christian life is a point which the contemporary doctrine of providence can find useful. It is in the primacy of the religious life, in the experience of God in the world, that the paradigmatic understanding of God's activity in the world is seen. In addition, the idea that we are activity engaged in making meaning in history as we participate in its flow is another insight that we can take from Bultmann as we attempt to construct a contemporary doctrine of providence.

However, without any concrete relation to history and historical activity, such existential views lose their contexts and meanings. Also, they are excessively individualistic and do not consider the real relations between people. Individual meaning is not the only criteria for activity—the social effects must also be considered. Individual meaning as such, without orientation to contexts, is not adequate for a contemporary doctrine of providence.

Indeed, it is precisely the almost total lack of content in Bultmann's view about providence that makes his reflection not the strongest foundation upon which to build. He shies away from pointing to any place at which God acts in history, and even holds that trying to find such a view would be illegitimate. Clearly, more reflection will have to take place before God's providential care can be adequately outlined and accounted for.

Barth's more content-rich view offers more concrete suggestions than Bultmann's paucity of content, but in the end it, too, is less than adequate for a contemporary doctrine of providence. Perhaps the most important point that Barth makes is that any discussion of providence will be a confessional one—that is, it will take place as an insider, rather than an outsider discussion. In part, the confession of the providential care of God for the world *is* what it means to be a believer. In addition, Barth, in and through his rich dialogue with the tradition, points out the benefits of seeing oneself as grounded in and conversing with the hosts of interpreters that have gone before. Such a sense of strength and the close attention to the question as detailed from a variety of viewpoints are certainly aspects that should be part of any contemporary doctrine of providence.

However, Barth, too, is ultimately not the answer as we seek to build an adequate understanding of God's activity in the world. This is primarily because much of his content, replete with royal and patriarchal language, is not available for many contemporary people who wish to describe God's activity in the world. Insofar as language about God as Father or King is unacceptable, much of Barth's doctrine of providence will be unacceptable as well. Indeed, the unacceptability of his language itself points to the narrowness of the method of the confession of revelation that Barth uses in detailing the divine activity. If such language is unacceptable, we must pay attention both to the fact of its unacceptability and to the suggestion that a wider method is called for. That the tradition outlines something like Barth's view is fairly clear, although it could be disputed. Also, that such language does not account well for contemporary experience of the divine activity is also exceedingly clear. Thus, some wider method will need to be engaged, that can account for the activity of God in and through all things, and also allow some critique of parts of the tradition that are unhelpful. In addition, Barth's view does not take fully into account the interdependent nature of creation and the covenant, and the fact that the ideas about one affect the other, and vice versa. Expecting the history of the covenant, *a priori*, to be the interpretive key of the understanding of the doctrine of providence is not adequate to the nature of the situation.

So we see that further reflection on the doctrine of providence demands several directions. First, it will need to account for the historical and historicized nature of human existence, by paying close attention to the facts of history as a context in which the providential activity of God takes place. It will also need to provide a method that can account for diverse points of view, both from within and outside the tradition. In addition, it will need to have a dialectical, processive orientation that will be adequate to religious experience, to the interdependent nature of history and its contexts, and to the availability of the content of such a doctrine to the contemporary believers. It must be adequate to the multi-faceted experiences of the contemporary mind. With these points in mind, let us turn to a thinker who pays very close attention to the processes and occurrences of history, and to the role that his understanding of "God" plays in them: William Dean.

3

Historicism
History as Theology, History without God

HISTORICISM AND WILLIAM DEAN[1]

IN WORKING TOWARD A contemporary doctrine of providence, the relation between God and history, the understanding of history needs to be taken extremely seriously—it is, after all, at least half of the discussion. The theological discussion of history has been rich and varied in the twentieth century, with Barth, Bultmann, Tillich, both Niebuhrs, Gilkey, Ogden, Pannenberg, Mark C. Taylor, and others weighing in with major contributions. While this study cannot hope to make a full inquiry into each of their views, an examination of at least one major thinker who has taken the impact of historical consciousness on theology seriously is necessary in order to see what impact a modern historical view has for a contemporary doctrine of providence. We will therefore examine William Dean's historicism that looks back to the radical empiricism of James and Dewey, the early Chicago School and the empirical theology that followed it for inspiration in elucidating the relationship between God and history. Dean's efforts can serve as a cautionary example: exemplary in his willingness to take the question of historical reductionism seriously and wrestle with the

---

1. A version of this chapter was published previously in the *American Journal of Theology and Philosophy*. Used by permission. See Zbaraschuk, "Not Radical Enough."

neopragmatists and deconstructionists espousing it; and cautionary in that he illustrates the difficulties of attending too closely to the strictly historical without taking into account moral, aesthetic, and religious experience.

There are many aspects of Dean's historicism that are attractive and helpful in thinking of the question of providence. Not the least of these is his insistence that any statements about God and religion be grounded in their historical contexts. Thus for Dean, his own statements will take into account American history, philosophy, and theology, and will attempt to answer the question, "To what extent will an American historicist concept of God make a practical difference in the lives of those who accept it?"[2] This attention to the actualities of history can provide a useful counterpoint to the more theological orientation of Bultmann and Barth, testing their theories against the historical record of the tradition and also challenging it. Dean's penetrating analysis of historical occurrences, his willingness to wrestle with the "methodolotry" of the postmodern relativists from the standpoint of radical empiricism, and his localism and specificity are all helpful emphases in working towards a contemporary doctrine of providence.

In the final analysis, however, Dean's historicism falls short of being much help in the quest to construct a doctrine of providence. This is primarily because his understanding of God as a "sacred convention" or "the spirit of history or "mystery" is too weak and morally ambiguous to provide a religiously satisfying doctrine of providence. Too much emphasis by Dean on the historical *characterization* of God leads to a loss of belief in God as such, and thus the ability to think seriously about any sort of relationship between God and history. Dean's attempt at "radical empiricism" is not radical enough—he does not take enough into account the moral, aesthetic, and religious intuitions that are at the heart of the Jewish and Christian religious traditions he wishes to historicize. God is swallowed up in history, and his attempt at an historicized theology becomes instead a history of theology.

THE UNREALITY OF GOD: CONVENTIONS, HISTORICISMS, ETC.

Dean's first work on the subject of an historicized theology is at first glance promising. In *History Making History: The New Historicism in American*

2. Dean, *History Making History*, 144.

Historicism

Religious Thought, Dean takes deconstructionists and neopragmatists to task for their lackluster doctrine of God—they can

> see no more in the concept of God than a heritage of lucky and unlucky guesses—lucky when they turn out to have some utility, unlucky when they did not. They offer no explanation for how those guesses were reached. Nor do they account for the religious person's crucial claim that, when they know God, they know something...[T]oday's new historicist would claim that theological research would have nothing to do with religious experience and everything to do with pragmatic tests of what must be subjective fantasies.[3]

For Dean, this is clearly not adequate. He would like to hold that there is something beyond pragmatically effective subjective fantasies in the idea of God.

Yet while condemning their efforts, he offers not much more himself. Instead of their distrust of the notion of God in totality, Dean's historicism would not move toward any

> effort to state the *a priori*, metaphysical or context-independent truths about God, [recognizing] the extent to which American thought about God is really the thought of a national community and that it can attain little more than a 'correspondence between theoretical statements and the facts as they are described' from an American context.[4]

What would the practical difference between the two views be? On the one hand, Dean's view has content—the historical writing that people say is about God. However, this writing is about a social construction, not an actual divine reality. What is the difference between a more generalized notion of God as "writing," the position of Mark C. Taylor that Dean critiques, and the specific writing done in an American context about God? Dean's viewpoint does not take into account his own criticism leveled at the deconstructionists and neopragmatists, that people who believe in God believe in something, except in this very minor way—if someone followed Dean's viewpoint instead of Mark C. Taylor's, they would attend to the pragmatic efficacy of an American construct of God rather than a European-influenced deconstructed one. However, the primary objection toward such a characterization of God is not the continental origin

3. Ibid., 142–43.
4. Ibid., 144.

and specific characteristics of the subjective (even if socially constructed) fantasy—it is the difference between fantasy and reality, between God as a human construct (no matter how pragmatically efficacious) and God as a living reality. This is not to say, of course, that our concepts of God are not constructed. Of course they are. But Dean's version of historicism gives no reason to believe that there is anything to which the construction refers any more than the other "new historicists" he critiques.

In fairness to Dean, his book *History Making History* is his self-described methodological statement,[5] in which he offers suggestions for a direction to move, rather than much specific constructive work of his own. That constructive work comes in his next book, *The Religious Critic in American Culture*, which is a theoretical statement of why he thinks religious criticism is important, why it is not practiced by many religious intellectuals in America, how it could be practiced more effectively in the present situation, and the case study/inspirational story of William James, who Dean sees as the "last great religious critic" of American culture. The inadequacy of Dean's doctrine of God, however, continues from his methodological statement to his constructive one. His idea of God as a "religious convention" and his insistence upon the moral ambiguity of the sacred convention are especially inadequate for a contemporary doctrine of providence. In addition, Dean's analysis of the role of the religious critic and his suggestions that she or he could best flourish in the non-university third sector undermine his ambiguous sacred convention and point toward a different notion of God than the one he espouses.

Let us first turn to Dean's notion of God as the "sacred convention" of American culture. Dean holds that conventions are the best way to understand the persistence of talk about rights and morals in an age of relativism,[6] and also offer an example of the best way to speak about God. "Conventionalism explains the coherence of what happens in most Western societies today, where normative worldviews are affirmed even though universal grounds for those worldviews are not."[7] Conventions are thought of as "real," in the pragmatic sense that they have effects. It is also a "reality apart from its effects, so that it is not simply what it is interpreted to be, even though what it is interpreted to be can alter its identity." It is a "mystery" in itself, although it is "not a person or a subject of any sort, nor

5. Ibid., xi.
6. Dean, *Religious Critic*, 102–4.
7. Ibid., 105.

Historicism

is it an object. Rather, it is a social, or relational, reality that exists not only in time but through time."[8] Thus, according to Dean, "conventionalism explains how religious critics can be relativistic, pluralistic, and historicist and yet be realists and work publicly" helping to "criticize and reconstruct the spiritual culture of a nation."[9] His example of a convention that operates in society is the American Constitution, that is real, has effects, has a sort of "life of its own," is interpreted, yet is not the sum of its interpretations and sometimes "takes initiatives" that are surprising.[10]

There is much of this analysis that is helpful to a doctrine of providence. Dean's insistence upon the constructed character of any conception of God (or as he prefers, "the sacred"), and his close analysis of its functions in society are points well taken. Surely it is true that concepts of God are historically conditioned by their philosophical, social, historical, and even personal contexts. The notion of social conventions as a way to look at certain aspects of traditions and examine the way they work is helpful in leading to greater understanding of the traditions in question. The question, though, of whether or not the convention is the best way to understand God is not answered by pointing to the existence of conventions in religious thought and practice. The real question is: are there conventions about God, or is God a convention? Dean would collapse the distinction between the two questions, insisting that we only have conventions. I would disagree, pointing to the reality of God beyond, behind, and in the transcendence of, the conventions about the Divine Reality.

That there is a reality behind the convention can be illustrated by the fact that religious experience does not always conform to the conventions of the society from which it comes. This is the point of novelty and advance in religious life and thought. From what does the inspiration for a new direction in the religious life of a society come? Why does a prophet, for example, write about the insistence upon morality rather than certain cultic observations? "I desired mercy, and not sacrifice,"[11] is a radical change in a sacrifice-oriented society. It could be that this novelty is based upon the genius and sensitivity of the individual, and the adequacy of their ideas to the situation the community finds itself in. But is that all there is in the religious life of an individual or a community? One empirical point is

8. Ibid.
9. Ibid.
10. Ibid., 136.
11. Hosea 6:6.

that many (not all) times, the person credits God (the reality) as being an inspiration for their ideas and actions. It could be that they are responding to the initiatives of their convention, and certainly they are to the degree that they are in conversation with their tradition. But in the cases in which those conventions are radically transcended, at pivotal points in the life of a tradition, it seems at least as rational to posit a reality behind the convention calling those participants to transcend certain aspects of it as to posit the convention as the only reality.

In addition to the question of the reality of something behind the convention, there is the question as to why Dean's historicism cannot abide any talk of a provisional theology beyond or behind the historical convention of the sacred. Certainly such discussions are part of the historical reality that Dean appeals to. Can one reduce a speculative theology to history? To do so would seem to so radically re-interpret the past statements that constitute the tradition Dean wishes to be in conversation with that he would make himself part of another tradition—that of Western atheism, rather than any kind of religious discourse. It would seem that he would need to take his own past more seriously.

Also, the idea of a convention fails Dean's own pragmatic test. An imaginary God is not efficacious, even if one talks about it as if it were real, if one really feels it to be imaginary. Dean, of course, would take issue with the label "imaginary," pointing to the Constitution as being very real. However, if God has only the same level of reality as the American Constitution, I do not think I err is calling such a God "imaginary," given the expectations people have of the word "God." Dean himself seems to recognize this lack of efficacy, as we shall see when we examine his later essay at the end of this chapter, which tries to correct the tendency towards a "pallid piety" in pragmatism and historicism. His own emphasis on historicism cannot provide for such a correction, however, because a sacred convention does not inspire worship or love, and certainly does not provide any basis for working towards a greater good, when it is understood as *nothing more* than a sacred convention.[12] The history of practice and doctrine is not a reason to change the world.[13]

---

12. The question, of course, is whether or not Dean believes that God is nothing more than a convention. He is coy about that, but I believe that he ultimately comes down on the unbelieving side. See his response to criticisms of his book in "Sheltering Skies: A Response," 98.

13. Both John Hick and John Cobb make this point in different ways. See Cobb, "In Defense of Realism," 196; and Hick, *An Interpretation of Religion*, 208.

Historicism

AMBIGUITY ALL THE WAY DOWN . . .

Perhaps the greatest challenge to Dean's usefulness for a contemporary discussion of divine providence comes out of his insistence upon the ambiguous nature of the sacred. Dean makes a powerful case for the consideration of the "moral ambiguity of God."[14] He criticizes John Dewey for not following through on his own radical empiricism and therefore for "[converting] dissonances that threaten the meaning of the whole into harmonies that preserve the meaning of the whole."[15] Dean maintains that there is no reason for this insistence in Dewey's own philosophy, and that it is an unneeded *ad hoc* argument that is the result of his liberal and positive approach to the subject, rather than an application of philosophical rigor.

In addition to the philosophical reasons for maintaining the ambiguity of the sacred convention he calls God, Dean also calls attention to evidences from the tradition that include evil in, or attribute evil to, God. He cites James Crenshaw's study *A Whirlpool of Torment*[16] which gives examples from the Hebrew Bible where God acts capriciously or unjustly. He approvingly cites Judith Plaskow's contention that "the denial of divine ambiguity is a denial of the real ambiguity of human experience or promotes a God unconnected with that experience" and her appreciation of her own tradition's "'refusal to disconnect God from the contradictory whole of reality.'"[17] He mentions Jesus' saying in the Christian New Testament: "I come not to bring peace, but a sword," and lauds Luther's and Calvin's recognition of "God's power and how this gave God a leading role in the dark side of history," calling their understanding mature and bold in its "willingness to find God, or whatever is ultimately important, not only in a sanitized portion of the whole of history, but in the whole of that history."[18] He points out that religious believers have given religious reasons for evil acts, such as slavery and the subjugation of women. Dean himself recognizes that such a characterization of God is a departure from even his own tradition of radical empiricism. Dewey, James, Bergson, Whitehead, Weiman—all these thinkers identified God with some form of good, in addition to or over against some notion of the whole. Dean calls attention

14. This is his term, not mine. Dean, *Religious Critic*, 140.

15. Ibid., 142.

16. Crenshaw, *Whirlpool of Torment*.

17. Plaskow, "Facing the Ambiguity of God," 70, cited in Dean, *Religious Critic*, 144–45.

18. Dean, *Religious Critic*, 145.

to the elements in the tradition and experience that speak otherwise, and decries any attempt to explain away the presence of evil in the sacred as not part of the "real" unity of ideals (Dewey) as "theological second-guessing." He holds that this doctrine of the ambiguity of God is "conventionalism's strength, not its weakness, for, in the last analysis, it lends historical realism to religious thought and encourages people not to rely entirely on the sacred and to be more responsible for religious developments."[19]

Dean has constructed a powerful challenge to the idea of the unmixed goodness of God. On the face of it, it appears that he has pointed out a major weakness in the tradition's characterization of the divine, and has a fuller, "rounder," picture of God and therefore God's relation to the world. However, on closer examination this proves not to be the case. Dean has not adequately addressed the philosophical and religious traditions from which he speaks, and cannot consistently hold positions inspired by his morally ambiguous God.

In arguing against Dean's morally ambiguous vision of God, we turn first to his examples from philosophy. Dean cites Dewey as a particular example of someone who got it *almost* right in his characterization of God. For Dewey, God is the "unity of ideal ends arousing us to desire and action"[20] giving us a sense of the mysterious whole and of our place within it. However, Dewey's God is also an "unambiguous force for goodness," rather than a force that promotes a sense of the whole as such. "For it [God] involves no miscellaneous worship of everything in general. It selects those factors in existence that generate and support our idea of good as an end to be striven for."[21] Dean finds no reason in Dewey's radical empiricism for such a separation between the good and bad in the divine convention, holding out the fact the historical traditions are morally ambiguous, and that the convention of the sacred must therefore be morally ambiguous as well. Dewey himself recognized much that was ambiguous in organized religion, and Dean points out that he should have attended to his own experience more closely.

Because he will only accept as evidence that which is historically based and conditioned, there is no possibility that Dean could recognize as "real" an orientation that inspires towards the good as such. His examination of the historical evidence would point out that it did not completely

---

19. Ibid., 143.
20. Dewey, *A Common Faith*, 42; cited in Dean, *Religious Critic*, 141.
21. Dewey, *A Common Faith*, 53; cited in Dean, *Religious Critic*, 142.

and at all times aim at the good, but at things which are considered evil. He thus considers any attempt to correct or criticize the mistakes of the past as "theological second-guessing."[22] This neglects a factor in experience that almost all of Dean's philosophical and theological forebears attended to as an important factor in their analysis of experience—the experience of *value* as a given in all experience.

Dean himself, in arguing against an epistemology of sense-data alone, cites Dewey, James, and Whitehead as favoring a radically empirical theory of knowledge that relies on "the full breadth of experience rather than on the five senses alone—on non-sensuous perceptions (the indirect, vague, and highly fallible experience of relations, values, affections) as well as on sense experience."[23] From Whitehead's perspective, there is no experience without its affective tone—we do not simply feel things as neutral, we feel them as good or bad, contributing to greater intensity or lesser, enlivening or deadening. "In its essence, mentality is the urge towards some vacuous definiteness, to include it in matter-of-fact which is non-vacuous enjoyment. This urge is appetition. It is emotional purpose: it is agency."[24] There is both loss and achievement, waste and satisfaction. Dewey, too, called attention to harmonizing rather than destructive attributes in his understanding of what God is.

This urge towards appetition, harmonization, with its concomitant assumption of value as an integral part of experience, argues against Dean's characterization of God as morally ambiguous. The reality of value within experience carries within it the assumption that there are states and things that contribute to value, and can affect it positively or negatively. Indeed, the experience of value as such orients the one who experiences that value toward preserving and increasing it. The idea of a good implies a morality that seeks that good. The urge to increase this value-in-experience is what the various thinkers Dean cites have identified with God, rather than the entire range of experience in all its ambiguous variety. Thus Whitehead separates the two ultimates of Creativity and God, Dewey's separate the "sense of the whole" from the "harmonious union of ideal ends" and James appeals to "the More" over against the mere addition of reality.[25] None of

22. Dean, *Religious Critic*, 143.
23. Ibid., 94.
24. Whitehead, *Function of Reason*, 32.
25. See James, *Varieties of Religious Experience*, 393–94, for a discussion of the "MORE." James' notion of the essence of religion is that there is an uneasiness in life

these thinkers confuse the whole of reality with the activity of God within that reality. An historicism such as Dean's, attending to the whole of the past tradition with uncritically equal weight, negates the experience of value in the present and the urge towards increasing that value in the future that are a great part of that tradition's ongoing life.

The next aspects of Dean's argument for the ambiguity of God is his citation of aspects of the tradition, both of Scripture and theological reflection, that have attributed evil to the divine. Again, upon a preliminary inspection, this interpretation appears to have some value—certain aspects of the tradition do in fact attribute evil to God. From an historicist and conventionalist view, this is the end of the matter. However, aside from the difficulties with the conventionalist view mentioned above, there are other considerations that oppose accepting the ambiguity of God within the tradition.

The first, and most obvious, of these considerations is that everything within the tradition does not count equally in formulating religious concepts. Even if one has Dean's methodology of attempting to accept the whole uncritically (and I have argued in the above section that this is untrue to his own radically empirical roots), there are elements in the tradition that call such formulations into question. The statement in the first Epistle of John stating that there is no darkness in God, and the elements in the Fourth Gospel about the identity of God and Love argue against an ambiguous God.[26] That both these statements emphasize the goodness of God, and others within the tradition attribute evil to God, are in the tradition is not in doubt—their substantive relation to one another is. It is too simple to say that because both statements exist in one's tradition God's nature is ambiguous.

Luther's concept of the "canon within a canon" offers an example within the tradition of downplaying certain elements to make a point. Luther wished to point out that aspects of the tradition that matched most closely with a certain theological orientation (namely, those that emphasized the sovereignty and grace of God) had priority over those that seemed to imply that humans were partners with God in some way, or could contribute to their own salvation. In developing such a doctrine, Luther illustrates clearly how and why certain theological emphases have more weight than

---

and religion is its solution, by virtue of the religious person's participation in the larger goodness, the "More."

26. 1 John 1:5; 4:8; John 3:16; 15:9–10.

others—because they conform with certain forms of religious experience. However, because Luther wants to claim that humanity is saved by the grace of God alone does not mean that the relation of God to humanity is just as he says, or more precisely that it is just as he says, and *also* that it is as his opponents say. The theological endeavor has not been, and is not, a practice of the addition of experiences and concepts. It has been, and is, a vast debate regarding the nature of God, the world, and humanity, and everything related to them. Dean's refusal to attend critically to an apparent disjunction in the tradition after identifying it is not a new theological methodology; it is simply his refusal to participate in the ongoing debate.

In a similar vein, his citation of people's use of religious reasons for acts that are later judged to be evil as evidence of the ambiguous nature of God is blind to what it means to be a religious participant in a tradition. Because one sees something that was done in response to a religious motivation as perverse or evil, it does not follow that God is evil or ambiguous. Dean's analysis of such an occurrence does not take into account the phenomena of mistakes and human fallibility. Dean, of course, calls this "reducing theology to second-guessing."[27] But I would maintain that it is precisely such "second-guessing" that constitutes one important strand of theological activity. In any theological endeavor that purports to be reformative of the tradition or oriented toward justice in society, the presence of which in the Jewish and Christian traditions cannot be doubted, the condemnation of the past activity in the name of God is the nature of the activity. Dean himself notes that "often historical societies prompted by a theological unity of ideals recognize—sometimes almost immediately—their impropriety," citing as examples the change in stance of some Israelis toward the Palestinians, some Christians toward other religions, and some Western religious traditions *vis-à-vis* women and blacks.[28] The recognition of and repentance from sinful mistakes does not signify divine moral ambiguity. Rather, it condemns the idolatry of placing human selfishness in the place of God's insistence upon justice and love. Certainly such an explanation would be in greater keeping with the understandings of the members of the traditions themselves.

After discussing the philosophical and traditional arguments for maintaining the moral ambiguity of God, Dean turns to cultural analysis to reinforce the notion. In one of the most interesting aspects of his argument,

---

27. Dean, *Religious Critic*, 142.
28. Ibid., 143.

The Purposes of God

Dean cites the world of American sports, wanting to point out the utterly ambiguous character of everyday existence. He does so in order to show that not only is there evil in the religious and historical realms, but that good and evil are so intertwined in commonplace events that there is no way to separate them and still have reality as it comes to us. He thus cites Joyce Carol Oates' analysis of boxing as highly metaphorical and morally ambiguous: "a powerful analogue of human struggle in the rawest of life and death terms"[29] ". . .in the brightly lit ring, man is *in extremis*, performing an atavistic rite or *agon* for the mysterious solace of those who can participate only vicariously in such drama; the drama of life in the flesh."[30] He also cites his own experiences at motor racing events and the brutality of professional football as other examples of ambiguous lived experience that are ignored by religious thinkers. "Too often American theology and public philosophy do what they can to isolate ultimate values from such evil and thus, to isolate religion and public philosophy from history."[31]

While Dean makes a good case for the ambiguous nature of historical existence, he makes the same mistake that he does in dealing with the ambiguity in religious traditions. To point out that everyday reality is ambiguous and has evil aspects does not mean that God ambiguous or evil. Certainly to "isolate religion and public philosophy from history" is one possible and historical response to the ambiguity of the world coupled with the doctrine of a good God.[32] Examples from the history of religion in America abound—the Shakers, the Oneida community, Seventh-day Adventism,[33] to name only a few. But Dean, with his insistence on historicism, should know that it is not the only one. There are also the Catholic modernists, the civil rights movement in the 1960s, even the religious right of the 1980s and 1990s, all of whom have a sense of evil in history, believe in a good God, and have chosen the route of historical engagement rather than isolation.

Those thinkers and activists who chose a life of engagement in history with an attempt to change or transform it illustrate their belief in a good God that attempts to do likewise. Those who believe in a good God do not

---

29. Oates, "The Cruelest Sport, 3; cited in Dean, *Religious Critic*, 147.
30. Oates, *On Boxing*, 116; cited in Dean, *Religious Critic*, 148.
31. Dean, *Religious Critic*, 148.

32. There is, of course, the question about whether these are the only reasons for such religious withdrawal from public life. I think that they are an important part of, but of course not the whole, story.

33. For a discussion of Seventh-day Adventism as an alternative to mainstream American life, see Bull and Lockhart, *Seeking a Sanctuary*, especially part II.

therefore deny the evil in the world—they affirm their belief in a God that is in constant communion with the world—not in the sense of *being* evil, but in *fighting against* it. Dean criticizes the empirical theologians for "making God's character independent of, and thus not truly interactive with, the dark or ambiguous side of history."[34] The religious believers who take their faith as a reason, even an imperative, to engage in history live out another option—that God does interact with the "dark side" by condemning it and working against it. They hold that God responds to the waste and evil in history by trying to ameliorate its effects and ultimately overcome it, not by "interacting" with it. God is *advocate*, not passive "interactor." This is perhaps the difference between the social function of "God" the convention, rather than God the Reality at the heart of every vision of goodness, truth, beauty, love, and justice that *is* religion.

To return to Dean's contention, then, that everyday reality is so thoroughly ambiguous that any theology or religious reflection that does not make its characterization of God also morally ambiguous is isolationist or not serious-minded, I have shown that his is not the only interpretation of the data of history, nor is it the response that best characterizes the responses of religious believers. His example of sports seems to be that we have boxing; it is morally ambiguous, and we shouldn't try to pretend that it's not. I maintain that his response is incomplete—taking something as it comes does not prevent someone from attempting to make a moral response to it and working for change in the future. Even Dean's example of boxing proves this point. People use gloves, limit their bouts to 15 2-minute rounds, and no longer fight to the death in professional prizefighting in today's world. In the Olympics, they use headgear and fight 3 rounds. There is a movement to ban boxing. Accepting reality as morally ambiguous does not mean that one should not strive to engage in moral action, and Dean's morally ambiguous convention-God provides no reason to do so.

THE RELIGIOUS CRITIC AS ULTIMATELY GOOD

This question of the morally ambiguous God failing the "pragmatic test" has two sides—on the one hand, there is the assertion that I have been making, that a morally ambiguous God provides no reason for acting morally, and that it is untrue to human experiences of value and engagement in religious traditions. On the other hand, there is the question of what an

---

34. Dean, *Religious Critic*, 77.

The Purposes of God

historically engaged project inspired by such a view of the divine would look like, and whether it would be consistent with its God. If Dean had a doctrine of providence it would be located here, at the level of human interaction with and the making of history is specifically informed by the ideas of God that the particular culture has and shares. In this case, his understanding of the role of the religious critic and her/his influence on history, by virtue of influencing others to appreciate the morally ambiguous "sense of the whole" that is the only God Dean recognizes, can be thought of as paradigmatic of the influence of God on history generally, Such a concept, we shall see, is self-contradictory as it does not do justice to the lived life of the traditions. Dean has provided us with suggestions toward such a project in his making the case that the home of the religious critic is in the "third sector" of American society, the non-profits, rather than in government or the university. His attempts at neutral language not withstanding, the constructive portion of his project has at its heart the sort of moral vision he denies at the heart of everything. Thus either Dean doesn't really believe in the morally ambiguous God, or chooses to ignore his characterization of the divine reality in his actual work that might impact history.

Such a consideration of the religious critic is necessary in order to see in the clearest possible fashion what Dean holds as the impact of God on history. He holds that the religious critic will, by virtue of her or his training and orientation, have the clearest view of what the "sacred reality," historically ensconced in the tradition, looks like in the historical sweep of things. Thus, the religious critic, by virtue of pointing out such activity (if it can be named as such in Dean's viewpoint), has the clearest vision and indeed can contribute to the activity of God in history. We will see that Dean's vision of God's activity and the religious critic's role in pointing it out and thus contributing to it is not in keeping with his own characterization and would indeed demand a different doctrine of God.

First, let us look more closely at Dean's suggestion that the "true home" of the religious critic is outside government, the private sector or the university, in the non-profit "third sector" of American society. This proposal takes into account his previous analysis of the separation and alienation of the university from the greater public life, due mainly to the professionalization and departmentalization of the university and its concern with "technical competence and status."[35] Dean links this professionalization with a loss of belief in American exceptionalism:

35. Ibid., 168; see also 20–21.

Historicism

> When American intellectuals lost their sense of participating in an American promise, they retreated into the university, became academic intellectuals, and largely abandoned public responsibility. They thought of themselves, not as those who might enlighten the citizenry of a unique democracy, but as physicists, philosophers, religious studies scholars, literary critics. Their talk was not now public talk but talk within an academic discipline and among academic intellectuals.[36]

Given these developments, Dean holds that the university is no longer a congenial place for those rare types who wish to speak to public life as a whole. Their duties are not oriented towards such endeavors, and they are not rewarded for it in an environment that is directed towards the goals of the profession. Neither will their natural home be in government or the private sector, with those organizations' emphases on votes or economic transactions, respectively. Instead, it will be in the "third sector" of non-profits, such as churches and charitable organizations, that the religious critic, who wishes to speak to something wider than the narrow specialization of a discipline, or the maximization of profit, or the maintenance of public order, will find her or his "psychological home." These organizations, while sometimes corrupt and/or wasteful, and not immune to the vagaries of poststructuralism, are still "by virtue of their organizational activities, inevitably more involved in public circumstances than universities are."[37] Dean cites a theoretical study of the third sector which maintains that its stock in trade, the way in which it interacts with the public, is best understood as "appeals to values," thus making it a natural fit for the religious critic, who wishes to appeal to a "sense of the whole" and further such a sense in public life. And, finally, being the good historicist that he is, Dean draws attention to a historical study that makes the case that "voluntary associations of the third sector have provided the historic wellspring of American social initiative."[38]

Dean's case for the natural home of the religious critic in the third sector is well-argued and historically sound, if not totally convincing. I am not as convinced as he is that the institution of government is only about the maintenance of civil order and is not also in some sense about the public good as well, and thus would also be a useful realm of activity

---

36. Ibid., 20.
37. Ibid., 167.
38. Ibid., 168.

for the religious critic. Nor does Dean's argument for locating the religious critic in the third sector support his stated intent of promoting a morally ambiguous God. His proposal for the new endeavor of the religious critic in the public sphere is filled with moral language. The main reason that he gives for a better fit between the religious critic and the non-university third sector is that "in the third sector, some vision of a common good is the highest order," whereas the university is "increasingly dedicated to professional activities that have little to do with the common good."[39] He posits that such third sector organizations will tend, because of their attempts to retain tax-exempt status, "to be conscious of their connection with a common good, even of their relation to the whole of society."[40] He cites the "third sector's imaginative appeals to value" that will "enable it to be the prime innovator, proving ground, and advocate for a society's evolving moral, aesthetic and spiritual life."[41]

In all these statements, and in his citation of the third sector as "the wellspring of American social initiative," there is a distinct orientation towards some idea of good, rather than evil. Of course, Dean could say that the "common good" is to be served not because it is moral, but because it is a term which does more justice to a sense of the whole. No one can argue that the concept of "common good" encompasses a wider range of vision and sense of the whole than academic arguments about an abstruse point regarding the theological orientation of 13th-century Christian mystics in Barcelona. However, such an appeal to the wideness of the term begs the question on two counts. The first is that such language is on its face the language of moral improvement. The second is that the use of aesthetic categories does not move one outside the language of morals.

Morality may in fact be subsumed in aesthetics—but perhaps a form of aesthetics that can best be spoken of in moral terms. Something like an appreciative awareness would be called for in order to examine in what direction the particular discussion should move, but this does not call morality as a binding and the best way to talk about experience into doubt. Dean's commitment, in a context of moral ambiguity, is to strive toward the good, even while recognizing the conditioned nature of "the good." He is not arguing for a-morality.

---

39. Ibid., 161.
40. Ibid., 163.
41. Ibid., 170.

Historicism

Dean's final definition of a sacred convention or God is one that "operates as an inspiration that prompts action"[42] towards a greater apprehension of "the whole." But it is not irrelevant to ask if that action is good or evil, even considering our discussion of morality and aesthetics above. Dean wishes to contribute to public life in America as a religious critic (or wishes to inspire others to do so), but he himself seems to think that both professionalism and deconstruction have hampered university people's ability to do so because of their amorality and limited vision. He advises these same university people to look to the non-university third sector precisely because of its emphasis on "the common good." If "the whole" is understood as Dean wishes it to be understood, than the action prompted by the inspiration of the sacred convention could be for the common evil. It seems difficult to believe that the religious critic would want to promote both the common good and the common evil at the same time, yet if one takes Dean's insistence on the ambiguity of God seriously, this is precisely what would happen. If ultimate reality is ambiguous, then action that wishes to orient people towards it will be ambiguous as well. Such a religious critic would probably not gain much more of a hearing in American public life than her or his deconstructionist colleagues.

All of this is not to take away from Dean's laudable intention to involve religious critics outside the narrow bounds of the university. Religious critics could be a tremendous public resource and could be of real benefit in realizing genuine good in the world, which is intimately related to God's providential plan for the world. It is primarily his doctrine of God as a convention which is itself morally ambiguous that has been the target here. Neither the radical empiricism that is Dean's intellectual heritage, nor the Christian tradition that is important to his project are favorably inclined towards the morally ambiguous convention-God. Neither does his insistence upon the ambiguity of everyday life exemplified in American sport necessitate the acceptance of evil at the heart of things—a justice-seeking view is at least as "historically realist" and also provides closer continuity with the tradition and is clear about the reasons for improvement. Dean's understanding of the divine reality is neither efficacious nor provides any reason for embarking on the very worthwhile project that Dean lays out, and a close analysis of Dean's own rhetoric shows that even he, although protesting otherwise, cannot escape the good God.

42. Ibid., 149.

The Purposes of God

THE "PALLID PIETY" OF THE "SPIRIT OF HISTORY"

Dean himself seems to recognize at least the pragmatic difficulties of his understanding of God. In a presentation to the American Academy of Religion in November 1999, Dean recognizes "pragmatism's pallid piety" and casts about for a "more effective God." Responding to a challenge from Richard Rorty that "religious thinkers are nostalgic and antiquated, that they refer to God only 'to link their days each to each' and that they fail to recognize that God is 'a perhaps obsolete name for a possible human future or 'an external guarantor of some such future,'"[43] Dean tries to show that his historicist/pragmatist view of God does not fall under those criticisms. He first attempts to show that many historical understandings of God have placed God inside history, rather than outside of it. He recaps his understanding of God as a social convention, re-baptizing that convention as "the spirit of history" that is responded to by religious people. Strictly from the historical manifestations of this God in history, it must be morally ambiguous, limited in power, transcendent (although Dean's use of "transcendence" is not always clear), living, and not an idol.[44] Thus far, Dean has not radically departed from his earlier work. However, he makes a surprising about-face when he concedes that "if these theoretical definitions tried to pass as accounts of what God actually is, they would never be capable of 'arousing us to desire and action' (Dewey's definition of God). In short, pragmatic theology's—and any theology's—theoretical God is pragmatically and religiously of very little use."[45]

Dean tries to get out of this dilemma by making the distinction between theology and religion, positing theology as theory and religion as the empirical study of actual religious belief and practice, in the manner of James' *Varieties of Religious Experience*. He proposes that one way to account for religion would be "to look for it at the bottom of historical reductionism" in the mystery that remains after the historical facts have been accounted for by historical analysis.[46] While he is deeply ambivalent about the process of historical reductionism that so much of his own theology depends upon, calling it "either trivial or absurd" he maintains that it goes on "making religions into social convention—mere products of a meaningless

---

43. Ibid., 1.
44. Ibid., 10–11.
45. Ibid., 12.
46. Ibid.

sequence of historical causes and effects, and depriving all religions of their claims to independent truth."[47] Nevertheless, Dean still contends that there is some sort of mystery in religious stories that cannot be accounted for in their historical antecedents. Quoting Flannery O'Conner, he says that there will appear "a depth where these things have been exhausted."[48] He appeals to the stories of Jesus and the community of Israel, pointing out that it is in their defeat by history that they transcend history:

> It was the stories of Jesus, of Israel and of other people sacrificed to history that transcended history and that suggested the spirit of history. It was stories that renounced hope of living beyond history, and that accepted history, that transcended themselves. . . . It is when God was reduced to becoming a product of history, a mere social convention of history, that God, in the language of the New Testament, became incarnate in history.[49]

God, according to Dean, is a mystery precisely because it is "reducible to and completely immanent in history. . .needed to make history meaningful in a way that history is not meaningful to itself." The history that "reduces God to itself is the history that acquires religious meaning."[50]

At first glance, this appears to be a major shift in Dean's thinking. After all, he does call his own historicist notion of God "pragmatically and religiously of very little use." I suppose that time will tell if this is a minor hiccup or the beginnings of a new direction in his work.[51] As it stands, however, the appearance of "the spirit of history" and "mystery" in Dean's theological reflection are of very little significance in terms of a substantive revision of his theological program. "The spirit of history," Dean's new term for God, does not escape the problems of moral ambiguity and the lack of pragmatic effect of the "sacred convention" discussed above. It is merely a restatement of his old themes. There is no reason to act for the common

---

47. Ibid., 13–14.

48. O'Conner, *Mystery and Manners*, 153; cited in Dean, "Pragmatism's Pallid Piety," 14.

49. Dean, "Pragmatism's Pallid Piety," 15. Quite similar to Hodgson's notion of incarnation in terms of the effect, but different in its insistence upon ambiguity. See Hodgson, *God in History*, chap. 5.

50. Ibid., 16.

51. Dean's later work remains ambiguous. See, for example, his *American Spiritual Culture*, where jazz, football, and the movies are plumbed for their spiritual depth, which, unsurprisingly, remains ambiguous.

good on the basis of the "spirit of history" when that spirit is so obviously ambiguous and lacking in actuality.

The question of his introduction of "mystery" is somewhat more complicated. While at first appearing to be something like the glimmerings of a genuine religious faith in a real God, "mystery" for Dean is not something like James' "More," a basic faith that there is meaning even if we cannot find it with our sense-organs. It is what is left over when any story is seen as the inexorable process of its historical antecedents, and still manages to move us. It is something like a wonder that these stories didn't get crushed into oblivion, or that we still remember them at all, or that they have the power to move us, even though we know that they are "only stories."

This seems to be a pretty paltry account of the heart of the vast diversity of life that is the religious endeavor. At the end of the day, Dean's project of religious studies would reduce every act committed in a religious framework down to its historical antecedents, occasionally find "mystery" in the elements that somehow transcend themselves, and call it a day. One wants to say, "That's it?" Is there no other point? What about joy, or love, or beauty, or goodness? The Psalms, the Song of Songs, Julian of Norwich, St. Teresa, St. John of the Cross, John Wesley, Gerard Manley Hopkins? An elusive speck of mystery smeared across the face of the jagged boulder of historical circumstance does not sound like any religion I know.

In the end, Dean's historicism with mystery is not substantively different from his historicism without it. His introduction of a very tiny elusive something at the heart of an historically reduced religious tradition has the same problems with the lack of any convincing reason for being a part of it—an actual God that is morally good. He may have convinced Richard Rorty that there is a possible characterization of religion that has "God" inside history. But even if he has, he will not have convinced many, even with the introduction of mystery, that this is a God that anyone will care to be connected to religiously.

DIRECTIONS FOR PROVIDENTIAL REFLECTION

What then, can we take away from this extended discussion of historicism exemplified by William Dean's work? In the final analysis, in spite of Dean's laudable emphasis on actual history and his close attention to the function of the conventions about God in history, his historicism and its ilk will have to be rejected in trying to formulate a contemporary doctrine of providence. His notion of God as a convention of social groups and nothing more ignores the experience of value and the reality of religious experience and new directions in religious thought. His insistence upon the moral ambiguity of God is untrue to the ongoing nature of the tradition he invokes, and cannot be maintained in a context of commitment to reform or justice. Of all the people that he cites, perhaps only Dewey would substantially share Dean's views, and even Dewey thought "God" was good. In his own constructive work, Dean violates his own principles of ambiguity and shows himself to be on the side of the good. Even his understanding of the mystery that remains after everything has been deconstructed out, although a hopeful sign, is still too morally ambiguous to be of use to the thinker who wishes to understand and participate in the action of God in history. At the end of the day, Dean's historicism is something like the history of theology, rather than a theological endeavor in its own right.

Dean's work, however ultimately inadequate in its final statement, points out several directions that any discussion of God and history must take if it is to pick a safe path in the jungle of theological and historical reflection on the subject. First, any discussion of God and history must be adequate to the actual historical occurrences. Dean does a brilliant job in attending to actual history, whether pointing out the ambiguity of the divine in the past tradition, or the role of the religious critic in American history. The social, cultural, historical evidence needs to be attended to in all its multiplicity. The question of God and history can only be addressed by looking at *both* topics. The richly illustrated examples of Dean's theoretical conclusions are the best parts of his books, and also the hardest to argue against, convincing by the weight of evidence rather than layers of rhetoric or deduction. Much work will have to be done to bring God back into the realm of the debate.

Second, any adequate discussion of providence will need to attend to the ambiguity of all experience, including religious experience. Tremendous evil and waste are a part of every person's experience, as are goodness and beauty. No argument about the nature of God can ignore the tradition's oppressive elements, as well as the reasons for their inclusion within that tradition. Even though one might not finally agree with Dean's conclusions, they must be addressed in such a way that their seriousness is taken into account.

Third, I am convinced that some form of a radical empiricism is necessary to move beyond Dean's historical reductionism. This will include the value-laden character of experience and the importance of such experience for positing the goodness of God and the theological critique of the past and the call to a new future. It will also argue for a God deeply involved in the ambiguity of the world. Much of this topic will be addressed in the next chapter, on Whitehead.

Finally, an analysis of historicism points us towards an insistence on participation in, rather than solely an understanding of, history. Historical reductionism is backward-looking, finding ultimately explanatory causes for historical concepts and conventions that continue to have effects in the present. But history is not only analyzed backward, it is also lived forward, with an appreciation of what has gone before, a feeling for the present choices, and an expectation of and hope for the future. Any analysis of history must take this dual character into account to be the basis of a satisfactory doctrine of providence. Much of this will be addressed in the forthcoming chapter on Hodgson.

A contemporary doctrine of providence, therefore, will have a philosophical basis that can take into account both the religious and moral intuitions of such thinkers as Barth and Bultmann, and also the historical specificity that Dean reminds us of. It will have an adequate grasp of the past, as well as an orientation to the future. It will attend to the ambiguities of historical existence, at the same time continuing to affirm a real, good God. Theology will thus neither ignore history nor give way to it in the ongoing endeavor to create a viable and vibrant contemporary doctrine of providence.[52]

---

52. Dean has responded in detail to this critique of his work in a response to a version of this chapter published as an article in *The American Journal of Philosophy and Theology* and at a conference of the Highlands Institute during the summer of 2010. In both venues, he expressed his extreme unhappiness with my characterization of his viewpoints, and critiques me for an extensive exercise in question-begging and for the "damaging use of hidden theological premises"; Dean, "Response to Zbaraschuk," 263. Perhaps those defects can be remedied by placing my critique in the context of the present work, of which it is a part, rather than the whole. Nevertheless, even given Dean's response, I see no reason to give up my critiques of moral ambiguity in God, and of the difficulties of considering God a convention for many, if not most, religious people. It may just be, as he tellingly points out, that we are in different strands of the relatively narrow tradition that we belong to—he with Niebuhr and Loomer, and myself with Wieman and Whitehead. That being said, I am grateful to Professor Dean, who was personally gracious to me and also provided an excellent conversation partner about this important topic. My philosophical disagreements with him in no way affect the personal respect I have for him and for his work.

4

Whitehead
God in the Processes of the World

In our discussion of God and history in the works of Bultmann, Barth, and Dean, we have seen some of the dead ends a discussion of providence can take. Too much emphasis on either God or history without paying attention to the other side can lead to either an irrelevant God who has no influence in the world where we live and move and have our being, or a world in which history is the only reality, and God is a concept that people talk about but has no real existence. The need for a more adequate conception is obvious. God and history are the subjects, and any discussion needs to take both of them into account.

At the same time, a doctrine of providence that is adequate to our experience must take into account the positive aspects that the accounts detailed above emphasize. Thus, Barth and Bultmann's emphases on a doctrine of God that provides meaning and is in some sense the center of the believer's universe, and Dean's careful consideration of historical reality, all must be taken into account. A doctrine of providence that hopes to supersede these powerful presentations must be at least as adequate they are—indeed, it must be more adequate, by virtue of its wider point of view. Such a view will account for the empirical facts of the world, and not try to make God a special case, immune to criticism from the world, and therefore finally unconcerned with it. In addition, it will be radical in its empiricism, taking into account not only sense data but also the component of value in all experience, and thus take religion, morality, and aesthetics seriously.

The Purposes of God

While there are many formulations of God and history that might do this, this chapter deals with Whitehead's philosophy of organism as a particularly fine example of a way to talk about the action of God in history. We will outline his theory of actuality, the role and directivity of God in it, and also his theory of 'Civilization,' which is his account of what the aims of God and their actualization in the historical world look like. We will explore in depth how this notion of the interaction between God and history is more adequate than the previous characterizations of Bultmann, Barth, and Dean. And, finally, we will point to sections of his thought that could benefit from a fuller elucidation, to give a greater cogency of argument and be more adequate to the ongoing process of God's action in the world.

REALITY IS PROCESS: THE WORLD, ACCORDING TO WHITEHEAD.

Many have tried to give a coherent account of Whitehead's exceedingly rich and evocative theory of actuality in a few pages. It is a somewhat daunting project. The theory is a complex construction, full of nuanced descriptions and insights, moving from the simplest to the most complex of things. Yet Whitehead strives for consistency across the range of actualities, trying to describe by a number of categorical statements the interactions between and among all levels of existence. It is, in its most stripped-down form, an account of two forms of existence, actual entities and eternal objects; their manner and mode of interaction; and the various complexities which arise from that interaction.[1]

Any discussion of the particularities of these two forms of existence needs to be conditioned by the prior explication of what Whitehead called the "Category of the Ultimate." This is Whitehead's description of the process of coming to be and passing away which is the ground and condition for the specific analysis of the types of actualities and their interactions. The "Category of the Ultimate" is composed of three notions: creativity; many; one. "One" means singularity and uniqueness rather than the integral number one—the sense in which something is itself and not just the conjunction of others. "Many" means that there are more "ones" than just

---

1. See Whitehead, *Process and Reality*, 22, 25. I am confining my discussion of the theory of actuality to *Process and Reality*, as I feel it is the most complete statement of Whitehead's thought on the subject.

a single entity—"there are many beings in disjunctive diversity."[2] The two terms presuppose each other. And creativity is "the universal of universals characterizing ultimate matter of fact. It is that ultimate principle by which the many, which are the universe disjunctively, become the one actual occasion, which is the universe conjunctively."[3] Creativity is therefore

> the principle of *novelty*. An actual occasion is a novel entity diverse from any entity in the 'many' which it unifies. Thus 'creativity' introduces novelty into the content of the many, which are the universe disjunctively.[4]

Creativity is the ebb and flow of each of the "ones" constituting themselves out of the felt influences of the "many" which are prior to them. It is in terms of these three notions that all further discussion of Whitehead's theory of actuality needs to be understood. The process of the "many becoming one, and being increased by one"[5] is for Whitehead the way in which the action of the universe is best described. It is with the "Category of the Ultimate" in mind—creativity, many, one, as the principles behind and beneath and through all things—that we turn to his more specific analysis of the forms of existence and their interactions.

As mentioned above, a simple statement of Whitehead's theory of actuality can be undertaken by characterizing his account of the two basic forms of existence, actual entities and eternal objects; their manner and mode of interaction; and the various complexities which arise from that interaction. The actual entity is what is meant by every thing/process/actuality that can be termed a unity in and of itself. Whitehead also refers to actual entities as the final realities.[6] They are the individuals-which-are. In the creative process of the many becoming one which is the background to this entire discussion, actual entities are what is coming to be, and passing away, and the processes from which the future actual entities will come to be.

The second basic form or category of existence in Whitehead's theory of actuality is the eternal object. He defines eternal objects as "Pure Potentials

---

2. Ibid., 21.
3. Ibid.
4. Ibid., emphasis original.
5. Ibid., change of verb tense mine.
6. Ibid., 22.

for the Specific Determination of Fact, Or Forms of Definiteness."[7] The eternal objects are any characteristics that can be abstracted from any specific actual entity. They are potentials that can be "ingressed" into the becoming of actual entities. An example would be the various colors, or ideas like goodness or truth. They can be understood as ideas or ideals or universals—Whitehead says the closest analogue in prior philosophy is the Platonic forms.[8] The question of *how* the forms get ingressed into the actual entities is a crucial one for a doctrine of providence, and we will deal with it more fully in the section on the directivity of God on the world. But first, we need to examine the manner and modes in which the eternal objects and actual entities interact.

As detailed above, the interaction between and among actual entities (the Category of the Ultimate as one, many, creativity) is the basic intuition on which the entire philosophy of organism is based. That each individual entity takes into itself and constitutes itself from the feelings of those entities prior to and in relation to it, including its own prior subjectivity projected into the future, is axiomatic for Whitehead. It is the "Principle of Creativity" discussed above. The question then arises as to what the various types of relations between actual entities and the potentialities available to them as eternal objects look and feel like. Whitehead speaks about the manner in which actual entities interact as "prehension." Indeed, the prehension of other actual entities, along with the eternal objects exemplified by those entities, is what in fact constitutes any actual entity in question. "The first analysis of an actual entity, into its most concrete elements, discloses it to be a concrescence of prehensions, which have originated in its process of becoming.[9] Prehension can be thought of as the internalizing of the feeling of other entities by the subjectivity which constitutes an actual entity. Concrescence can be thought of as the process of concretizing those prehensions, those feelings, into a unity. It is a subjective process, which is aiming at a satisfaction. The aim will figure prominently in our later discussion of the directivity of God in the world.

So far, this description is a recipe for determinism. If this were the complete theory, then each actual entity would be nothing more than the sum of its parts, the aggregate of its feelings, so to speak. Whitehead,

---

7. Ibid.
8. Ibid., 44.
9. Ibid., 23.

however, insists on the *free* subjectivity of each actual entity.[10] He holds that there are three factors in each prehension: the prehending subject, the datum prehended, and the "'subjective form' which is *how* that subject prehends that datum."[11] It is in the subjective form of each prehension that elements of subjectivity enter into the equation. Certain feelings are either muted or excluded altogether. Exclusion results in what Whitehead calls a negative prehension.[12] Both positive and negative prehensions, however, have a subjective form, which can perhaps best be understood as the emotional tone that contributes to the chord (harmonious or otherwise) of the final satisfaction of the subject, which is the concrescing actual entity.

Continuing the discussion of the manner and mode of interaction between and among the actual entities and eternal objects will lead us to Whitehead's understanding of propositions. Propositions are not the linguistic constructions of logicians, but are possibilities for feeling[13] presented for ingression into various actual entities. They are not the pure potentials of the eternal objects, nor the concrete realities of actual entities, but are "lures for feeling"[14] for the actual entities. They are the data for prehensions, constituting in what manner particular eternal objects are related to particular actual entities. In its abstract form, a proposition is "a manner of germaneness of a certain set of eternal objects to a certain set of actual entities."[15] In the contrast of "what is" and "what could be" constituted by propositions as lures for feeling is the origin of both novelty and consciousness. Novelty arises when the subject of an eternal object actualizes one rather than another of a set of possibilities. "Fact is confronted with alternatives."[16] Consciousness arises when the contrast between what could be and what is becomes very intense, or complex. Propositions are the potential relations of actual entities and eternal objects that are grounded

---

10. By subjectivity, Whitehead does not mean consciousness or personality or the experience of the senses. Electrons are not little human beings. What he does mean is that there is some form of experience at all levels of existence, with some form of decision involved. See Cobb, *A Christian Natural Theology*, 27, 39.

11. Whitehead, *Process and Reality*, 23, emphasis original.

12. Ibid., 41.

13. By "feeling," Whitehead does not mean feeling distinct from judgment or belief—these are categories of feeling for Whitehead. See *Process and Reality*, 187.

14. Whitehead, *Process and Reality*, 185.

15. Ibid., 188.

16. Whitehead, *Science and the Modern World*, 288; quoted in *Process and Reality*, 189.

The Purposes of God

in fact. This is in contrast to the subjective forms, which are the elements of subjectivity in how actual entities prehend the feelings which arise through other actual entities, eternal objects, and propositions (and their complex interaction). Here we have the last element of this "nutshell-distorted" explication of the manner and mode of interaction between the basic elements of reality in Whitehead's theory of actuality—the propositions. They are the elements of potentiality in the relation of the other elements, actual entities and eternal objects, to one another.

Of course the basic forms of existence and their manner and mode of interaction are not the description of the whole complex which is reality. There are also the various complexities that arise from the interactions of the basic forms of existence. In Whitehead's understanding of actuality, there are three divisions of these complexities—nexus, multiplicities, and contrasts. Nexus are what Whitehead calls "Public Matters of Fact,"[17] or a "particular fact of togetherness among actual entities."[18] They can be understood as the "unities of actual entities" which make up most of the concrete experience of reality. Multiplicities Whitehead calls "Pure Disjunctions of Diverse Entities."[19] Nexus are aggregates of actual entities, which exemplify the category of "one" in the category of the ultimate discussed above. Multiplicities are examples of the "many." And "Contrasts," are "Modes of Synthesis of Entities in one Prehension, or Patterned Entities."[20] They are the actual experience of contrasts of eternal objects in one prehension. Whitehead uses the example of the contrast between red and blue, but it is obvious that the majority of experiences are a series of much more complicated contrasts. Nexus, Multiplicities, and Contrasts make up much of what humans consider important in their own experience and will figure more prominently when we discuss God's aim for the cultural world. However, for purposes of outlining this theory, they can be thought of as the complexities that arise in the interaction of actual entities and eternal objects. They are the result of "creativity" embodying greater and greater levels of complexity in the world. Such a definition is sufficient as we turn to the next topic of this chapter, the directivity of God on the world.

17. Whitehead, *Process and Reality*, 22.
18. Ibid., 20.
19. Ibid., 22.
20. Ibid.

THE ROLE AND FUNCTION OF GOD

Now we come to the crux of the matter—the question of the role and function of God within Whitehead's vision of reality. As might be expected, it is in the indeterminacy of the concrescing subject, the actual entity as it comes to be, that the influence of God is felt. As detailed above, each subjective reality, what Whitehead calls an actual entity, feels or prehends the past, including its own immediate past, and those feelings are concretized into a new satisfaction of feeling. This satisfaction of feeling, the concresced actual entity, in turn affects its successor actual entities, providing the basis for the occasions that will succeed it as it fades. The process of concrescence is where the influence of God is felt.

God, according to Whitehead,[21] provides the ordering and graded relevance of the eternal objects to a particular actual entity. This happens as the occasion in question feels God's purpose for it, as well as feeling the feelings of the actual entities that immediately preceded it with those it its personally ordered society (if any) and those of its wider universe. As the actual entity begins to move from reception to active integration or harmonization of its data, its subjectivity conditions not only its feelings of prior actual entities (the "subjective form"), but also the aim at satisfaction itself. To put it another way, each occasion of experience not only feels the universe subjectively, but also "creates" itself with an element of subjectivity as well. Thus every actuality has a "subjective aim" at a satisfaction—it is a particular aim at a particular type of satisfaction, which is dependent on the possibilities inherent in the occasion and its situation. The initial stage of this subjective aim at satisfaction is "an endowment which the subject inherits from the inevitable ordering of things, conceptually realized in the nature of God."[22] Thus we see the role and function of God in the ongoing advance of creativity which is the ultimate reality according to Whitehead:

> God is the principle of concretion . . . he [sic] is that actual entity from which each temporal concrescence receives that initial aim from which its self-causation starts. That aim determines the initial gradations of relevance of eternal objects for conceptual feeling; and constitutes the autonomous subject in its primary phase of feelings with its initial conceptual valuations, and with its initial physical purposes. Thus the transition of the creativity from an

---

21. I am here referring to the ideas about the divine that Whitehead elucidated in *Process and Reality*.

22. Whitehead, *Process and Reality*, 244.

> actual world to the correlate novel concrescence is conditioned by the relevance of God's all-embracing conceptual valuations to the particular possibilities of transmission from the actual world, and by its relevance to the various possibilities of initial subjective form available for the initial feelings.[23]

Put rather crudely and anthropomorphically, God sets the valuation of the world by setting each entity in motion as it decides how to constitute itself by giving it a "push" toward certain ideal aims depending on its particular circumstances.

How this happens in Whitehead's scheme is evident: God's purpose for each actual entity is in the form of a proposition, which, as stated above, is the possibility for feeling the contrast between the actual and the possible. The occasion is the subject of the proposition, and appropriate eternal object is the predicate.[24] The possibilities presented by this felt proposition are how the subject feels God's purposes for it.

All of the above discussion is in reference to what Whitehead calls the "primordial nature of God," also called the "secular function"[25] of God or the "principle of concretion"—how ideals get translated into actuality.[26] It is not particularly comforting—Whitehead can refer to "what is inexorable in God, is valuation as an aim towards order" and speak of the "chaff being burnt" and the "ruthlessness of God" in this context.[27] There is another part of Whitehead's doctrine of God that also deals with the directivity of God on the world in something more like what the Western religions will call the care of God for the world, or the love of God. This is the "consequent nature of God." While the "primordial nature" of God is the "envisagement" of the eternal objects in graded relevance for each actual occasion, with an eye toward order and intensity, the "consequent nature" of God can be thought of as "the divine receptivity," in which God feels the world with perfect acuity and preserves the world in the "divine memory," and therefore shapes the aims for the world according to the world's past as well. Whitehead

---

23. Ibid.
24. This is detailed in Cobb, *A Christian Natural Theology*, 157.
25. Whitehead, *Process and Reality*, 207.
26. By "secular" Whitehead does not mean that it is a "proof" of God's existence or that this discussion will somehow convert modern secular atheists. Rather, it is an explanation of a particular intuition of reality—the intuition of a definite kind of order in the universe. When Whitehead uses the word "religious" for an idea, he is by and large referring to the historical religions and their doctrines, concepts, and/or practices.
27. Whitehead, *Process and Reality*, 244.

calls this the "love of God for the world" and "the particular providence for particular occasions."[28] God is not only the urge toward order and novelty, but is also the "fellow-sufferer who understands."[29]

It remains to be seen, of course, how this quite general understanding applies more specifically to the human cultural world. In the next section, we will examine Whitehead's vision of historical progress—the concept of civilization.

"CIVILIZATION": THE VISION OF HISTORY

General principles, by definition, do not admit of special cases. They must apply, with degrees and applications appropriate to the entity in question, to all levels of actuality. In addition to applying to forces and particles, the general vision of God's activity in the world must apply to the cultural world as well. God's influence is felt by sub-atomic particles and by historical forces.

Whitehead's treatment of God's aim for history is scattered throughout various sections of various works. As the question of order and novelty and how they come to be is one of the core subjects of his thought, and as he ultimately saw the role of God as the urge to order and novelty, nuggets on the subject are strewn throughout his work. I will confine myself, however, to the two sections where he gave most systematic attention to the subject of God and the cultural world, dealing with what he calls religious and moral intuitions—certain sections, especially Part V, of *Process and Reality*, and the section on "Civilization" in *Adventures of Ideas*.

Some preliminary remarks are in order. First, the outline which Whitehead presents in these two sections is along the lines of a persuasive essay—he meant them as "suggestions as to how [the question of religion] is transformed in the light of [his metaphysical] system."[30] But these suggestions are based upon an "unsystematized report" of the existent religions and he also held that his metaphysical constructions were "confessedly inadequate."[31] Thus he was not at all dogmatic in his presentation of how he viewed God and the world interacting—he held that "any cogency of argument entirely depends upon elucidation of somewhat exceptional ele-

---

28. Ibid., 351.
29. Ibid.
30. Ibid., 343.
31. Ibid.

The Purposes of God

ments in our conscious experience—. . .religious and moral intuitions."[32] Thus, Whitehead's view is that our religious and moral intuitions give ideas as to how the metaphysical system operates, and also that the metaphysical system must have a place in it for religious and moral intuitions. In the selected sections of *Process and Reality*, he deals with the first, and in *Adventures of Ideas*, the second. Also, Whitehead's conception of the purpose of philosophy to show how generality arises from the facts—and the generalized forms his statements take—show the high level of abstraction and the distortion necessary in any discussion characterized by symbolic reference.[33] Thus as I comment on Whitehead's work, I do so not with the idea of correcting the entire viewpoint, but of offering some suggestions which will give greater "cogency of argument" by slightly closer attention to certain moral, aesthetic, and religious intuitions. In the main, I find Whitehead's theory of providence to be quite adequate. I hope to "flesh out" some of the areas he either left untreated or did not explore adequately, without calling into question the main system.

With these reflections in mind, let us now turn to Whitehead's treatment of God's aim for the cultural world in *Process and Reality*. In this massive work, Whitehead is concerned with describing in general terms how the whole of reality—nature and culture, physical and metaphysical—operates. The aims for the natural and the cultural worlds are thus, in the broad sense of the term, the same. This aim, which the primordial nature of God is luring the world toward at all levels, is *intensity*.[34] This is where Whitehead's conception of God most resembles a "principle of order." God's aim for each entity (and the world collectively, by implication) is "depth of satisfaction as an intermediate step towards the fulfillment of [God's] own being."[35] "God's purpose in the creative advance is the evocation of intensities."[36] Of course, how this ideal will work itself out takes a mind-boggling variety of forms, as the massive complexities of natural forms and cultural manifestations demonstrate upon even a cursory examination. But Whitehead holds that all of the above manifestations can be understood in terms of the seeking of greater and greater intensity of experience.

---

32. Ibid.
33. See, Whitehead, *Process and Reality*, Part II, chap. 8, and also *Symbolism*.
34. Whitehead, *Process and Reality*, 105.
35. Ibid.
36. Ibid.

Thus he holds that the two great principles toward which all levels of actuality, including the cultural, are being called are "Permanence" and "Flux." These can also be seen as "order" and "novelty." Far from being antithetical to one another, however, they presuppose and need one another. Whitehead calls attention to this as he points to a religious intuition in the hymn: "Abide with Me/Fast falls the Eventide" which he offers as an example of the notion of clinging to a permanence in the flux that surrounds an individual.

> Ideals fashion themselves around these two notions, permanence and flux. In the inescapable flux, there is something that abides; in the overwhelming permanence, there is an element that escapes into flux. Permanence can be snatched only out of flux; and the passing moment can finds its adequate intensity only by its submission to permanence. Those who would disjoin the two elements can find no interpretation of patent facts.[37]

This is one of the specific points where Whitehead uses a religious intuition to illustrate his understanding of the interaction between God and the world at all levels of existence.

For example, far from keeping to a discussion of the natural world in his treatment of permanence and flux, Whitehead ties this understanding of their interrelated character specifically to the cultural world. He points out that as societies stifle their aims at novelty and zest in the name of order, they tend to bore themselves out of relevance, and therefore existence.

> The history of the Mediterranean lands, and of western Europe, is the history of the blessing and the curse of political organizations, of religious organizations, of schemes of thought, of social agencies for large purposes. The moment of dominance, prayed for, worked for, sacrificed for, by generations of the noblest spirits, marks the turning point where the blessing passes into the curse. Some new principle of refreshment is required. The art of progress is to preserve order amid change, and to preserve change amid order. Life refuses to be embalmed alive. The more prolonged the halt in some unrelieved system of order, the greater the crash of the dead society.[38]

But societal order is not only a conservative, suffocating element. There is the "contrast between order as the condition for excellence, and order

---

37. Ibid., 338.
38. Ibid., 339.

as stifling the freshness of living."³⁹ Order is necessary for the evocation of greater intensities. Also, it is the fundamental building block upon which novelty and intensity come to be: "The old dominance should be transformed into the firm foundations, upon which new feelings arise, drawing their intensities from delicacies of contrast between system and freshness."⁴⁰ Order and novelty are "but the instruments of [God's] subjective aim which is the intensification of formal immediacy."⁴¹ These intensities of contrast are the aim of God for the cultural world, as outlined in *Process and Reality*. Such a general view, however, begs for a more specific treatment. In the fourth part of *Adventures of Ideas*, Whitehead fills out his view of cultural progress as he deals with the concept of "Civilization."

Whitehead holds that the idea of "Civilization" is somewhat baffling: "[it] is one of those general notions that are very difficult to define."⁴² We tend to "pronounce upon particular instances. We can say *this* is civilized, or *that* is savage."⁴³ Whitehead maintains that much of what is counted as "civilized" is an imitation of the classical societies of Greece and Rome, but that we are entering upon a new epoch, in which the imitation of the past will no longer hold the weight it once did. Although he does not speak much about God in his discussion of civilization, his points about the ideals striven for in a civilized society presuppose the ingression of ideals discussed above in *Process and Reality*, and God is *the* integral part of the ingression of ideals in the general system.⁴⁴ The theory of "Civilization" is Whitehead's more specific spelling out of what the influence of God on the world during our epoch of human history looks like. It is not only in religious institutions that the influence of God is felt—God works in and through all cultural institutions. There is no split between sacred and secular.

> Churches and rituals, Monasteries with their dedicated lives, Universities with their search for knowledge, Medicine, Law, methods of Trade—they all represent that *aim at civilization*, whereby the

---

39. Ibid., 338.
40. Ibid., 339.
41. Ibid., 88.
42. Whitehead, *Adventures of Ideas*, 273.
43. Ibid., emphasis original. Here Whitehead in indebted to a more general view of society, common in Victorian England, that societies progress through stages. Frazer and Tylor outline two such versions of this view.
44. Cobb holds that *Adventures of Ideas* is Whitehead's most religious book.

conscious experience of mankind preserves for its use the sources of Harmony.[45]

The "sources of Harmony" are the ideals presented in graded relevance to human beings in their individual and communal existence, with the urge toward satisfaction. Once again, the final aim is at greater intensity through greater and greater contrasts.

After examining some of the particular instances of "Civilization" and discussing them, Whitehead presents a "general definition" of civilization: "a civilized society [exhibits] the five qualities of Truth, Beauty, Adventure, Art, and Peace."[46] Ultimately, all the others will be subsumed into Adventure and Peace, and, finally, Peace alone. That does not mean that the others are not important constituents of the final realities. All these ideals are mutually intertwined constituents of one another. This continues Whitehead's elucidation of Permanence and Flux as the ultimate ideals, Adventure and Peace being their cultural forms. But, in the final analysis, Adventure and Peace are the final ideals which the other ideals serve. Let us examine Truth, Beauty, and Art first to see what they are in Whitehead's understanding and how they fit into his overall cultural scheme.

The first of the qualities which Whitehead sees in a civilized society is Truth. Whitehead consistently defines Truth as the "conformation of Appearance to Reality."[47] This seemingly simple statement is not as simple as it appears—much like Whitehead's understanding of civilization. In the section on Truth, Whitehead teases out meanings about Appearance, and points out that our seemingly clear apprehension of reality in sense perception is not at all as true, in his sense of conforming to reality, as we assume much of the time. But he points out, too, that there is an urge that moves us to search beyond untrustworthy Appearance. Science, for example, urges us to the truth beyond the immediate sense perception: Does the sun actually "rise?" In the face of such urges, Whitehead postulates within nature a "tendency to be in tune, an Eros urging towards perfection."[48] This urge cannot be discussed in terms of truth alone, but points beyond it towards the ideal of Beauty.

---

45. Whitehead, *Adventures of Ideas*, 272, emphasis supplied.
46. Ibid., 274.
47. Ibid., 241, 250, 281.
48. Ibid., 251.

The idea of Beauty, according to Whitehead, can be characterized as "the mutual adaptation of the several factors in an occasion of experience."[49] And, as Whitehead points out, "adaptation implies an end."[50] This end is a Harmony and a Strength of Beauty, in which various factors within an occasion of experience are held in some kind of an harmonious tension. This is in keeping with the discussion of "contrasts" leading to more intense experience above. All of the factors in an occasion of experience cannot be harmonized into a Strength of Beauty, however—there is also what Whitehead calls variously "discord" and "Aesthetic destruction."[51] He maintains that such discords cannot necessarily all be harmonized, but are part of the urge toward "Adventure" which will attempt to find a new solution which will solve this discordant relation. This is where "Truth" and Beauty" can come together—in their juxtaposition, they can (it is not necessary) lead to the search for new forms of harmony, leading to Adventures of Ideas (hence the title of the book). This harmonious tension is an example of the ideals of Permanence and Flux working themselves out in the realm of history.

Whitehead uses Art as an example of the Adventure of Ideas that can result when Truth and Beauty encounter one another in a subjective occasion of experience (like a living person). Whitehead defines Art as "the purposeful adaptation of Appearance to Reality."[52] Note the combination of the definitions of Truth and Beauty—Beauty as a "mutual adaptation of several factors in an occasion of experience" and Truth as "the conformation of Appearance to Reality." Thus, "the perfection of art has only one end, which is Truthful Beauty."[53] It is only when the two are in concert that great art can be achieved. Art for Beauty's sake alone has what Whitehead calls the "defect of massiveness"[54] which can be thought of as variety of detail without purpose.[55] And "in the absence of Beauty, Truth sinks to triviality."[56] It is only when they are together that they constitute an Adventure of Ideas that can lead to fresh insights and novel solutions to felt discords in individuals and societies.

49. Ibid., 252.
50. Ibid.
51. Ibid., 256.
52. Ibid., 267.
53. Ibid.
54. Ibid.
55. Ibid., 253, 267.
56. Ibid., 267.

Thus we can see how, in Whitehead's theory of cultural progress, Truth and Beauty are brought together in Art as an example of Adventure. Adventure, in a more general sense, however, is Whitehead's concept of a society being in tune with the character of the universe. In his mind, "Advance or Decadence are the only choices offered to mankind [sic]. The pure conservative is fighting against the essence of the universe."[57] His discussion is based on three basic metaphysical principles. The first of these is that reality *is* process—there is *no* static perfection, according to Whitehead.[58] "The process is itself the actuality, and requires no antecedent static cabinet. . . .The process is [the past's] absorption into a new unity with ideals and with anticipation, by the operation of the creative Eros."[59] The second metaphysical principle on which he bases his identification of Adventure with the nature of the universe is that "every occasion of actuality is in its own nature finite."[60] Putting the two principles together, one sees that the process that is the actuality is finite. There is no "steady-state" for a society in which every thing is in balance. There is either progress or regress. The third metaphysical principle is that of individuality, which has to do with Harmony. It is the harmonious feeling of the process that is reality, most powerfully expressed in individual instances. The various discords, discussed above in the section on Art, also contribute to the conformation of the appearances of the social organization with the fundamental urge to novelty, the Eros leading to Adventure. When a society stagnates, "Adventure is essential, namely, the search for new perfections."[61] When trivial variations on existing cultural forms no longer excite the members of the society, "Bolder adventure is needed—the adventure of ideas, and the adventure of practice conforming itself to ideas."[62] This notion of practice conforming itself to ideas is one area which will bear fruitful reflection in bringing Whitehead's understanding into conversation with Hegelian-influenced thinkers, and their helpful emphasis on praxis, in later chapters. In addition, we see how Permanence and Flux are woven through the very fabric of the realities that comprise the Adventures of Ideas that are the progress and regress of societies. Permanence is a necessary condition for

57. Ibid., 274.
58. Ibid.
59. Ibid., 276.
60. Ibid.
61. Ibid., 258.
62. Ibid., 259.

the novel forms of Flux that come out of it, and Flux is often in the service of a lasting Permanence.

Thus we see how the notions of Truth, Beauty, and Art are subsumed into the concept of Adventure in Whitehead's theory of cultural progress. But there remains one final ideal aim for civilization that completes it—Peace. This is the most difficult concept in Whitehead's theory of civilization—it is in some sense the ideal opposite of Adventure, and in some sense subsumes it as well and is itself the "ground and aim of aims." Whitehead speaks of Peace as "that Harmony of Harmonies which calms destructive turbullence [sic] and completes civilization."[63] He holds that

> It is not a hope for the future, nor is it an interest in present details. It is a broadening of insight due to the emergence of some deep metaphysical insight, unverbalized and yet momentous in its coordination of values.... It is primarily a trust in the efficacy of Beauty.[64]

It seems that Peace is the feeling and trust that allows discord to ultimately be used as a goad to adventure, rather than an ultimate condition of things.[65] "Peace is the understanding of tragedy, and at the same time its preservation."[66] Whitehead thinks of the experience of Peace as a gift,[67] something not in the nature of human beings to come up with on their own. It is something like faith that there is an order and meaning to things in the face of the tragic nature of existence: "This is the secret of the union of Zest with Peace:—that the suffering attains its end in a Harmony of Harmonies. The immediate experience of this Final Fact, with its union of Youth and Tragedy, is the sense of Peace."[68] Peace is the final aim toward which God directs the world—a kind of trust that there is a meaning and a purpose, even if we do not completely understand it.[69]

Does Whitehead's vision, then, propound the victory of permanence over flux? Not in an *ultimate* sense. The more general ideals of permanence

---

63. Ibid., 285.

64. Ibid.

65. Whitehead, *Adventures of Ideas*, 285: "It preserves the springs of energy, and . . . [avoids] paralyzing distractions."

66. Ibid., 286.

67. Ibid., 285.

68. Ibid., 296.

69. This is actually akin to the insight that Bultmann makes into his entire vision of providence, or Barth's insistence on God's governance "Nevertheless."

and flux are both subsumed in the wider cultural ideas of Adventure and Peace. Adventure entails both Truth and Beauty, Harmony and Intensity, and uses the permanence of order and ideals to aim at the larger goals of Adventure. And Peace, far from being a cessation of Flux, is itself the ground from which aims at novel forms of Flux (Adventures) can be attempted. So they are as integrally intertwined as are Permanence and Flux in the Whiteheadian vision of the civilization.

A WIDER, STRONGER, MORE ADEQUATE VIEW

In the preceding discussion, it has thus become evident that Whitehead's understanding of God and God's interaction with the world provides a more complete way of thinking and talking about providence then either the Christian existentialists Barth and Bultmann, or the historicist William Dean. A philosophical understanding such as Whitehead's is able to take moral and religious intuitions seriously and also integrate them conceptually with the ambiguous ongoing process of the world in a meaningful fashion. This is so for many reasons.

First, in Whitehead's vision of the world, God is integrally built into the structure of the way the world operates. The world would not be what it is without God. All order, from the loose organization of particles to the highest complexity in the artistic and cultural achievement of human beings, have God as an integral source, calling them on to be what they are. Such an understanding is surely more adequate to the experience of the religious person than an attempt ground providence only in a revelational and confessional mode (a la Barth); and is also more adequate than having the "modern worldview" of Bultmann, where history has no meaning, and value and meaning are found only in the existential decisions of human beings. As outlined above in Chapter II, if God is outside nature and history, or if God can only be thought of in the terms of the tradition, then God either ultimately becomes meaningless, a panacea in the face of the dark, uncaring world that surrounds us (like Rorty's idea of God as a nostalgic, antiquated notion to "link our days each to each"[70]), or is not adequate to our contemporary experience. Whitehead's vision of God as the true reason why there is order, novelty, and existence at all in the world is more adequate to our religious experience of dependence on God than the more narrow theories put forward by either Bultmann or Barth. Instead of trying

---

70. See discussion in Dean, "Pragmatism's Pallid Piety."

to save God by placing the divine reality outside of history, Whitehead's understanding of how the world works has God at the very heart of all action, from the sub-atomic to the cultural. Instead of consigning God to the realm of individual human beings, God is understood to be acting throughout the natural, personal, and historical/cultural worlds, offering aims to the varying degrees of actual entities, calling them on. Surely this is more adequate to the realm of religious experience, that has God at the heart of all things.

By insisting on God's influence in the natural and historical world, through all levels of reality, Whitehead's conception of the action of God in history can escape Bultmann's psychologizing explanations. Although it is true that such a conception has its own dangers, like the danger of the "God of the gaps," it at least holds God at the center of existence, rather than making the divine reality a private hypothesis that can be dismissed when history crowds out such peripheral hypotheses.

And, finally, a conception such as Whitehead's gives a basis for a moral and aesthetic vision that allows judgment and discrimination between and among acts, while Bultmann's conception is only concerned with abstract "meaning" divorced from the context and results that constitute the act itself. Bultmann provides no way of judging the concrete results of the act, as the only question that he is concerned with is whether or not it has meaning. Whitehead's conception, on the other hand, with its evocation of Flux and Permanence, Harmony and Intensity, and Adventure and Peace, all embodied in concrete historical realities that are themselves the proving ground of the ideals advocated, provides ways of talking about moral actions and concrete historical realities that are not purely subjective. Thus, they are more adequate to our experience in the matrix of human interactions that constitutes history.

In the same manner that Whitehead's understanding of the action of God in history is more adequate than Bultmann's existential understanding, it is also more adequate than Barth's overly-anthropomorphic Christian triumphalism. Barth is so tied to royal and patriarchal metaphors[71] that he falls into the danger of giving God the attributes of Caesar,[72] that is, of reifying hierarchical human-human relations and calling them divine-human ones. Whitehead's vision of God, as the source of ideas/ideals, the urge towards intensity, the divine Eros, doesn't fall into the same traps. God

---

71. See the discussion by Hodgson, *God In History*, 25–28.
72. The phrase, of course, is Whitehead's; see *Process and Reality*, 342.

is still intimately involved in all aspects of all beings, but is not understood so anthropomorphically.

In addition to being less open to anthropomorphizing, Whitehead provides a better answer to the problem of evil in history than does Barth. Barth tries to deny the seeming lack of divine control with his notion of "Nevertheless"—confessing that God rules even though we can't perceive how it is possible. Whitehead, through his emphasis on the free character of all levels of existence and the tremendous impact of the past, has a better answer. Simply put, there is the massiveness of the past, which excludes miraculous possibilities, and there is the freedom of the creature, which means that sometimes the ideal aims of God for the world do not get fully actualized. God is involved, God points the world toward Truth, Beauty, Love, Goodness, Harmony, Intensity—but the possibilities for actualization are limited somewhat by the fixed character of the past, and, in addition, the world is free to not respond, thus setting the stage for the possibilities of tragedy and suffering.[73]

One could even make the case that such emphasis on the freedom of the creation is a better explanation of the traditional language about God and human relations (including God and history) than any kind of "divine totalism." The same point that many process-evangelical or so-called "openness of God" theologians make about God and individual human beings also holds for God and history: that a conceptuality accounting for real freedom is truer to their traditional language about sin and repentance, worship and spirituality, than the kind of "divine rule" insisted upon by Barth.[74] We can even look back to the Augustinian/Pelagian controversy, or the Arminian/Calvinist debate, and side with the Pelagians and Arminians in their insistence that the only thing that explains the traditional understanding of sin and repentance is enough freedom to make mistakes.[75]

In addition to providing a better answer to the problem of evil in history, and being better able to account for the experiences leading to traditional language in the Bible and Christian reflection about sin and repentance, Whitehead's vision of the world and God's role in it makes it

---

73. For a more detailed discussion of a Whiteheadian response to the problem of evil, see Griffin, *God, Power, and Evil*.

74. See, for example, Pinnock et al., *The Openness of God*. Their collective essays present a fine overview of the so-called "open view of God," a conservative/evangelical dialogue with process thought.

75. For Pelagianism, see Brown, *Augustine of Hippo*, especially chaps. 29–31; for Arminius, see Gonzalez, *The Story of Christianity*, 2:179–83.

The Purposes of God

possible to talk seriously about God and history in the same breath. As we showed in chapter II, Barth radically separates the two by taking God's rule out of empirical consideration, by making nothing able to count either for or against it in an ultimate sense. Whitehead, on the other hand, understands God as acting in and through all levels of actuality; and history, intimately connected with the natural processes upon which it depends, it is shot through-and-through with the influence of God. By keeping empirical discussion an integral part of the discussion about God and history, Whitehead makes a meaningful discussion of the two possible.

It is thus evident that Whitehead, in his ability to make sense of the "stubborn facts" of the world, is better able to hold together both the intuitions of the religious life and the empirical happenings that constitute history in one conceptual scheme, without insisting on the un-reality or meaninglessness of either. He thus offers a more complete, coherent, and satisfying doctrine of providence then either of the Christian existentialists.

Looking to the other side of the empirical/existential split outlined in the preceding chapters, Whitehead is also clearly more adequate then Dean's more historicist understanding in his presentation of the interaction between God and history. This is so for several reasons.

First, Whitehead's aesthetic vision provides a way of talking about the goodness of God that evades the irrelevance of Dean's weak doctrine of God. Instead of being limited to descriptions of what aspects of the tradition have said about God, Whitehead's understanding of God, through the presentation of ideal aims to every actuality at its level, provides a way of talking about God's goodness that cannot be reduced to its historical antecedents. Because Whitehead accounts for the valuational character of experience, he is able to find a way to talk about God that is not purely talking about past characterizations of God—it makes the language of the living, loving, acting God (while metaphorical, like all language) plausible, rather than an artifact of the past. In short, Whitehead's language about God provides for a real understanding of present spirituality, where religious people are on the side of a good God, rather than a conventionalist and historicist analysis of past theological concepts.

In addition to providing a basis for affirming a good God, Whitehead's theory of reality can at the same time account for the ambiguity of historical existence in a more complete fashion than Dean's. Dean's vision holds that reality (including, of course, the divine reality in whatever form it takes) is utterly and completely ambiguous, and that somehow affirming goodness in God is a betrayal of the insight of ambiguity in historical existence. Whitehead's vision of reality, by holding that all actual entities are made up of their past experiences, modified by an ideal aim, better accounts for our experience of an ambiguous past along with insights that call us to transcend such a past and work towards a better future. Dean's work holds no such promise.

Along with being able to emphasize the goodness of God in an ambiguous world, Whitehead's concept of God is also more religiously satisfying than Dean's. If spirituality is, as David Griffin and others suggest, something like "being in tune with the character of the universe,"[76] then God as the actual source of all that is good, of the order that makes life possible at all, of the novelty that makes life worth living, of the truth and beauty that we not only define for ourselves, but feel in our bones as we experience the world; then this conception is more adequate to the spirituality that is at the heart of all religion. If, without being too anthropomorphic, we can say that God is really at the heart of these things, rather than that God is something like the U.S. Constitution, an utterly human construct that is real, has effects, and "acts" in surprising ways, then we do have a more religiously satisfying God. It is a matter of removing the quotation marks from the verb "act"—Whitehead's God is continually acting in everything, whereas Dean's could be said at most to be "acting" in our minds. In one important sense, we are trying to be truer to our experience.

All this prior discussion, of course, brackets the question of how concepts and practices are interrelated. There is no question that concepts affect practices, and vice versa. A spirituality that is controlled by the vision of God as Lord/King/Ruler leads one to submit. Or, is it the other way around, that spiritualities that lead one to submit lead to kings and lords? The truth is probably somewhere in between. To take a Whiteheadian approach, the truth of our finiteness and vulnerability can lead to such institutions as kings, and such institutions certainly can affect our spiritualities as well. Appearance is partially conformed to reality, and thus a partial truth is expressed.

However, the whole truth is not expressed. Thus, in addition to the urge to express a finiteness, there is also the urge to express control, to celebrate the human power to modify the environment in order to "live, to live well, and to live better."[77] William James' division of the world into

---

76. The provenance is from Whitehead, *Adventures of Ideas*, 251.

77. The function of reason, according to Whitehead. There must be a way to celebrate

two types of "religious personalities," the "once-born" and the "twice-born" expresses this insight to some extent. The once-born celebrate and practice their ability to modify their environments, and spiritualities of justice and action in the world result. The twice-born, feeling deeply their own finite character, celebrate and practice their own insignificance, and spiritualities of contemplation and withdrawal are the result. Appearance tries to conform with reality: people try to tell the truth. The whole truth, however, shows a discord between opposing viewpoints. A wider view, on the other hand, shows the partial truth of both, and therefore points toward the necessity of a new formulation. This new formulation will have more in common with Whitehead's method and description of finding truth than with William Dean's.

WHAT ABOUT JUSTICE? POSSIBLE MODIFICATIONS . . .

While I am hopeful that Whitehead's conceptuality can be a stable base from which to build an adequate and vibrant contemporary doctrine of providence, I do have some specific points at which I think that Whitehead's particular theory of cultural progress could benefit from some suggestions. I have doubts that every ideal aim hinted at by our moral and religious intuitions can be adequately accounted for as a function of Permanence and Flux, or of Truth, Beauty, Art, Adventure, and Peace. One example is the intuition of the necessity of pursuing Justice as such. Is Justice an Adventure in the pursuit of Art? Such language does not seem to express the felt urgency of the matter. Yet is a society civilized when it is not just? That, too, seems to stretch the meanings of the terms. We could then, offer something like this as a modification of the Ideal scheme to include Justice in the following manner:

A civilized society not only exhibits the qualities of Truth, Beauty, Art, Adventure, and Peace, it will also exhibit the quality of Justice if it is to be worthy of the name. In one sense, a Whiteheadian vision could subsume the ideal of justice as an exemplification of the ideal of Truth, with the apparent disjunction between appearance and reality being the driving force behind the urge for justice. The disjunction in question would be between the apparent necessity of an unjust action under the laws of a society and the reality of the unnecessary suffering entailed, for no particular good reason.[78]

---

such an urge, in spiritualities. See *The Function of Reason*, 8ff.

78. Whitehead seems to be pointing in this direction in his discussion of the question

Thus it could serve as a goad to further adventure—the attempt to fashion a better, more just society in order to better tell the truth. There is much to be said for such a formulation. Among other advantages, it illustrates how, perhaps, injustice serves as a spur to better attempt "impossible" or "unthinkable" projects, like the aforementioned dissolution of slave societies.

Such a formulation of justice as a subset of truth is, however, unsatisfying in a larger sense. To make justice serve truth, or beauty, or adventure ignores the radical call to change that is part of the experience of injustice. It undermines the felt necessity of action. It is almost a "gnostic" sort of solution to the problem of suffering: we understand its function, and that understanding somewhat mutes the force of the empathetic feeling of "suffering-with." Also to right an injustice for the ultimate purpose of bringing about greater intensity of feeling seems to cheapen the suffering itself. Justice demands action in and of itself, and speak of it as being a part of truth or beauty could take away from the urgency of the felt injustice, and therefore the will to act for its righting.

Whitehead himself seemed to note this danger in emphasizing the ideal aims without some sort of a larger frame of reference. He pointed out that the ideal aims of beauty, truth, etc., cannot be pursued for themselves alone, or they run the risk of becoming "ruthless, hard, and cruel . . . and thus lacking in some essential quality of civilization."[79] Whitehead maintained that the sense of Peace was necessary to temper and give context and meaning to the other ideal aims. Thus, following Whitehead's intuition, I would propose that the reason for the necessity of Justice as an ideal aim in a Whiteheadian scheme is not because it is an incomplete telling of the truth, but that injustice is a violation of Peace and thus a civilized society cannot stand without Justice.

Close attention to the nature of radical unnecessary human suffering that itself constitutes injustice is important to see why this is so. There are at least two different responses to human suffering: a blunting and numbing of human feeling, and a resolve to work against it regardless of the consequences. The first can be illustrated by certain examples from Elie Wiesel's *Night*, as Jewish people are radically oppressed by the Nazis on the way to the concentration camps, they lose their feeling for and with the human beings who suffer with them, culminating in the man who beats his father to

---

of slavery in the second chapter of *Adventures of Ideas*.

79. Whitehead, *Adventures of Ideas*, 284.

death for a few mouthfuls of bread.[80] Sustaining any sense of a "harmony of harmonies" in such a situation seems impossible. There may be exceptional cases that can manage it,[81] but on a broader cultural level, it would be hard to call the society that allowed such things "civilized."

The second response, that of an identification with the sufferers and a resolve to end such suffering, can in one sense be thought of as part of the further goad to adventure in that it is a discord. However, massive injustice, by virtue of its interruptive character,[82] moves us outside of our explanatory schemes and forces us to the praxis of suffering. Interruptive means, in this case, the end of a vision of Peace, of the Harmony of Harmonies. To use a Whiteheadian type of example, it is the "It cannot be borne!" of grief and rage that accompanies great loss or tragedy. An analogy with the experience of overwhelming pain in the human body and the effect on the human mind can illustrate this point further: In the same way that a hammer-blow on the finger blots out other experience because of the immediacy and intensity of the pain, the feeling of the suffering of oneself or others in radical injustice also blots out other considerations, making Peace, Adventure, Art impossible until something has been done.

A fine example of the destruction of peace through injustice, and the compulsion for action that it entails, can be found in an essay by Pacific Northwest writer David James Duncan, "Beauty/Violence/Grief/Frenzy/Love: On the Contemplative Versus the Active Life."[83] Duncan outlines his own transformation from award-winning novelist to environmental activist at the age of forty, writing opinion pieces and satire to try to save some of the remaining wilderness in the Pacific Northwest:

> I became a nonfiction writer . . . not out of a sense of calling, but out of a sense of betrayal, out of rage over natural systems violated, out of grief for a loved world raped, and out of a craving for justice.[84]

Duncan writes about the end of the contemplative life that sustained his novel-writing, as corporate and government interests systematically destroyed the ecosystem where he lived. He illustrates Whitehead's emphasis

---

80. Wiesel, *Night*.

81. See Frankl, *Man's Search for Meaning*. Saints are ideal examples, not expressions of cultures.

82. This is following the analysis of Chopp in her *Praxis of Suffering*, anticipating its discussion in the chapter on Peter Hodgson.

83. Duncan, in *My Story as told by Water*, 167–79.

84. Ibid., 167.

on the ideal aims as states of individual, rather than the social or political, emphasis, while at the same time pointing out that such individual aims also have social and political contexts and outcomes that in turn affect the individual in question. His topic, in this context of destruction is "the grief and frenzy that daily invade every sincere human's attempts to simply pursue a vocation that expresses gratitude and respect for life."[85]

In the essay, Duncan holds an imaginary dialogue between Thomas Merton, the great American contemplative, and activist Montana writer Rick Bass. He points out Merton's warning against the "pervasive form of contemporary violence to which the idealist . . . easily succumbs: activism and overwork" that "neutralizes his [sic] work for peace," even "destroy[ing] his [sic] inner capacity for peace. . .[and] the fruitfulness of his [sic] own work, because it kills the root of inner wisdom that makes work fruitful."[86] Whitehead himself could have written such a warning of not attending to the Harmony of Harmonies, the Peace that is at the heart of the world. He would have approved of this attitude that would keep the priorities in their proper places, by virtue of referencing everything to the aim of Peace.

Bass, however, replies to the above quote, in a hand-written note in the margin:

> Yes. but NO
> Can't do it! Not yet.
> Not _now_

Then Duncan imagines the two men going on a walk together in the woods, first in the wooded hills of Kentucky where Merton made his contemplative home at Gethsemane Monastery, and then in the deforested mountains of northwestern Montana where Bass makes his. If they should encounter the same kind of destruction being visited on the northwestern forests, Duncan claims that

> [t]here is little doubt in my mind that this kind of alteration, inflicted upon the forests of Gethsemane, would induce in the nature-adoring Trappist the very state his contemplative self abhors: *the frenzy of the activist.* When your heart's home is being annihilated, your peace and serenity are in deep shit and that's all there is to it.[87]

85. Ibid., 172.
86. Quoted in ibid.
87. Ibid., 177.

If the very conditions of life and beauty and love are being systematically destroyed for nothing more than more money in some already wealthy person's pocket, Peace, in Whitehead's sense of a trust in the efficacy of beauty, is an early casualty.

It is interesting that Whitehead chose Peace as an ideal aim, complementary and in some senses opposed to Adventure. In common parlance the opposite of Peace is not Adventure, but War. Injustices on large scales, with their repression and savage acts, undermine the sociological conditions necessary to contemplate and dialogue on philosophical and religious topics.[88] In large populations, injustices often lead to armed resistance, which easily escalates into war. The point at issue here is not to enter into the large and varied literature on the possible (and possibility of) justifications for war but to point out that insofar as injustice is a contributing factor in leading to large-scale armed conflict, it undermines both the conditions for and the expression of Peace.

Of course, one could argue that Whitehead was not talking about the actual state of Peace as a sociological and political condition, but as an ideal aim toward which individuals and societies are called.[89] This is, of course, true, but the exemplification counts as we consider the ideal aims and their effect in the world. Injustice runs counter to Peace as a felt reality of the character of the universe, in that it destroys both the ability to feel as such and the pursuit of art, adventure, and peace. It is also counter to the exemplification of the ideal aim in societies, in that it undermines the conditions for the possibility of peace on the large scale. In both senses, Justice is a necessary component of True Peace in the world.

MOVING ON: FREEDOM AND PRAXIS

Another Whiteheadian area that could benefit from further exploration is the idea of freedom as an ideal in and of itself. Whitehead speaks of freedom and liberty as an extension of the other ideal aims for a civilized society. For example, he holds that "the social value of liberty lies in its productions of discords"[90] ostensibly for the purpose of furthering Adventure. And he also

---

88. It destroys both the "leisure and libraries" that philosophers need for their work, according to Richard Rorty—see Dean's analysis in "Pragmatism's Pallid Piety."

89. See, for example, the discussion in *Adventures of Ideas*, 274.

90. Whitehead, *Adventures of Ideas*, 257.

maintains that freedom can be seen as one of the outcomes of the insistence upon individuality that is one of the characteristics of the universe that the Adventure in civilized societies are trying to emulate.[91] It does seem to me, however, that the notion of freedom could bear more reflection than Whitehead accords it. How would it fit into the general conception of the world? Can freedom, like justice, be adequately accounted for as a furtherance of intensity of feeling? How are freedom and justice related? Do they presuppose one another? It is specifically with the aim in mind of exploring some of the implications of justice and freedom and their shaping role in history that we turn to another concept of God in history– that presented by the Hegelian Peter Hodgson in his *God in History: Shapes of Freedom*.

---

91. Ibid., 281.

5

Freedom and Praxis
Peter Hodgson's Fuller Vision of History

Whitehead's theory of actuality was presented in the previous chapter as a more adequate way of accounting for the influence of God on the world than either the historicizing William Dean, the existential Bultmann, or the confessional Barth. Whitehead's vision of the world, presenting a picture of the world as conditioned by its past yet being lured toward ever-new goals and purposes at all levels of actuality, which we as human beings both describe and participate in, is a particularly rich and evocative basis for a doctrine of providence. This "Platonic realism"[1] accounts for the fixed character of actuality and its encounter with and partial actualization of an ideal presented to it, which in turn becomes a new actuality. This continuing development, in which reality is always presented with new aims in a continuing process of self-and-other creation, has myriad possibilities for development.

One fruitful (and obvious) affinity that such a formulation holds is with modes of theorizing inspired by Hegel.[2] The encounter that we will develop in this chapter is with another "contextualized idealism" presented by Hegelian-influenced theologian Peter Hodgson in his brilliant treatment of the doctrine of providence, *God in History: Shapes of Freedom*. We

---

1. The term is Whitehead's; see *Process and Reality*, 42, 50.

2. See John Cobb's note in *Process Theology as Political Theology*, 19, that any mode of theology that emphasizes process/event over substance is process theology, specifically citing Hegel as being as much process thought as Whitehead.

will first outline Hodgson's basic understanding of God's influence on the world, the trinitarian formulation of God as triune figuration, History as deconfigurative process, and Freedom as transfigurative praxis. We will then discuss the relation of his dialectical view of God in history to Whitehead's theory of "civilization" outlined in the preceding chapter. Hodgson has an ongoing dialogue in his text with both Whitehead and Whiteheadian-influenced thinkers, most notably John Cobb, and both his specific statements and overarching similarities and differences will be dealt with. After having discussed Hodgson's view of God and its relation to Whitehead, we will address what is particularly helpful in Hodgson's formulation as opposed to Whitehead's: a richer analysis of history as such; a fuller understanding of *human* freedom; and, most compellingly, an insistence on the central role of praxis and the specific shapes that God's presence takes in history. This discussion of what the shapes and forms of God's action with the world in freedom looks like will lead us into a discussion of what "the beginning of the history of freedom" might look like from one perspective, in terms of "freedom *for*," in the chapters to follow.

GOD IN HISTORY AS FREEDOM: A "NEW TRI-UNITY"

Hodgson begins his treatment of God's role in history with an historical introduction showing how the very idea of "history" itself has become problematic in the contemporary situation.[3] He first deals with the "end of salvation history" as it has been classically understood, outlining the philosophies of history in the Scriptures, the early Latin theologians, Augustine, Aquinas, Calvin, "modern" (17th-18th century) thinkers, and Barth, and while picking up insights from all of their formulations (most notably Barth's doctrine of God as "the One who Loves in Freedom"), he finds them all to be ultimately unable to convincingly present an idea of God's action in history for contemporary readers. He then moves on to the "post-modern" thinkers such as Derrida and Foucault, along with a/theologian Mark C. Taylor, and their attack upon the categories of "history" and "God" as such—their contention that the idea of a single, comprehensible aim for history has disintegrated. Aims and goals seem to be entirely conditioned

---

3. This is a brilliant strategy for dealing with nihilistic postmodernism. There is nothing like showing the historical development of an idea which purports to trumpet the "end of history" to demonstrate its flawed character.

by social contexts, and the loss of belief in a transcendent ground of such aims leaves one ultimately aim-less, with a paralyzing loss of direction and meaning. Hodgson acknowledges the rhetorical power of the critique while questioning its substance, faulting especially Taylor (whom he sees as paradigmatic) for taking an "all-or-nothing" approach and for constructing an elaborate straw man. That we can no longer point to a text or a civilization and say "this is God's will" does not mean that there is no action of God in history—it simply means that we need to look harder and in a different place for it. Hodgson examines the categories of "God, History, and Freedom" and their interactions "in light of both the postmodernist challenge and of the empowerment experienced in a particular kind of praxis, which [he designates] as 'emancipatory,' 'liberating,' or 'transfigurative'"[4] as a way of engaging in the "hard labor" of teasing out an adequate way of speaking of the presence of God in history which is both a critical deconstruction and re-appropriation of the tradition.

Hodgson takes his conversation with the tradition seriously, as evidenced by his ultimate use of Trinitarian categories (with an Hegelian twist) to characterize the shapes of God in history. Following Barth's formulation of God as the "One who Loves in Freedom," Hodgson re-presents God as triune figuration, History as deconfigurative process, and Freedom as transfigurative praxis. God is conceived not as the absolute, unrelated, impersonal Other, but in the tradition of Hegel (and interpreters of Whitehead and Hartshorne, I would add) as an Absolute that is "not static substance but dynamic, living, infinite intersubjectivity"[5] in which "the world in general, and human history in particular, are an essential moment in the divine life."[6] Hodgson does not rest with Hegel's construction, however, but wishes to push the discussion to further emphasize the "real difference" between God and the world, with the concomitant attention paid to "the ambiguities, struggles, contradictions, and unfinished character of history."[7] God will ultimately be understood as Trinitarian Spirit, but less as a Trinity of knowledge than as a Trinity of praxis.

God, according to Hodgson's re-visioning, "is a process or event of triune figuration appearing in three primary figures, shapes, or modes."[8] The

---

4. Hodgson, *God in History*, 42.
5. Ibid., 45.
6. Ibid., 44.
7. Ibid., 45.
8. Ibid., 93.

first of these three figures/shapes/modes of God is the One, also thought of as "God," what is emphasized in the tradition as the immanent Trinity, or the moment of *identity* in the divine life. God is God's own intersubjective reality for the sake of the world, and the world's freedom. The second of the three figures/shapes/modes in the divine life is Love, or "World," or the moment of *difference* from the One of the previous moment. This is the moment of genuine otherness, "no longer simply the One but the 'All in all.'"[9] It is because the world is not God that it can become a moment in the dynamic ongoing divine life at all, and that it can be "saved from its annihilating nothingness."[10] For Christians, the relation between the first two moments are paradigmatically understood by considering the superimposed images of the *basileia* and the cross of Jesus, in which God's presence of love was manifested in community and led to suffering and redemption in the world, not outside of it.[11] The world is freely its own, in order to be from God and freely for and within God as well. The third and final shape of Hodgson's Trinitarian re-formulation is Freedom, or Spirit, or the moment of "mediation" in which the shapes of God become manifest in the world in distinct, though always incomplete, forms. "God is 'Spirit' insofar as God is present to, active in, embodied by that which is other than God, namely, the natural and human worlds."[12] "The triune figuration of God culminates in the third and final figure, which is also the name of the whole God: God as Spirit overreaches and encompasses God as God and God as world; the Spirit is the trinity of one, love and Freedom."[13] God is Spirit when the moment of identity is mediated in the difference of the world, and what results are various shapes of freedom.

In a sense, Hodgson's trinitarian formulation of God provides a blueprint for the remainder of his argument: the triadic understanding One, Love, and Freedom manifested in God, World, and Spirit is the outline for the rest of the book. God really is the "All-in-all" in Hodgson's formulation—having outlined "God" as triune figuration, he will give greater attention to the categories of World and Spirit in the sections on history and freedom that follow. The three, however, *are* dynamically interrelated in his formulation, and (just as his understanding of God contains substantial

9. Ibid., 103.
10. Ibid., 106.
11. Ibid., 107.
12. Ibid., 111.
13. Ibid., 112.

reflection on history and freedom), he will continue to develop theological themes in the sections on history as de-configurative process and freedom as liberating praxis.

Hodgson's chapter on history is the most wide-ranging and difficult in the book, moving from Hegel and Troeltsch through other modern and post-modern philosophies of history, exploring the relationship between narrative construction and historical construction, and finally moving toward characterizing history as an ambiguous process which can be accounted for in a variety of competing ways. In the first general division of the chapter, Hodgson explores what he calls the "con-figuring" elements involved in sketching an outline of history, mainly drawing on and explicating the philosophies/theologies of history of Hegel and Troeltsch. He finds much that is interesting and useful in their characterizations, including distinctions between "levels" of history, "soft relativism" (in which a truth is seen to be relative in its context, but still true), and the religious basis for maintaining a teleology (however faint and ill-defined). Certain intuitions of narrative constructions of history, most notably from Hayden White and Paul Ricoeur, also emphasize the moral and religious basis for an ultimately comic (as opposed to tragic) mode of emplotment in history, as well as the constructive character of history itself. These insights show the "con-figuring" character of history—the way in which it shapes and forms the raw facts of existence into a comprehensible and meaning-giving unity.

The narrative analysis of history, however, is a two-edged sword, pointing out both that history is configuring and also calling into question the basis of that configuring character. Certain narrative understandings of history question the relation between the ideological commitments of the author and her or his emplotment of history, wondering whether or not the author/critic finds what she or he looks for. Hodgson also discusses the poststructuralist critics of history, such as Derrida, Foucault, Taylor, and Gillespie. While Hodgson is skeptical of the completeness of their analysis in characterizing history as abyss, genealogy, or fiction, he acknowledges the force of the critique brought about by these critics' attention to an hermeneutic of violence and domination in the historical realm: "Who today after Nietzsche and Freud, after Hitler and Stalin, after Verdun and Dachau can still believe in the triumph of reason? How can we avoid the conclusion that not reason but unreason rules in history?"[14] "It is not easy to dispute the claim that the only drama ever staged in history is 'the endlessly repeated play of dominations.'"[15] History has de-figuring as well as con-figuring elements, and is therefore ambiguous in character.

Hodgson's final characterization of history as a "de-configurative process" is both an admission of this ambiguity and an attempt to point beyond it. He points to the analyses of Paul Tillich, Paul Ricoeur, Ruth Page, and David Tracy, as affirming and fleshing out the highly ambiguous nature of our historical existence. He approvingly quotes Tracy's quest for a stronger term—"ambiguity may be too mild a word to describe the strange mixture of great good and frightening evil that our history reveals"[16] but notes that "for the time being it may be the best we have."[17] Hodgson finally enlists Rebecca Chopp's analysis of liberation and political theologies as both a confirmation of the deeply ambiguous character of history and as pointing to a way to find a point of reference from which to engage in positive action. Her insight is that suffering is interruptive "because of its 'nonidentity' character: that is we lack the ability fully to express and comprehend it; we cannot fit it into an interpretive schema by which we might make some sense of it."[18] Chopp holds that such suffering demands a "praxis of suffering," which entails solidarity with the sufferers. Hodgson agrees wholeheartedly, but also points out that such an analysis needs a counterpart in working out the presence in history of liberating elements as well, if we are not to give into nihilism in the face of such interruptive horror. Instead

---

14. Gillespie, *Hegel, Heidegger, and the Ground of History*, 114, quoted in Hodgson, *God in History*, 168. It is interesting, however, that the force of the post-structuralists' critique of history is strongest when they are presenting not the end of history as such, but an alternative vision of history as tragic or grotesque, an appeal to the horrifying reality rather than the optimistic unreality. Thus, their strongest arguments are *substantive* rather than de-constructive of meaning as such. Foucault is more convincing as a revisionist historian than a cultural theorist. There seems to be an implicit condemnation in his "dispassionate" analysis of the horrors of history—an almost "Enlightenment" naiveté that understanding of the "truth" will lead to a better society.

15. Hodgson, *God in History*, 179.

16. David Tracy, *Plurality and Ambiguity*, 73, quoted in Hodgson, *God in History*. 181.

17. Hodgson, *God in History*, 181.

18. Ibid. In a certain sense this is similar to John Roth's and D. Z. Phillips' critiques of attempts to "solve" the problem of evil, in that any "solution" is a muting of the radical character of the suffering, which demands to be alleviated, not comprehended or explained. See Roth, "A Theodicy of Protest," 18; and Phillips, "The Problem of Evil," 192.

of giving in to "a this-worldly hedonism or an other-worldly indifference" Hodgson presents the possibility of

> turn[ing] back to history with a renewed determination, with a sober, almost defiant hope that possibilities for transformation do exist within history despite the terrible interruptions, that the praxis of suffering can issue in the praxis of freedom. Suffering, poverty, and oppression are not ends in themselves, they are abominations, evils, that must constantly be resisted and combated. The praxis of suffering is a negative work; it must be converted into a positive work, the praxis of freedom.[19]

The very disintegrative character of the radical suffering which is the greatest challenge to any sort of historical formulation points to the necessity of engagement within that historical process for the actualization of God in the World as Freedom.

Actualizing God in the world in the shapes of Freedom demands, in Hodgson's view, a turn from theory to praxis. In the face of the ambiguous character of the analysis of history, he holds that "the determination to act can have a salutary, clarifying, releasing effect, overcoming the inertia and uncertainty that frequently burden a purely theoretical weighing of alternatives."[20] He enlists four major twentieth-century thinkers behind this thesis: Gadamer, Habermas, Rorty, and Arendt.

In addition to these major figures in the field of philosophy, Hodgson finds corroboration of the turn to praxis among theologians as well. He cites both Johann Baptist Metz and Gustavo Gutiérrez as examples of this turn. Metz provides a broad emphasis on praxis by insisting that theory and praxis are in a dialectical relationship, and by opposing what he sees as a prior trend in theology of the "nondialectical subordination of praxis to theory."[21] Hodgson appreciates this viewpoint, but thinks that Gutiérrez comes closer to the mark when he proposes that "theology is critical reflection on a praxis that always in some sense precedes it."[22] Hodgson agrees with Gutiérrez, but points out that in addition "creative theology can itself be an act of praxis. . .surely Gutiérrez's is."[23] He then posits that praxis can be understood as a "concrete totality" (something akin to Hegel's

---

19. Hodgson, *God in History*, 182–83.
20. Ibid., 186.
21. Metz, *Faith in History and Society*, 50, cited in Hodgson, *God In History*, 189.
22. Hodgson, *God in History*, 190.
23. Ibid., 191.

"concrete universal") which captures "within a single concept all the essential dimensions of human being . . . The category of praxis brings into play all the dimensions of human existence simultaneously."[24] Something like praxis is necessary to bring "God" and "history" together for Hodgson: "God and history are conjoined at the point of praxis—not indiscriminate, amorphous praxis, but praxis of a distinctive sort, namely, free, liberating, emancipatory, transfigurative praxis. Such praxis *is* the concrete universal—God and history together in the shapes of freedom."[25]

Hodgson has one final point to make about praxis. Once again following Bernstein's analysis, he points out that all of the major philosophers who advocate praxis over theory presuppose communities where a type of solidarity, which makes praxis possible at all, exists beforehand. Arendt speaks of the way in which action for public freedom arises "miraculously," and Habermas of the resiliency of communicative reason "even when it is violated and silenced again and again."[26] Hodgson points beyond Bernstein to the religious source of such a vision, positing that it is in this vision that God's shapes arise and are known and form history. His next section will explore both how he views God acting in history and the paradigmatic ways in which Christians have understood the shapes of God in history in the form of Jesus' life, death, and resurrection.

How God acts in history is, of course, the crux of the matter. In Hodgson's eyes, it is at the point of dialectical intersection between "two interacting factors: ideal and real, possible and actual, universal and particular, transcendent and immanent, divine and human"[27] that the shaping influence of God on historical process can be perceived. The central metaphor is that of shapes and shaping, as opposed to idea or ideal. "Shape" is more concrete than "idea." Hodgson draws on a volume edited by Owen C. Thomas[28] to examine contemporary thought on God's activity in the world, outlining briefly the theories which he finds less helpful ("personal action," "primary cause," and "two perspectives and languages), and with more depth those he finds congenial to his notion of "shaping"– "uniform action" and "process." While appreciating the emphasis on God "acting" through

---

24. Ibid.
25. Ibid.
26. Bernstein, *Beyond Objectivism and Relativism*, 228, cited in Hodgson, *God in History*, 193.
27. Hodgson, *God in History*, 194.
28. Thomas, ed., *God's Activity in the World*.

being God in a dynamic interrelationship with the world, Hodgson worries that such a formulation is too vague. What does the shape look like? It takes the shape of transfiguring, liberative praxis.

As mentioned above, Hodgson holds that understanding the activity of God in history is best expressed as a shape, rather than an idea or a person. A shape is not tied to one person, and can take multiple forms and permutations throughout time. It is the expression of Spirit: Hodgson follows Hegel in insisting there is never *Geist* without *Gestalt*. Also, the divine "idea" without a "shape" would remain simply an abstract idea. Hodgson argues convincingly that the "'divine idea' or 'rational-ethical values' do not appear in history as a theoretical principle or set of ideals but as a structure of praxis, a pattern or gestalt that guides, lures, and shapes historical process."[29] Once again, the question of what specifically that shape looks like rises, and Hodgson here answers confessionally: "for Christians the person of Jesus of Nazareth played and continues to play a normative role in mediating the shape of God in history, which is the shape of love in freedom."[30] This love in freedom is understood paradigmatically in the gestalts of the *basileia*, the cross, and the resurrection of Jesus. The *basileia* is the community of open wholeness that surrounded Jesus in his life; the cross shows the violent response of the economies of domination to such a community; and the resurrection shows that even death cannot keep such divine shapes from coming to be in the world again and again. These are the ways in which Christians see the influence of the divine Gestalt in the world.

All of these gestalts or shapes are seen by Hodgson as contributing to greater and greater freedom. His trinitarian theology comes full circle as he reflects on the final term in the understanding of God as the One who Loves in Freedom. After examining the etymological roots and meanings of freedom, Hodgson points out that various clues from Hegel point us to move beyond intersubjective understandings of freedom to the "objective, institutional" level of "universal freedom,"[31] in which communities are shaped by the ideas of justice or "right." He examines Habermas' theory of "'communicative action,' which is a type of social interaction mediated by discourse and oriented toward reaching understanding,"[32] and, while

---

29. Hodgson, *God in History*, 208.
30. Ibid., 209.
31. Ibid., 219.
32. Ibid., 220.

Freedom and Praxis

finding it suggestive, wishes to move more in the direction of praxis rather than understanding. Thus Hodgson proposes a theory of "communicative freedom" which is oriented toward "emancipatory praxis."[33] He grounds such a theory theologically, in which liberation is experienced as an "empowerment from within. . .which makes it possible for us to think and act anew, to break through distorted communication, to shape communities of freedom afresh, when all the resources at our disposal have been exhausted."[34]

This understanding of communicative freedom and emancipatory praxis grounded in the historical process can account for the partial nature of liberation—it is a process, not an endpoint. Hodgson cites both James Cone and Rosemary Radford Ruether as pointing out in their work how the process of liberation is an uneven one, impeded by the "powers and principalities" aligned against it, but how it is a real liberation nevertheless. Such an understanding of "a plurality of partial, fragmentary, ambiguous histories of freedom"[35] concerned with shaping "fragile syntheses of values and praxis. . .which achieve momentary, relative victories over chaos and tyranny through a process of confrontation and compromise"[36] is nearer to the truth than any false triumphal march of the old salvation history. As such, it is an "open teleology" rather than a determined one, and can be used to craft a new understanding of the "history of freedom" accordingly.

This "open teleology" gives the possibility of beginning to craft a new "history of freedom" beyond the totalizing discourses of past treatments. Hodgson suggests two metaphors from Hegel that could be profitable in shaping new cultural syntheses: the work of art and the helical spiral. The work of art is a unity in itself, occupying time and space, but with a character open to myriad interpretations. The work of art depends as much on the observer as on the artist for its effect. It is intersubjective, non-exclusive (there are many works of art), and open toward the future. The other metaphor is the helical spiral that points out the undulating pattern of movements of freedom and justice, rather than a linear progression.

---

33. There is an important line of argument that Hodgson deals with here—that of the question of the unredeemed suffering of those who are sacrificed in the cause of freedom. While he takes the question seriously, he holds that even such a radical question does not mean that we can avoid speaking of praxis in history. Death is not final, nor is it the whole of life.

34. Hodgson, *God in History*, 229.

35. Ibid., 233.

36. Ibid.

Both of these metaphors point Hodgson toward postulating the "shapes of freedom" as the goal of history, and to call for an attempt to outline the "history of freedom within history."[37] The shapes of freedom that call us to liberating praxis are the shapes of God in history.

Before taking up Hodgson's suggestion of attempting to elucidate a small part of the history of freedom by outlining what one or two "shapes of freedom" look like in the contemporary world, we will first return to Whitehead's understanding of the interaction between God and history to compare and contrast it with Hodgson's, hoping for some fruitful interaction between these two thinkers. A closer examination of parts of their respective analyses will shed light on both theories, and will lead to a more complete understanding of the relation between history and the Divine.

WHITEHEAD AND HODGSON: PROCESS, FREEDOM, AND THE END(S) OF HISTORY

In this section, we will first examine the specific points at which Hodgson discusses Whitehead and Whiteheadian thinkers in relation to his own view. We will consider how Hodgson has used Whitehead, and will suggest, based on an analysis of the concept of freedom in both thinkers, that they can offer mutually correcting analyses, illustrating the limits of each other's thought and pushing both thinkers' concepts to a more adequate view of the interaction between God and the world. This will lead to a more prolonged discussion of "nature" and "history," in which I will maintain that both concepts should be seen as on a continuum, rather than separate from and opposed to one another. And, finally, Hodgson's emphasis on praxis and the participatory quality of historical existence, exemplified in "shapes of freedom," will lead us into the following chapters.

There are many points at which Hodgson's and Whitehead's theories of God and history are very similar. This is, as pointed out earlier, one consequence of both Whitehead and Hegel emphasizing event over substance in the general philosophical scheme of things.[38] Thus Hodgson's characterization of history as deconfigurative process would not be at all strange to Whitehead or anyone influenced by him. The idea in Whitehead's *oeuvre* that all of actuality, including history, is in process is obvious to the most

---

37. Ibid., 246. There are echoes here of Barth's history of the covenant that provides the interpretive key to understanding the remainder of history.

38. Cobb, *Process Theology as Political Theology*, 19.

cursory inspection: after all, Whiteheadian-influenced thought is often called *process* thought.[39] What Hodgson aims at by the term "de-configurative"—an appreciation of the ambiguous character of history and an insistence upon its tragicomic character—is also emphasized by Whitehead.[40] Even an insistence upon the character of evil as pointing beyond itself to a moral vision, so important for Hodgson's understanding of history, is alluded to by Whitehead as well.[41] It is in the question of the characterization of the source of this moral vision—in the doctrine of God—and in the question of God's interaction with the world that Hodgson feels that he differs from Whitehead and Whiteheadian thinkers.

Hodgson has three points in his essay at which he dialogues with Whitehead and Whiteheadian thinkers. The first of these is in his discussion of the nature of God, and while appreciating much of what process theologians have said about "God's relativity vis-à-vis the world. . ., how God acts in the world. . ., rethinking the question of evil, and . . . affirming the open, unfinished character of history" he chooses instead to "explore the possibilities of a different conceptual framework"[42]—that of Hegel. He wishes to explore possibilities that have not yet been explored, and also has "an intuitive conviction that a triadic dialectic is better able to account both for reality as experienced and for divine process than a dipolar one."[43] So in his first treatment of Whitehead, Hodgson agrees with the Whiteheadian insistence upon process and the real relations of God with the world, while differing with the characterization of it. It is mostly a detailing of the Whiteheadian position on God and its permutations through Cobb, Lewis Ford, Langdon Gilkey, Charles Hartshorne, and Schubert Ogden, without much discussion or evaluation. He takes a different path and leaves it at that.

The second point in Hodgson's essay where he comes into conversation with Whiteheadian ideas is in the section on the activity of God—where exactly the point is where we can say "God was here," so to speak.

---

39. A few concrete examples among many of the insistence upon process in Whitehead's thought are *Adventures of Ideas*, 274–75; *Process and Reality*, 208–15; and *Modes of Thought*, 86–104.

40. See, for example, *Religion in the Making*, 17: "The fact of evil, interwoven with the texture of the world, shows that in the nature of things there remains effectiveness for degradation."

41. See ibid., 17, 97; and *Adventures of Ideas*, 286.

42. Hodgson, *God in History*, 81.

43. Ibid.

The Purposes of God

Here Hodgson engages more fully with the Whiteheadian thinkers, finding Ogden's suggestion that God "re-presents" the universal divine presence in "'certain distinctively human words and deeds'"[44] akin to his characterization of God as the gestalt of freedom in history. He also is appreciative of Cobb's understanding of God as "unitary actuality of cosmic scope and everlasting duration that in every moment confronts us with new ideal possibilities"[45] and of Cobb's discussion of the "real influence" of God that is not coercive.[46] He worries, however, that the formulations of the process theologians (influence, presence) are not definite enough to provide a concrete understanding of God's action. He prefers his notion of shape/gestalt. I would interject at this point that Ogden's insistence upon the significance of Jesus[47] is anything but indefinite. Be that as it may, Hodgson seems to think that he is saying something substantially different than the process theologians when he says that "What God does in history is not simply to 'be there' as God or to 'call us forward,' or to assume a personal 'role,' but to 'shape'—to shape a multifaceted transfigurative praxis."[48] But is this the case? Certainly the words are different—Whiteheadian "adventure" is not Hodgsonian "transfigurative liberating praxis." But there are more similarities than meet the eye.

When Hodgson states that God shapes the world "by giving, disclosing, in some sense *being* the normative shape, the paradigm of [transfigurative] praxis"[49] he is not that far removed from the Whiteheadian notion that God acts by presenting ideal aims to each individual actuality which gets ingressed or not into the makeup of that entity. What Hodgson has done is describe more fully what the process looks like in human history, most specifically with reference to freedom. If

> God is present in specific shapes of patterns of praxis that have a configuring, transformative power within historical process, moving the process in a determinate direction, that of the creative

---

44. Ogden, *The Reality of God*, 164–87, quoted in Hodgson, *God in History*, 201.

45. Cobb, "Natural Causality and Divine Action," 207–22, quoted in Hodgson, *God in History*, 202.

46. See Hodgson, *God in History*, 202, for a basic agreement with Cobb's point: "These metaphorical *gestalten* are not empirically visible but they have a real power to shape the world..."

47. "Jesus... is God's decisive act in human history," in Ogden *The Reality of God*, 186.

48. Hodgson, *God in History*, 205.

49. Ibid.

unification of multiplicities of elements into new wholes, into creative syntheses that build human solidarity, enhance freedom, break systemic oppression, heal the injured and broken, and care for the natural,[50]

then Hodgson's characterization of God can be thought of as a particular exemplification of Whitehead's more general notion of God. Certainly, all the ethical work done by Cobb on the subject of the environment and economics[51] points in a definite direction of "new cultural syntheses" that are liberating and transfigurative, having as their goal solidarity, freedom, the end of oppression, healing, and care for the natural.

Indeed there is consonance between Hodgson and Cobb in on many levels. This can be seen most clearly in their understandings of what sorts of activities are ongoing in the praxis of liberation. I here take my clue from Marjorie Suchocki's contention that John Cobb does indeed develop a pneumatology alongside his theological and christological works of *A Christian Natural Theology* and *Christ in a Pluralistic Age*. However, this pneumatology is not a single volume. Instead, it is implied in major works on ecology, economics, politics, education and interreligious dialogue. These comprise his doctrine of the Spirit. Her point is that his realization that "it is no longer simply sufficient to reinterpret faith, one must transform it for the sake of the transformation of the world"[52] becomes the work of the Spirit participating in the ongoing processes of life.

The Spirit, in Suchocki's creative interpretation of Cobb, is "the creative transformation realized in the world that is offered by "Christ" —the initial aim and Logos of God; she holds that "insofar as we instantiate that aim, the Spirit is born in us, becoming one with us in the creation of community."[53] As Suchocki points out, "the Spirit combines God and the world. . .in human history. Taking the event of Jesus to be the paradigm instance of such a revelation, those of us in the Christian tradition recognize God's incarnate Spirit wherever the Spirit may emerge."[54] Such a characterization fleshes out the discussion of the work of the incarnate

---

50. Ibid.

51. See, Cobb and Daly, *For the Common Good*; Cobb, *Is It Too Late? A Theology of Ecology*; and Cobb and Birch, *The Liberation of Life*.

52. Suchocki, "Spirit in and through the World," 177.

53. Ibid., 184.

54. Ibid., 186. Again, very similar to Hodgson's notion of the incarnation of Jesus and its function in the world.

Spirit in the world: in liberating praxis, in concern for making the world a better place in line with the ideal aims of God—Truth, Beauty, Art, Adventure, Peace (and also Justice, following our discussion in chapter four)—the Spirit works in each and every concrete act that contributes to these goals. As Cobb demonstrates, in and through the content of his (according to Suchocki) pneumatological works, the shape of God is in economic and ecological work, in education, in religious dialogue and pluralism, and in political and ethical work. Cobb's reflection and creative work *is in fact* part of the work of the Spirit, the praxis of liberation, participating (*a la* Tillich's notion of symbolization) in that towards which it points.

Of course, it is perhaps natural that Whiteheadian-influenced Christians will have much in common with Hegelian-influenced Christians, so more examination of Whitehead proper will throw more light on the consonance between the two. But first, let us examine the last point at which Hodgson deals specifically with Whiteheadian ideas.

This concluding point is in Hodgson's "final analysis" where he points toward the need for an "open-ended" teleology (as opposed to either a loss of teleology altogether or a "closed" teleology where the end is already presupposed, as in Pannenberg), citing Cobb as an eminent example of such a presentation in contemporary theology. He differs from Cobb's affirmation of Whitehead's vision of adventure and peace in *Adventures of Ideas*, choosing instead to highlight his own synthesis of Hegel, Troeltsch, and others in the service of freedom. He does think, however, that he and Cobb are fundamentally similar in their call for an open-ended teleology. The question then becomes, which teleology? Once again, Hodgson and Whitehead's teleological visions are not opposing so much as they are complementary, each mutually illustrating the other's analyses and offering insights that correct each other's omissions.

The best example in pointing out how this mutual correction can be done is in each thinker's treatment of the topic of freedom. Whitehead and Hodgson have very differing visions of what freedom is, although each operates under a similar theoretical understanding of the way the world works. They share an emphasis on the ongoing nature of the world process, as opposed to any notion of static categories, and both also share an emphasis on the religious viewpoint as giving a hint to what the ultimate

Freedom and Praxis

purpose of the world is all about.[55] On the surface, however, they could not be more different in their conceptions of freedom. For Hodgson, "freedom" means human freedom, and freedom in the interpersonal and historical realms. His treatment of the topic is based on literature that is philosophical (like Hegel) and political/historical (like Jaspers and Arendt). His emphasis on emancipatory praxis gives a clue as to what his final understanding of freedom is. It is a contextualized freedom, based upon the circumstances of the individuals and groups in question, but still deals almost exclusively with human questions of freedom within the realm of history.

Whitehead, on the other hand, conceives the question of freedom much more broadly. In his specific treatment of human freedom in *Adventures of Ideas*, he blasts the literary treatments of freedom as "dealing mainly with the frills."[56] What Whitehead is concerned about is freedom from hunger and cold, and from being locked into a static repetition of patterns. "Freedom of action is a primary human need."[57] This emphasis on freedom from the constraints of sheer meaningless repetition is something that pervades Whitehead's characterization of the world-process. Thus freedom is not only freedom within the human condition, but also in relation to and from the unrelenting processes of the natural world. Increasing freedom of action for the masses of people is a good, but the various ways of organization to achieve this end are seen in the context of the achievement of the freedom of organic processes from the repetition of inorganic ones. Indeed, Whitehead's most basic categories of existence, the actual entity and the attendant processes which compose it (see Chapter 4) can be thought of as explaining the processes of the actualization of freedom at its most basic levels. George R. Lucas has convincingly argued that the locus of freedom in Whitehead's metaphysics is in the category of the subjective aim of the actual entity.[58] It is at this point that non-determinism and the orientation toward ideal aims takes place, and thus freedom is in Whitehead's theory all the way down. Of course, a similar doctrine of metaphysical/ontological freedom is present in Hegel as well, but Hodgson's treatment of

---

55. Whitehead's treatment of the ideal opposites in *Adventures of Ideas* and *Process and Reality* finally comes down to a religious vision and trust in the goodness of the world-process, something very like the religious basis for an open teleology and trust in the ultimate comic vision of history detailed in Hodgson's treatment of history as deconfigurative process.

56. Whitehead, *Adventures of Ideas*, 66.

57. Ibid.

58. See Lucas, *Two Views of Freedom in Process Thought*, 15–52.

it is mostly from the side of culture, rather than a broader category which would include nature as well. The treatment of freedom in Whitehead's work is thus a multiple treatment—freedom as a basic component of all levels of actuality, freedom from inorganic staticity, increasing freedom within organic life, culminating in human existence, and finally increasing or decreasing freedom of human persons within societal organizations, evaluated on moral and aesthetic intuitions. The recognition that freedom is not only a process within history, but also within a natural context, has various positive consequences.

The first of the positive consequences of such a broader conception is the consideration of persons and things which fall outside the traditional scope of "history" as a construct. John Cobb, in a critique of Johann Baptist Metz' political theology, has pointed out that the very categories of "history," "politics" and "civilization" are oriented to urbanization and industrialization:

> Unconsciously, perhaps, the subsistence farmer, and even the peasant village, are assimilated to images of an unhistorical nature which serves civilisation [sic] and industrialisation [sic] but has no inherent reality. After all, history and sociology are written by urban people. Rural areas are viewed as remote and backward. Primitive cultures are studied by anthropology, not sociology. History belongs to the city.[59]

While Cobb faults Metz' Kantian anthropocentrism for the narrowness of view which leads to this neglect of vast areas of population and environments in a way that does not necessarily apply to Hodgson's Hegelianism[60], much of Hodgson's discussion focuses upon the purely cultural to the exclusion of the natural context of the historical process. One gets the impression, although it is not explicitly stated nor philosophically necessary, that the "public freedom" founded by the "emancipatory praxis" that Hodgson speaks about is primarily for communities of people who have come to some consciousness of their state of oppression within the larger system

---

59. Cobb, *Process Theology as Political Theology*, 120.

60. Cobb finds the exclusive Kantian emphasis on the subjective side of the subject/object divide at fault for the discounting of nature in the work of Metz and other political theologians. Hegel's more complete analysis of freedom as an ontological category, and his insistence upon the dialectic all the way down does not admit of the same critique. However, Hodgson does deal mostly with the same sorts of themes that Metz and other political theologians deal with: "history" as an urban story, or the story of the triumph of the city.

of economic and political exploitation. Indeed, his mentions of the natural world are cursory and feel almost like an afterthought in his discussion of the role of history, or the condition by which history is able to continue.[61] Whitehead's broader vision of freedom as an integral part of all existence reminds us that we are natural creatures, and that culture is so embedded in nature that they are separated at their peril. Historical freedom is an extension of natural freedom.

A continuing question that is central to this discussion of providence, the role of God in relation to the world, is the relationship between nature and history. In one especially clear example, the "argument from design" works beautifully at the level of descriptive "laws," forces, and molecules, but not so well at the level of societies of living beings "red in tooth and claw" competing with or parasitizing upon each other. Is nature merely the "stage" or medium within which history plays itself out? Is history "nature writ large," a more intense and dramatic illustration of the general principles that seem to form and shape the basic categories of nature? How best to understand that relationship, nature as an analogy/hermeneutical clue for history, or vice versa? And the role of God? Is it different for nature? For history?

There are (at least) two considerations here: 1) We are thoroughly embodied beings, and to split us into a "body" from the realm of "nature" and a "soul," that interacts with other "souls" to form "history" seems artificial at best. The fragile chemistry of our minds, so easily sent awry, would seem to argue for a unitary vision of humanity. Also, the degree to which culture, the realm of "history," is intertwined with and dependent upon "nature" seems to demand a theory that can be consistently held across both realms (if indeed there are two). To understand history-within-nature on the analogy of person-in-nature, intertwined with one another, dependent upon one another, shaping one another, a single expression, seems most adequate to our experience of it.

2) The difference between "nature" and "history" can be seen to be one of degree, rather than of kind. Of course, the "degree" amounts to a great deal: the difference between the fragile coalition to preserve peace in Western Europe based on economic and communicational relationships since 1945 is vastly different from the inner workings of the Golgi apparatus in

---

61. See, for example, Hodgson, *God in History*, 237; see also Hodgson's discussion of Ruether's vision of a society in which human and non-human systems are harmonized (ibid., 232–33) is introduced without comment, although this aspect of the natural is a significant departure from the strictly historical discussion preceding it.

The Purposes of God

the cells of all the living beings involved. Ultimately, however, we could not have history without the Golgi apparatus, or something like it, and thus the interaction of God with the world would need to take into account both the wonder that life and the systems that preserve it came into being at all, and also the series of tragedies and triumphs in history that has been the result of that life. The doctrines of creation and providence can be seen as a single doctrine, with expressions appropriate to the character of the beings discussed. Whitehead's discussion of freedom at multiple levels of existence reminds us to keep the discussion of "God-in-history" focused in its broader, "natural" context.

At the same time that Whitehead reminds us to focus on a broader context in discussions of God and freedom, Hodgson's emphasis on praxis as the primary category to understand God's work in the world offers a "corrective" to Whitehead's at times more detached view of human action in history. The vision of Adventure and Peace (a Peace which is based on Justice!) or Permanence and Flux in Whitehead is a starting point, not an end. In one sense, the placement of these categories at the end of Whitehead's books is unfortunate, because it can imply that they are the final word on the subject. If the scheme that they describe is at all true, this is not the case. They are *ideals*, the beginning and end (*telos*) of the action that continues in an ongoing process. How these ideals are worked out, in ongoing praxis, is what life will in fact look like. Whitehead does seem to recognize this as he points to "the economic interpretation of history"[62] as an advance over previous understandings—the conviction that how life works itself out in commerce and daily life is the place at which the real debates take place—in lived practical life, not contemplation of ideas. Perhaps this is a re-ordering of "Adventure" and "Peace" in Whitehead's vision—the primacy of Peace seems arbitrary, so why not the primacy of Adventure, informed by a religious, aesthetic, moral vision? Perhaps in view of the tremendous destruction and waste that takes place at the historical level of reality, the cry must be "Peace? There can be no Peace!" Action, engagement with the historical world, Hodgson's category of praxis, is required.

Hodgson's emphasis on praxis can be seen as a shift from Whitehead's "contemplative" vision to a more "action-oriented" one. This is not to say that the contemplative vision is not important—Hodgson himself points out that such a religious and moral vision is necessary to overcome irony

---

62. Whitehead, *Adventures of Ideas*, 66.

Freedom and Praxis

and meaninglessness at the heart of history.[63] But the vision is not an end in itself. The end is to actualize the just society that one has envisioned. Hodgson brings a fresh reminder of and emphasis on the creative, active nature of human being, in addition to the contemplative nature. Indeed, he makes the case that this active, creative, part of human nature is primary to who and what we are.[64] Praxis takes the vision of adventure and peace and tries to flesh it out—in the specific attention to specific shapes of freedom Hodgson points beyond Whitehead.

Such an analysis, is, of course, not final. Indeed, Hodgson himself points out that his analysis is another beginning, not the last word on the subject. In calling his concluding chapter "The Beginning of the History of Freedom?," Hodgson issues a challenge for further reflection on the topic of freedom and the shapes of freedom, with specific attention to specific communities and persons and situations to see what "love in freedom" really means. Is "Freedom" as such the end? Does the divine spirit move in other directions? Can aesthetic pursuits be reduced to a function of freedom? Although greater actualization of freedom can be a goal in and of itself (thinking in the cultural world of freedom from slavery or freedom as expressed in Beethoven's 9th Symphony), it seems to me that consideration of the goal which freedom serves is at least as important as the consideration of freedom as such. Hodgson points in this direction with his characterization of "love in freedom" as the shape of God in history. Freedom needs to be *for* something. This is not a criticism of Hodgson, but an attempt to take what he says seriously. What would the shapes of Freedom in history look like?

---

63. See Hodgson, *God in History*, 158.

64. Of course, Whitehead's scheme does have something like this same understanding in the insistence upon the self-creativity of every being—see *Process and Reality*, 47–48. Hodgson brings out more clearly what this activity will look like at the level of culture than Whitehead does.

6

Freedom for Beauty and the Other
Contexts, Objects, Subjects

As we have seen in the last chapter, one way to formulate a contemporary doctrine of providence is to follow Peter Hodgson's analysis. He asserts that the influence of God in history is in the "shapes of freedom" that become incarnate, leading to (hopefully) new shapes and so on in a never-ending, ever-expanding history of freedom in the world. He does not spell out what those shapes are in detail, pointing only to the tantalizing "beginnings of a history of freedom," looking back and forward at the shapes that have occurred, calling for efforts to try to begin to interpret and document the progress of the consciousness of freedom in the world. However, freedom *as such* is a difficult concept. Freedom, as mentioned in the conclusion of the previous chapter, is necessarily a contextualized and conditioned thing. We are free *from* things, people, social constructs; and we are free *for* things, people, social constructs. Freedom always has a context and an object. Hodgson, of course, knows this well. His book is mainly on setting some theoretical boundaries and establishing the possibility of the discussion of freedom in a milieu that is less and less hospitable to such a conversation. He calls for the specifics and leaves the door wide open for those who will follow. In response to that call, this chapter is an attempt to contribute to the discussion of the forms and shapes of freedom in history, which are, following Hodgson's analysis, the incarnation of the Spirit of God in the world, which constitutes God's providential activity. We will call attention to certain objects, contexts, and subjects of freedom. They cannot be considered entirely separately, of course, as they intertwine with and affect one another.

First, we will examine the way in which freedom must be for something or someone, and hold up Gustavo Gutiérrez' insight that freedom is for "the other." We will also insist that freedom must be for oneself at some level as well. Following this discussion of freedom for the self and the other, we will move into a consideration of the various contexts of freedom—natural, social, and political—and its objects in those contexts—the self, the other, and the poor. And, finally, we will call attention to the subjective nature of freedom, building on Hodgson's insight that the point of praxis is the key by which to understand and participate in the action of God in history. Thus the contexts, objects and subjects of freedom for the self and the other will be considered, maintaining throughout the emphasis on the shaping force of God in history. Following this, we will point the discussion toward a consideration of beauty and its relation to freedom.

This discussion is meant to be suggestive, not exhaustive. Discussions of beauty and freedom will hopefully go on forever, finding new shapes and new expressions in their contexts and for their subjects. God and history, after all, seem to be realities that continue to fill our lives. Others will certainly have other points of view, other ideas of what freedom is from and for, and what beauty is, and how the two fit together in the realm of history, and how God is related to all three. This chapter offers suggestions as to what those shapes of freedom and beauty will look like in our own time and place—what the aim of God for the world in our cultural situation might be.

FREEDOM FOR THE OTHER, FREEDOM FOR THE SELF

In considering the question of providence, of God in history, of the shapes that freedom takes in the life of the world, it is good to consider who or what freedom is for. Gustavo Gutiérrez, in discussing the theological meaning of liberation, cites St. Paul's insistence that Christ liberated us in order to make us free; and then answering his own rhetorical question as to what we are made free for, answers, "Free to love."[1] Expounding further on this insight, he quotes Dietrich Bonhoeffer:

---

1. Gustavo Gutiérrez, *Liberation*, 24.

> In the language of the Bible, freedom is not something man [sic] has for himself but something he [sic] has for others . . . It is not a possession, a presence, an object, . . . but a relationship between two persons. Being free means 'being free for the other,' because the other has bound me to him [sic]. Only in relationship to the other am I free.[2]

These insights call important attention to the relational meaning of freedom—that freedom, like everything else in human experience, does not happen in a vacuum. There is no such thing as "freedom as such,"—every aspect of freedom, considered concretely, has an aspect of "freedom from" and "freedom for." Gutiérrez and Bonhoeffer call attention to the interpersonal and socio-political contexts of freedom, insisting that part of the Christian experience of being made free from sin is considering what that means for those around us with whom we are in relationship. Thus Gutiérrez can rightly claim that "[t]he freedom to which we are called presupposes the going out of oneself, the breaking down of our selfishness and of all the structures that support our selfishness; the foundation of this freedom is openness to others."[3] Freedom does not occur without a social context, and it is a relational category.

Such an understanding presupposes and builds upon the understanding of God's activity in the world detailed in the previous two chapters on Whitehead and Hodgson. Without the understanding of the possibility of freedom in the metaphysical vision of Whitehead, freedom as such would be an illusion. Without an orientation to value characterized by something like Whitehead's ideal aims, or Hodgson's praxis of freedom, talk such as Gutiérrez' and Bonhoeffer's is vain. In fact their orientation toward a particular type of freedom, freedom for the other, is an important incarnation of the moments of identity and difference in the divine life and therefore the shape of freedom as the Spirit in the world that Hodgson understands as the activity of God. Such a discussion of the object of freedom is not exhaustive, however.

There is still one important caveat that must be dealt with before we proceed any further: being free for the other does not mean sacrificing one's very self. This is a new oppression, not freedom. Several feminist authors have pointed out the dangers of a self-abnegating spirituality for those in disempowered positions in society. Those in power can easily exploit the

---

2. Bonhoeffer, *Creation and Fall*; quoted in Gutiérrez, *Liberation*, 24.
3. Gutiérrez, *Liberation*, 24.

Freedom for Beauty and the Other

powerless by calling on them to sacrifice further or by "elevating" their suffering, while continuing to enjoy their own power and privilege. Thus Susan Nelson Dunfee points out that it is not Reinhold Niebuhr's sin of pride that North American Christian women have been especially prone to, but the sin of hiding.[4] It is not out of selfishness but rather self-negation that many women have acted and continue to act, and their denial of self has primarily benefited those in power—in this context, men. There is a world of difference between having the freedom truly to be for an other and having those in power encourage or dictate what one will be or will not be for. Freedom for the other may only make sense in a world in which the subject is concretely and subjectively already in some sense free. Gutiérrez is speaking to a privileged community—those who have the leisure to read and write theology. For the poor about whom he speaks, freedom for oneself is perhaps the primary objective.

An example from Nobel Prize-winning author Toni Morrison's novel *Beloved* illustrates this point. One of the main characters, Paul D., after walking down a street in New Jersey a free man and working for money rather than because he was a slave for the first time, decides that "to eat, walk, and sleep anywhere was life as good as it got."[5] His focus is on experiencing being free—working for wages, eating, sleeping, and loving where *he* wishes to, and then moving on. While this could be seen as living only for himself, being free for oneself is an integral part of being free at all. The radical negation of freedom in the institution of slavery, with all of its concomitant horrors, leads to freedom for oneself being the primary focus of life, rather than freedom specifically for others. Hegel's point about the progress of the consciousness of freedom ending up where *all* realize that they are free[6] is germane to the topic. People must be free for themselves in addition to being free for others.

The freedom for oneself is as much an exemplification of the shaping force of God on history as the freedom for the other. Without something like Whitehead's God, it is futile to speak of freedom at all, at least, to speak of freedom as a *good*, something beyond mere indeterminacy. The strongly felt character of the betterness of freedom for oneself, rather than subjection (or slavery, in the case of Morrison's novel) has no sense without some

---

4. Dunfee, *Beyond Servanthood*, chap. 4.
5. Morrison, *Beloved*, 269–70.
6. Hegel, *The Philosophy of History*, 17–19.

grounding in the ideal aims of Whitehead or the "One" of Hodgson.[7] Freedom is not chaos, but a better state of existence.

The preceding discussion of freedom for oneself and/or others shows that neither can happen in abstraction from one another. Gutiérrez and Bonhoeffer insist that Christian freedom is freedom for the other. Nelson points out the reality that in certain conditions of oppression, the self can be lost in the insistence upon the other. And Morrison's story illustrates that sometimes living out one's own freedom is the only proper response to the massive structural violence that enslaves both body and soul. Surely the truth must take all of these insights into account. To be free must mean that one is free in some sense for one's own self, and that being free for oneself is an irreducible part of being free for the other. At the same time, to be free only for oneself, without consideration of the social context in which one finds oneself, can and does lead to institutionalized selfishness and further oppression of those further down the socioeconomic scale. So both insights must be taken seriously, and accorded their proper due. Both insights point to the various contexts in which freedom for the other and the self take place as the primary consideration to take into account. Consideration of the context is a good first step in weighing the needs of self and other in their appropriate relationship.

THE NATURAL CONTEXT OF FREEDOM

The variety of contexts in which freedom operates is rich and multiplex, and will of course vary with each individual. No characterization will be absolutely adequate to every individual's experience. Nevertheless, there are certain points in terms of the contexts of each individual that allow us to see better what we are talking about when we discuss freedom for the other. These contexts will to a large extent shape the possibilities for the actualization of freedom that are open to individuals and social groups. Such a consideration of contexts allows us to take seriously the radically historical nature of our experience, as William Dean has reminded us is so important. Any freedom at all means being part of various contexts and

---

7. Morrison herself made the passing remark that almost all African-American people believe in God. While this might have sociological explanations, it also can be referenced to the clear experience of increased value in moving from a subjugated to a more free state in American society (of course, much work remains to be done on this front as well). "Trouble in Paradise."

Freedom for Beauty and the Other

communities—natural, interpersonal, and socio-political—and a discussion of these will make it clearer what the shape of freedom will look like.

The first context within which the freedom of the individual for the other is actualized is the *natural* context. In our mechanized and technological world this understanding of ourselves as first and foremost natural creatures, animals, in a context that either sustains or damages our physical bodies is often pushed into the background. We often consider ourselves to be "thinking animals" or "conscious animals" or "members of a society" or "*human* beings" with the emphasis on the constructs of our minds and cultures. This is in many senses appropriate, as our social interactions are our most intense and meaningful ones, and do shape the decisions we make to a far greater level than any other. Nevertheless, before moving on to the interpersonal and social contexts in which our freedom operates, it behooves us to consider ourselves as physical bodies, affected by and affecting natural contexts. Such a consideration will ground our discussion of freedom, and also provide some oft-neglected points of consideration in terms of what our freedom is for.

We are first and foremost biological forms of life. This means that, like all other biological forms of life, we have a finite lifespan, having a definite time of birth, experiences of life, and a point at which we will cease to be. Our finitude, bounded by the edges of our life, is the fact at which freedom comes to an end. History is a cultural and social concept, and as such transcends this finitude to a certain extent, but all of its participants are biological life forms with these same constraints. History, too, will one day either come to an end or so radically transcend its physical character as to no longer be history at all. So even a discussion of history has these same limitations. In addition to the finite limits of an individual human life, there is also the biological context needed to sustain each physical body. Each of us needs food, water, air, sleep, and companionship in order to continue to function. Bertrand Russell is supposed to have said that if everyone would eat three square meals a day and walk for six miles,[8] taking care of the animal part of ourselves, we'd all be much better off. Although this comment betrays a certain insensitivity towards those who don't have the abundance of food or leisure to engage in such activities, it calls attention to our nature as physical selves, with physical needs, that are the context and basis of all other social and cultural discussions, including those of freedom.

---

8. I have searched and searched for the reference to no avail.

What, then, does our nature as biological beings have to do with freedom, besides being its ultimate constraint? To a large degree, much of the discussion of freedom has been about being free from the various natural and biological constraints placed upon us. Hegel asserts that one prime directive of human culture is to transform the material world in order to make us freer from it.[9] William James talks about a "war against nature"[10] in order to transform it for human needs. Whitehead holds that "the primary function of Reason is the direction of the attack on the environment" with the purpose "to live, to live well, and to live better."[11] There is tremendous truth in such insights. From the beginnings of agriculture to the newest technological gadget, much cultural energy has gone into making us free from the constraints of our natural, bodily limitations. To a large degree, this effort has been successful, at least in the so-called "first world." We now have inoculations to prevent the childhood diseases that since the dawn of time were a "natural" part of human existence. We live in heated or cooled environments, and it is possible for the most affluent to travel around the world in hours. There are even discussions now about preserving individual humans for 200–250 years in a relatively robust state.

Recent attention, however, has been given to the negative effects of such single-minded concentration on escaping the "natural" limitations of the human being. A culture so concentrated on escaping from the natural constraints of biology does not often look to the cost of the measures it enacts in order to be free. Much contemporary reflection on the ecological crisis points out that it is a consumer society bent on convenience regardless of the costs that does so much damage to the environment.[12] In addition, the search for the "freedom" of more consumption by the affluent is often at the expense of more basic freedoms, such as the freedom from starvation or freedom from exploitation, of the poor. Without a consideration of the effects of the freedom from natural limits, affluent members of technological societies can pursue great personal freedom at a cost of ecological devastation and social exploitation. Freedom for some is at the expense of

---

9. See entry on Hegel, *The Encyclopedia of Philosophy*, 3:438.

10. In James, "The Moral Equivalent of War." See 299: "To the coal and iron mines, to freight trains, to fishing fleets in December . . . to road-building and tunnel-making, to foundries and stoke-holes, and to the frames of sky-scrapers would our gilded youths be drafted off . . . [They would] have done their part in the immemorial human warfare against nature . . ."

11. Whitehead, *The Function of Reason*, 8.

12. See, for example, Ruether, *Gaia and God*, 88–89.

Freedom for Beauty and the Other

freedom for most, and threatens, in the form of ecological holocausts, the freedom of all.

Once again, paying attention to the ideal aims and goals of freedom will bring these issues into sharper relief. A praxis that has justice as one of its ideal aims cannot abide freedom only for the privileged few. Such a society destroys the conditions for peace, and will ultimately undercut its own reason for existing at all. It is manifestly contrary to the vision of open love that Hogdson holds out as the *basiliea* of Jesus—the paradigmatic shape of God in history for Christians.

In addition to the natural context of the individual as a biological entity, we see that there is also the consideration of the individual as an entity in an ecosystem, as a member of an ecological context and community. This is in addition to the interpersonal and social communities that we will consider in more detail later. But the individual's exercising her or his freedom, or working toward greater freedom from their natural context, always has consequences for that natural environment. This is *not* always bad. There is a tendency in much ecological literature to point out the terrible effect humans have on their environment just by existing.[13] What these nay-sayers neglect is the nature of life, that it is a catalytic agent that greatly increases the rate of entropy as a trade-off for increased intensity.[14] We are going to burn things up. The point that more reflective observers tend to make is that human beings do have real choices regarding the extent of the damage they will do. If human beings neglect the web of life that sustains them either through greed or ignorance, they will destroy the basis of life altogether and commit suicide. Rosemary Radford Ruether makes this point emphatically in relation to dietary practices in Western-influenced countries:

> One result of this expansion of the meat, especially beef, diet is the excessive grazing of animals, which is destroying forests and polluting streams though failure to recycle animal excrement. A large segment of humans today is starving or malnourished, and this is partly related to the fact that a Western elite is eating high off the food chain.

She then moves from analyzing the effects of these actions on the contexts of their perpetrators to the ethical solution called for:

---

13. See, for example, Manes, *Green Rage*.
14. See Whitehead, *Process and Reality*, 105–6.

> Both inter-human justice and a sustainable relation to the rest of nature demands that humans return to feeding themselves primarily from the first stage of the food chain, from the food produced by plants.[15]

The question of dietary practices is a classic example of the need to examine contexts when considering questions of freedom. Who can be against people getting better nutrition? As we noted above, proper care of the human body is a necessity for life itself and therefore for the discussion of human freedom at its most basic level. Yet when considered in the wider framework of the natural and social contexts of human life and freedom, the difficulties become clear. The privilege of the wealthy few impinges upon the basic freedom of the poorer many, and destabilizes the natural environment upon which both depend. Such a relation is not just. The shapes of freedom must be considered together with their natural backgrounds, and not in abstraction from the contexts which constitute them.

One final point on the natural context of freedom that has already been suggested by the preceding discussion: human freedom is actualized and has effects not only in the realm of the biological person or in the local ecosystem, but as part of a global system as well. This is a natural extension and broadening of the previous discussion. An analysis of the effects of actions on the immediate local context is not enough. Humanity has achieved such power in its pursuit of the freedom and leisure of the wealthy that the consequences of actions have effects far beyond the immediate environs of the actor. The perhaps classic example is the nuclear fallout from the Chernobyl disaster, affecting milk supplies throughout Europe and Asia. Other examples are global warming and the depletion of the ozone layer, situations that have consequences for all life and are mostly the product of the industrial practices of a few wealthy nations. Here again, attempting to be free from one's natural circumstances can lead to a breakdown of those circumstances itself, and thus of the conditions for the further actualization of freedom.

What then can finally be said regarding the relation of freedom to its *natural* contexts—those of the human person as a biological form of life, as a participant in a local ecosystem, and as a participant in a global ecosystem? First, let us address the question from the position of being free from various constraints. The first and most obvious question of "freedom from" is in terms of the biological nature of the human body. Freedom can

---

15. Ruether, *Gaia and God*, 52.

scarcely be discussed without some mention of the needs of the physical body—freedom from cold, hunger, thirst, etc. Such a consideration underscores the nature of the human being as a biological life form, and paradoxically points to one of the major constraints that human beings are *not* free from: death. As biological beings, human beings are firmly within, not outside of, nature, and "in nature death is not an enemy, but a friend of the life process."[16] All life depends upon death of some sort, and the attempt to be free from death may be a major contributor to the "inability of cultures to create sustainable ecosystems."[17] We will explore this point in more detail later in considering the social context of freedom.

But human beings not only struggle to be free from oppression of whatever kind in their natural context, they are also, as Gutiérrez reminds us, free *for* something if they are free at all. Freedom is directed toward a goal; it is not merely the squirming out from under some unfortunate condition. In the natural context, what is freedom directed toward? In the first place, it is directed towards the freedom of the individual self from the overwhelming grasp of the natural world. Again, because we have become so technologized in the last century, it is easy to forget precisely how dependent upon nature we are. Natural disasters remind us over and over again of our individual and cultural powerlessness in the face of nature. But it does not take a natural disaster to illustrate to what extent nature has power over, and is ultimately indifferent to, each of us on an individual and collective level. Swimming in the ocean on a sunny day and being caught in a riptide is an uncomfortable reminder of the tenuousness of our natural life. Is it any wonder that we build boats and wear life jackets? Freedom for the self is one orientation of freedom in the world.

Another, as Gutiérrez reminds us, is freedom for the other.[18] Within the natural context of freedom, it is specifically the non-human forms of life that we are free for, in addition to ourselves. Rosemary Radford Ruether points out that much contemporary thought on nature has taken a hierarchical, militaristic vision of nature as the "other" to be vanquished, annihilated, with all too predictable results. She insists upon the need for a consideration of the "others" of nature as "members of a biotic community

---

16. Ibid., 53.

17. Ibid.

18. We will deal specifically with the others that Gutiérrez is most concerned with, the poor, in the forthcoming section on the social context of freedom.

upon which we depend for our life."[19] In this case, being free for the other and free for ourselves, indeed the very basis of our freedom, is one and the same thing. Freedom for the non-human other is thus as much a part of freedom as freedom for the self or for other human beings.

THE SOCIAL-POLITICAL CONTEXT OF FREEDOM

In addition to the biological and ecological contexts of freedom, there are also the social and political ones. This is not to say that they are distinct from one another, of course—they are in fact so intertwined with one another that distinctions, when closely examined, seem to be matters of degree rather than kind. As Ruether reminds us, "even to differentiate 'social' from 'natural' reflects too much the modern dualism."[20] In addition, the mutually interdependent nature of natural and social contexts insist that any analysis that claims to be adequate to the human situation consider each in terms of the other. Nevertheless, our interpersonal and political contexts are in many senses *the* way in which we see the world. To this end, without forgetting the natural contexts of freedom, we now turn our attention to the social and political contexts of freedom, to see how these too illustrate the working out of the shape of God in history as freedom.

In the first place, our nature as human beings is, at our deepest level, to be social beings. Our sociality is the most important part of ourselves. A mere glance at some recent psychological literature makes this concept almost beyond dispute. "Classical" psychoanalysts such as the Freudians, ego psychologists, and object-relations theorists, all stress early childhood experience as pivotal in childhood development.[21] Others stress the role of peer groups over the influence of parents in children's personality.[22] However, both groups agree that social influence is the most important factor; they disagree only about which group is doing the socializing.

Even the recent physicalist trend in psychiatric treatment, emphasizing the role of malfunctioning brain physiology and chemistry and its pharmacological treatment, serves to emphasize the social nature of human being.[23] What is most difficult in psychotic patients with schizophrenia, for

19. Ibid., 57.
20. Ibid., 209–10.
21. See. Mitchell and Black, *Freud and Beyond*, especially chaps. 1–5.
22. See Harris, *The Nurture Assumption*.
23. See Shorter, *A History of Psychiatry*, especially chap. 7, "The Second Biological

example, is that their malfunctioning brains cause them to see and hear a different reality from everyone around them. Precisely because so much of reality is socially constructed, they soon realize that no one else shares their terrifying world, and understandably become paranoid. One of the saddest aspects of mental illness is that the people who suffer from it are often utterly alone.

In addition to the testimony of the psychological literature, recent anthropological literature from a variety of philosophical and theological orientations stresses the social nature of human beings. For example, Jean Mouroux, the French Neo-Thomist points out, in the non-inclusive language of 1948, the absolutely social nature of the human personality:

> As a unique and specified image each man has to realize some hitherto unknown aspect of humanity by way of the development of his own personal resources and values. He can do it only by entering into union with others, and by thus setting up this community, extended across space, charged with live and meaning, nourishing and expressive, which we call society. . . .Whenever he falls back into himself he feels his ties with the human community, he discovers there the call of the whole species, and that is why his essential power is the natural love of the Whole. He is a member and a part; he is defined by his significance for, and his position and role in, the species.[24]

In a similar observation from a radically different philosophical perspective, the Barthian pastoral theologian Ray S. Anderson holds that social identity is prior to individuation:

> What we call singularity of being may be said to be social before it is psychological. . . .[I]ndividuality as a form of human being is a result of differentiation through relation with another. The differentiation which constitutes the determination of humanity as a singular experience is a *history* of the self in encounter—this is the radical social nature of humanity.[25]

And, finally, the "multi-dimensional" and "realist" anthropology championed by Latin American feminist María Pilar Aquino, insists upon the social dimension of women's and men's being over against an "idealist" and "one-dimensional" anthropology. Speaking of the bodily existence of

---

Psychiatry."

24. Mouroux, *The Meaning of Man*, 120–21.
25. Anderson, *On Being Human*, 46–47; emphasis original.

women and men, she emphasizes its social elements: "Women and men have no other way of being persons except in their bodily existence. This is how they relate, interact, communicate, and express their lives."[26] Relating, interacting, communicating, and expressing all imply someone to do such activities with or to—for Aquino, as for the other theologians mentioned above, human reality is social reality at a profound and affecting level. Each theorist, despite differing philosophical and theological perspectives, affirms that human existence in the singular is largely constituted by human existence in the plural.

Both Mouroux's and Aquino's analyses, however, point us beyond the purely interpersonal to the realm of the organized social context of humanity, that is, the political. The distinction between social and political is fuzzy, and may only reflect a difference in size and in the level of organization. However, some discussion of purely political realities in addition to social ones will benefit our characterization of the contexts of freedom. It is in terms of the political realm that much of the enormous literature on freedom has been written. "Freedom," indeed, has nearly always meant freedom in a relation to another social group. This has often meant that people have only considered freedom in terms of some kind of legal arrangement, instead of permeating all levels of society. Laws, of course, are vastly important, reflecting the formal rules by which a society will live. The manumission of slaves in the European and American societies in the nineteenth century was a hugely significant event. But, as further analysis of the condition of Americans of African descent in the late nineteenth and twentieth centuries has shown, freedom is not simply a matter of changing the laws. It is a cultural effort that needs to take place at all levels of society. Gutiérrez calls it "the continuous creation, never ending, of a new way to be human, a *permanent cultural revolution*."[27] Subjective commitment, in addition to consideration of the contexts and objects of freedom, is necessary in order to actualize freedom in the world.

All abstract theorizing about the political context of freedom is, of course, useless without attention to the particularities of the situations discussed. Political (and social and natural, too, of course) situations must be considered in their specificity. It is at this point that the liberation and feminist theologians, with their emphasis on experience—especially of the poor and women—as primary, and the tools of the social sciences they use

---

26. Aquino, *Our Cry for Life*, 89.
27. Gutiérrez, *Liberation*, 21.

to analyze and critique the existing power structures, are the best examples of contextualizing freedom in the social and political realms. The precise context that Gutiérrez, for example, has in mind is Latin America, with its radical inequality in terms of the distribution of the material needs of human life. Thus Christian freedom calls him in his context towards working for the liberation of the peoples of Latin America from unjust social structures, and toward the establishment of more just ones.

This Christian freedom, the call of God for Gutiérrez, has shape, form, reality in and through his activity, and the activity of others that he analyzes and allies himself with. This is a prime example of the doctrine of providence as a call to make the world a better place in and through our own activity, a response to the call of God. God presents possible solutions to the felt inequality, and also provides the impetus to work towards their transformation into something new and better—more just, more equitable, more beautiful.

This discussion of freedom in its particularity of social and political contexts, calls us back to the consideration of what freedom is from and for in the social and political senses, just as in the natural realm. In the first place, as we mentioned above, much of the discussion of freedom has been in terms of the political sense of being free from oppression. Whether this has taken the form of having the "inalienable rights" of the U.S. Constitution, such as the right to keeping the police out of one's home unless they have a warrant, or some other conception of freedom from oppression, this is the primary way in which theories of freedom have been formulated.

It behooves us, however, to examine slightly further what this freedom in a social and political context would entail, taking into consideration examples raised from some of those most concerned about it. "Oppression" is such a general category that there is a tendency among those who have not experienced it firsthand to attribute it to the imaginations of those who are oppressed.[28] Thus, a few concrete examples are in order, to illustrate the struggle for freedom in the political and social realm. And this struggle for freedom is precisely what Hodgson points towards in his emphasis on praxis. It is in and through this struggle, the socio-political one, that the shape of God in history is mostly clearly seen. As women and men respond to felt injustice, observe possibilities for new values in their social and po-

---

28. Witness, for example, the passage of anti-affirmative action legislation in several Western American states, due mainly to the majority white position that "the playing field is level" now, and that no impediment to women and minority advancement exists any longer. Women and minorities, of course, seem to feel differently.

litical situations, they feel the orientation toward actualizing these goals. They feel that call of God to make a better world. This struggle for and actualization of freedom is precisely one shape of God in the world. Let us examine more closely what actualizing the aim of God entails.

Women and men are striving to be free from violent death. This is forgotten by those who live in countries that by and large have the rule of law, such as North American and European countries, or that have not fought a war in recent memory.[29] Violent death is a real possibility for the vast majority of the world's people, either from repression on the part of a government or government-sponsored group, such as the death squads in El Salvador, or on the part of criminals that take advantage of a lawless situation, or a cultural habit of violence such as of men against women. In addition, war has been the largest threat of violent death to the largest number of people throughout history. In a nuclear age, this threat is exponentially greater. In much the same way that people at a base level seek to be free from the whims of nature in providing the basic needs for their bodies to stay alive, they also seek to be free from the most pressing dangers of threat to their physical health in the social and political realm. Violent death, either from war, government repression, cultural practices or simple chaos is an ever-present threat to the lives and therefore freedom of most of the world's population.

The aim of God in orienting the world to such social structures that lessen the possibility of violent death is a prime example of the shape of freedom in the world. Violent, untimely death (as opposed to the ultimate destiny of all living things), as well as the social conditions that create it, are antithetical to the aim of God for freedom in the world. In the first place, because when people are dead they cannot experience freedom, and their intensity of feeling is lost to both themselves and to the divine life. And, secondly, because the conditions of chaos and lawlessness that are the conditions for wide-scale violent death do not lead to greater freedom in the social and political realm, but (by and large) to repression and further violence. Once again, freedom is not chaos.

Aside from violent death, which has a finality to it that gives it a primary consideration, there are other oppressions that people strive to be free from in their concrete social and political situations. One of these

---

29. Although it is not forgotten in the case of minorities in those societies, who can be just as susceptible to violent death at the hands of the authorities as members in other areas of the world. The Rampart scandal in Los Angeles, with most of the victims of police brutality being African-American or Hispanic, is a case in point.

is non-lethal violence, especially as perpetrated against women by men. In the United States, one out of every three women will be abused in her lifetime by a father, husband, or intimate partner. In Latin America, some surveys suggest that the level of violence against women is as high as 70 to 80 percent.[30] To be free, in the social and political context of being a woman around the world, needs to include being free from suffering systematic or occasional violence at the hands of whatever man happens to be in a familial relationship with her.

Freedom in a social or political context also is freedom from starvation. Although this might seems like part of the natural/biological context of freedom mentioned above, human starvation in the contemporary world is a political problem. Ever since the so-called "green revolution" of the 1960s and 1970s, most if not all famines have been either political or economic in nature, with those who have the food withholding it from those who do not. From the Ethiopian famine in the 1980s brought about by various warring factions using hunger as a means to subjugate the enemy, to the combination of pride and fear that kept North Korea from getting relief in the late 1990s, the reason for human starvation is greed or hatred, rather than lack of food.[31] To be free in a social or political fashion must mean to be free from starvation.

Freedom in a social and political context, however, must also mean to be free for people, passions, activities, as well as having a minimal level of security for one's body and family. It is in this context that some of the best work on freedom in a social context is done. Much of the above discussion on the freedom for the other, while at the same time not neglecting the freedom for one's own self, is relevant here. Freedom for one's self and for the other must be a part of any notion of freedom considered concretely. However, the "generalized" other is not sufficient to describe or evoke the shape of freedom in history. Juan Luis Segundo reminds us that not every "other" is the same:

> I do not believe that there is any other way of expressing the option for the poor concretely than to say that it is God's compassion for the most afflicted. When I say "for the most afflicted," I should not wish this to be understood as meaning some very sophisticated or subtle kind of suffering. The gospel is clear, even materialistic, in its indications of the priorities of suffering. I know very well that

30. Aquino, *Our Cry for Life*, 100.
31. See Ruether, *Gaia and God*, 92–96.

a wealthy person can suffer deeply and profoundly. But if I see a poor person drowning and I am speaking with the rich about their suffering, I would immediately go to the aid of the person drowning and would leave the suffering of the rich for some later time. The option for the poor is an option for those in whom the lack of humanness appears before us as the clearest priority to be addressed.[32]

The "preferential option for the poor" reminds us that freedom for the other means, in a Christian context, freedom for the poor precisely from their poverty. Indeed it means for those of us in a more affluent situation, the "conversion to the other." It is not merely an ideological or political "stance," or a concept that is intellectually held: it is a way of life that is lived out in concrete solidarity with the poor. Thus Jon Sobrino can say that "the Church of the Poor,"—that is, the church which has really and truly taken the preferential option for the poor and is living that option—"finds the historical site of conversion, *the place of the other and the force to become the other.*" Thus freedom can be seen in this case as illustrating its true nature—it is not an abstract "concept" to be worked out, a "belief" to be held, a "theory" to be elaborated. It is a way of life, an orientation, a social movement, that lives and breathes in the concrete existences of those whom it grasps and changes them forever: "And the most important thing, although it is apparently trivial in terms of mere conceptual reflection, is that it consequently happens in good measure."[33] The conversion to the other, even becoming the other, in a concrete fashion for the purposes of liberation, is the most important result that freedom brings in its social/historical context. Indeed, it is itself an instantiation of the shape of freedom, the providence of God, insofar as nothing transforms society (and therefore history) more radically in the orientation of justice and peace than such a conversion.

In addition to the freedom for the other as the preferential option for the poor, there is another aspect of the directivity of freedom that must be considered in order to have a fuller picture of its social and political context. Although it may be redundant to the very ideal of freedom as a social reality, the reality that freedom is freedom for the future merits discussion. Besides the emphasis on final causality and its implied "open teleology" discussed in the previous chapters on Hodgson and Whitehead, with the orientation

32. Segundo, "The Option for the Poor," 125.
33. Sobrino, *Resurrección*, 163; quoted in Segundo, *Signs*, 79.

to the possibilities for the future being pivotal in their discussion of the progress of cultural life, a few more points relating to the concrete relation of the social and physical aspects of freedom as freedom for the future are in order. The first of these is that in social terms, freedom for the future is freedom from the past. This does not mean that the past is somehow forgotten, or minimized, or held as unimportant. On the contrary, it is out of the past that the future is made, and in that sense the past does determine the future. Put concretely in terms of our previous discussion relating to freedom for the poor, there have been, for example, atrocities perpetrated by the government of El Salvador. However, *the future is open*. That there have been atrocities shapes what is and what will be, but it does not determine it. The atrocities in El Salvador can cease. Environmental degradation can be decreased. We do not have to continue on our destructive course. In this sense, we are not doomed to repeat the past. Trends in history may run differently, but it is not necessary that the mistakes of the past are a never-ending cycle of despair: "an endlessly repeated play of dominations." We *can* move in a different direction, and that we can is a great step in thinking that perhaps we *will*.

Such openness to the future, along with the ideal aims are the call to actualize them, are indeed the work of God in history. Indeed, history as such depends upon some sort of openness to the future, like that described by Whitehead and Hodgson.[34] God is the ground of such openness; the presentor of the options, and the lure towards actualizing the good, true, and beautiful in that open future.

One final comment on the social and political contexts of freedom: Juan Luis Segundo, speaking to the demands of an orientation that sees one as a participant in rather than an observer of history, calls attention to the distinction made by Jesus between those who wanted a "sign from heaven" and his own insistence on reading the "'signs of the times,' [or]. . .concrete transformations effected by himself in the historical present and then entrusted to his disciples both for the present and the future."[35] Segundo takes as primary, therefore, not the concern about "rightness" from an abstract or theological point of view which is then applied to the concrete historical situation, but instead holds that "Jesus' theology completely rules out applying any theological criterion to history *except the direct and present*

---

34. This is not the same orientation to the future championed by Wolfhart Pannenberg. This future is a possibility, not an actuality.

35. Segundo, "Capitalism-Socialism," 29.

evaluation of happenings here and now." The criteria for evaluating action in regards to liberation in the world is thus *"historical sensitivity, . . .* [or in] the Synoptic Gospels, . . . the 'heart'— . . . the hard and closed heart [or] the open, sensitive heart."[36] Any analysis of freedom will miss the point of freedom itself if it does not consider it from the perspective of the actual liberation or lack thereof taking place in the historical situation.

This underlines and makes clearer both the social and political contexts and the object of freedom in relation to another factor—the subject of freedom. Freedom, especially when thought of in terms of liberation for the someone, cannot be simply a question of a cold analysis of factors in the economic makeup of a situation. Freedom is a commitment to the working out of actual processes in history, with the subjective transformation this process requires. It is a matter of having one's heart open, and being willing to be moved and to act on what one's heart feels, without having to make sure that the actions are in line with some preconceived abstract notion of justice or compassion. This is not to say, or course, that there is no place for conceptual analysis or evaluation in choosing how to act for the cause of liberation. Of course there is. But it comes from the subjective willingness to be an actor in history, being moved by the context to work for freedom. The "signs of the times" are the union of the context and object of freedom, demanding the engagement of each subject's free action.

BEAUTY, FREEDOM, LOVE

One particular group of "cultural shapes" combines contexts, objects, and subjective action in a concrete totality. It includes freedom, but also could be viewed as a goal of freedom. I speak, of course, of beauty and its creation in the world. If the totality of our lives is about anything at all on the cultural level, it must be about beauty, in the creation and contemplation of beautiful things and ways of being. Beauty is not a cipher, the concept of which is more or less independent of context. The creation of a work of art necessarily is set in time and place, has definite parameters, has material constitution, and has a "meaning" for the time and place and persons by and for whom it was created. It cannot spring out of nothing and for no one. It must have natural, social, and political contexts. Let us consider the creation and contemplation of beauty as an aim for God in history, one of the shapes of freedom for the human epoch.

36. Ibid.; emphasis original.

Freedom for Beauty and the Other

Both Hodgson and Whitehead offer contributions on the subject of beauty and art that can advance the discussion. Hodgson invites us to consider the shape of "love-in-freedom," or the action of God in history, on the analogy of a work of art. The consideration of the totality of contexts, subjects, and objects that make up the continuing action of freedom in the world can be better understood in such a characterization. The work of art has a material context that has a meaning, but that meaning shifts according to the person making or experiencing it: "The art work gathers time and space into a meaningful presence, but the perfection it achieves is dialectical rather than univocal. . . .It is a specific temporal shape that does not enclose or enframe but rather opens out into infinity." In addition, beauty is not exclusive: "The perfection of one work of art does not exclude that of another."[37]

Hodgson, of course, is not discussing beauty as such, but is offering the analogy of a work of art as a way to understand the making of cultural shapes and forms that fashion history in a positive way as the continual, ongoing action of God in history. Nevertheless, such an imaginative connection highlights the consonance between the terms and offers illustrative power. In the making of art, as in the making of history, the aesthetic and moral considerations are primary.[38] And such aesthetic and moral criteria have their grounding, as we have seen, in the activity of God. There are contexts which make up, and yet do not exhaust the meaning of the art. And it is always capable of new interpretation, and can take new directions.

Whitehead has much to say about Beauty and Art that is germane to our discussion. He holds that Beauty is the point of everything, natural and cultural: "The teleology of the Universe is directed to the production of Beauty."[39] The endeavor of life has an aesthetic justification. The human effort to produce beauty has a special place in the human cultural realm: "The work of Art is a fragment of nature with the mark on it of a finite creative effort, so that it stands alone, an individual thing detailed from the vague infinity of its background."[40] Whitehead holds that art evokes vividness of life without the difficulties: "The secret of art lies in its freedom. The emotion and some elements of the experience itself are lived

---

37. Hodgson, *God in History*, 242.

38. For a discussion of morality and aesthetics as the criteria for historical judgment, see Harvey, *The Historian and the Believer*, especially chaps. 2 and 3.

39. Whitehead, *Adventures of Ideas*, 265.

40. Ibid., 270-71.

again divorced from their necessity. The strain is over, but the joy of intense feeling remains."[41] Freedom is not only for beauty, but beauty also is for freedom. Both aspects imply and mutually enhance each other, leading to "Adventures of Ideas," or civilization.

Both Hodgson and Whitehead insist on art as the paradigmatic way in which to understand the human "urge to beauty." And to a large degree, art is, as Whitehead says, "the consciously determined pursuit of beauty."[42] However, a danger in attending too closely to the cultural as opposed to the natural context of beauty can have a distorting effect. Whitehead ignores his own dictum that "the teleology of the Universe is the production of Beauty" when he denigrates the cultural value of natural beauty: "A sunset is glorious, but it dwarfs humanity and belongs to the general flow of nature. A million sunsets will not spur men on to civilization. It requires Art to evoke into consciousness the finite perfections which lie ready for human achievement."[43] Such an attitude does not appreciate the immense liberative effect of the beauty of the natural world on the human psyche. Nature as well as art can evoke and inspire freedom in the cultural world.

The role of nature in inspiring freedom can be illustrated by invoking a variety of sources, from the Romantics to environmental activist/novelist/philosopher Edward Abbey. One amazing example of the natural world inspiring freedom when every human institution has failed to do so can be discerned in the pages of Nobel Prize-winning author Toni Morrison's novel *Beloved*. In the harrowing accounts of the lives of the ex-slaves in Morrison's book, the natural world seems to intrude itself at some of the most horrifying times, with a reminder that, in spite of the tremendous suffering and lack of recourse of the sufferers, that there is still something more, and that not everything good has been destroyed. The very beauty of the world is a reproach to the human horrors perpetuated on it. Sethe, the character around whom the story revolves, always sees Sweet Home, the plantation where she lived in Kentucky, as a beautiful place, even though she cannot stand to remember it as such and hates herself for doing so:

> there was Sweet Home rolling, rolling, rolling out before her eyes, and although there was not a leaf on that farm that did not make her want to scream, it rolled itself out before her in shameless beauty . . . [she saw] Boys hanging from the most beautiful

41. Ibid., 272.
42. Ibid.
43. Ibid., 271.

sycamores in the world. Try as she might to make it otherwise, the sycamores beat out the children every time and she could not forgive her memory for that.[44]

It is the trees upon which children were hung that intrude upon her memory, and they are still beautiful even as they have been defiled by being used as a gallows. And even though Sethe cannot forgive herself for remembering their beauty, that same beauty still, in the face of all the horrors for which it is the setting, cannot help but be seen as what it is—beautiful. That she can see beauty at all in the world is reminder that there can still be something for which to love and live.

Paul D., the main male character of the book, has a similar relationship with the natural world—its beauty keeps trying to evoke love from him, even though he has buried all his feelings in the rusted-shut "tobacco tin" which he feels has replaced his heart. Every time he escapes from slavery (he has five abortive tries before the Civil War ends),

> he could not help being astonished by the beauty of this land that was not his. He hid in its breast, fingered its earth for food, clung to its banks to lap water and tried not to love it. On nights when the sky was personal, weak with the weight of its own stars, he made himself not love it . . . Anything could stir him and he tried hard not to love it.[45]

He cannot help himself from loving, as a response to the world, even though he feels he has to "love small . . . [the] grass blades, salamanders, spiders, woodpeckers, beetles, a kingdom of ants."[46] But that small love, which is all he feels he can manage, keeps the habit of loving alive, and helps him begin to open his "tobacco tin heart" at the end of book.

For both Sethe and Paul D., the beauty and the love it inspires lead towards freedom. The beauty of the world is what keeps the hope of freedom alive for both of them as they are progressively violated by institutions of destruction. The beauty of the natural world is in spite of and in the face of the horror of the cultural one. The only culture they know is the one that tells them that they are not their own people, whereas the beauty of the natural world calls forth a response from them that eventually proves to be

---

44. Morrison, *Beloved*, 6.
45. Ibid., 268.
46. Ibid., 162.

their salvation—it inspires them to never give up as they search for freedom and wholeness in a broken world.

From a consideration of beauty in the natural world and its effects, let us move to examine beauty in the cultural world and its interaction with and effect upon freedom. The first point is that this discussion of beauty is not a narrow aestheticism. It is rather an orientation toward the beautiful that takes place in all socio-economic aspects of life. Whitehead points out that "the teleology of the Universe is the production of Beauty"— beauty is the point at all levels of natural and cultural endeavor. Even to use the examples of art and "high" culture is to distort the discussion. It is more like an aesthetic orientation to life. This orientation is contingent upon the form that it takes, and visual art is only one form of its expression. Thus beauty is understood as one of the fundamental activities of human being, as the transformation of material to meet human needs,[47] it must take place not only on the level of "high" culture but throughout all levels of society—cooking, folk art, music, dance, etc.[48] Venezuelan feminist theologian Gladys Parentelli, in her study of the "natural" ecofeminist practices of the poor women of her country, emphasizes this orientation in the ways in which such women live their lives: "Women take advantage of the tiniest piece of earth, an empty can or jar to plant vegetables, spices, beans, even a fruit tree so that there are always sweet-smelling herbs and fresh, medicinal spices to give flavor to soups and salads."[49] In addition to utilization of scarce resources for aesthetic ends in the realm of household work, Parentelli also points out that these women create visual beauty out of their difficult circumstances as well: "A truck tire, filled with earth, becomes a flower bed . . . A vine from a flowering plant [planted beside a path] delights a passerby."[50] An orientation toward creating beauty for themselves and for others is basic to all socio-economic levels of existence. Such practices show how the poor women of Latin America live out an aesthetic orientation in their circumstances of life.

Of course, there are conditions in which it is not possible to even try to attempt these measures. Parentelli makes the distinction between "poverty"

---

47. Again, this insight is from Hegel, see above.

48. See, for example, Langer, "The Cultural Importance of Art," 75: "The ancient ubiquitous character of art contrasts sharply with the prevalent idea that art is a luxury product of civilization, a cultural frill, a piece of social veneer."

49. Parentelli, "Latin America's Poor Women," 33.

50. Ibid., 35.

and "misery." Thus, following on Parentelli's example of poor Latin American women, they must have access to seeds and earth and truck tires in order to enjoy even the minimal aesthetic fulfillment of planting flowers. They must have food before they can prepare it with attention to making it flavorful and healthy. Our attention is called back to the precise point of much liberation theology: the goal is providing minimal concrete social conditions for the poorest of the poor in and through concrete subjective and political engagement.[51] Such engagement is key to providing the social and natural possibilities for an aesthetic orientation to be actualized at all.

PROVIDENCE AS THE SPIRIT IN THE WORLD

Finally, then, in relation to our discussion of providence, we have explored the importance of the contexts and the objects of freedom in the world, the action of God in history. Attention must be paid to the specific contexts—natural, social, political—that freedom is actualized in. Also, the goals of freedom are as important as the contexts: what freedom is for is at least as important in recognizing its shape as where it comes from. And, finally, the engagement of each human subject in her or his context with her or his goals is a vital ingredient in the discussion of freedom.

What is left, then, to consider in trying to come to a contemporary and vibrant doctrine of providence? In the previous chapters, we have dealt with existentialism and historicism, process thought and Hegelian and liberation theology. In the final analysis, what is the action of God in the world? All of our contributors have valuable reflection on the subject—God acts on human lives, in the Christian tradition, inside as well as outside history, and for beauty and freedom. What remains is to provide a synthesis that incorporates the various important points regarding the action of God in the world, that takes into consideration the contexts, objects, and subjects in and upon which God moves towards the divine purposes in history, and also points us to the future, opening us to the action in the present for the future. In the next and final chapter, we will attend to the theological conception of the Spirit in the World as a way in which to understand God's activity in and through and for history.

---

51. Thus Anselm Min reminds us that liberation theology has chosen a dialectical vision of theology precisely because it offers the possibility of creating concrete social conditions for the poor "in which they too can enjoy liberty, equality, and justice." See Min, *Dialectic of Salvation*, 60.

7

The Spirit in and through the World

INTRODUCTION

MUCH OF THE LAST chapter has attended to the "shapes of God in history"—what, considered from the viewpoint of a Whiteheadian-influenced Hogdsonian liberation-oriented praxis of freedom, we could point to as the trace of God in history. We have attended to natural, social, and political reality, asking what the aims of freedom are, orienting them with regard to their contexts, objects, and subjects. Now at the end of the discussion, however, we will attempt to move full circle to attend once again to the question of God, and examine, in the light of our previous discussion, what we can and will say as we describe the divine reality and its interaction with the world.

Throughout this work I have attempted to show the insights and inadequacies, the possibilities and shortcomings, of various contemporary theological writers, with the hope of leading towards an adequate, vital, believable doctrine of providence—in short, an account of God's action in the world that is both contemporary and credible, that is not archaic and yet maintains a continuity with tradition, basically, what we can really mean when we say "God's hand in the world is seen *there*."

This has not been an easy process. In order to put my thoughts on paper, I have had to question what I really mean, and ask if I can *unambiguously* say that I believe that there is a God that acts in the world, or in history. My final answer is: I cannot. I cannot say with the same certitude that I have that I exist, that God exists, or that God's action in the

The Spirit in and through the World

world is clear and unambiguous. It is something that must be teased out and discerned, and is often a matter of interpretation and the judgment of faith.[1] Nevertheless, although I still at times fear Freud and Feuerbach, I do find the action of God in the world and on history, something that I can still ambiguously affirm. The question then is, how to speak about it in the most meaningful way? All languages are not created equal. In a compelling example, the language of *hypostases* and *ousia* in the classical formulation of the doctrine of the Trinity not only needs translation from its original Greek to make sense, but also needs cultural translation; even then is somewhat puzzling, as even those who used it admitted.[2] Given the impossibility of simply continuing to parrot the tradition, and also the discussion in the preceding chapters, what is the best possible language to speak about the action of God in history? What words give us the best sense of what we think to be the case?

Throughout this essay, we have explored something of the conceptual framework of what an adequate notion of the contemporary doctrine of providence might be. At this point, we will revisit the central point of Barth and Bultmann's exploration of the ideas of God in history—that life lived according to a vision of God provides the historical and empirical demonstration of such a belief. It is individual human beings and their communities, living out their authentic convictions, that matter in the religious/moral/ethical discussion of God's interaction with history.[3] While much time and energy was spent discussing the shortcomings of their existentialist views in chapter two, it is in particular the content (or lack thereof in Bultmann's case) that is objected to, rather than the contention that it is in the lives of people and communities that the discussion of the doctrine of providence will have its primary locus.

In addition to the key role religious and moral experience play in our construction of a doctrine of providence, such a doctrine must be adequate to the ambiguities of the historical record. As our discussion of William Dean's historicism showed us, any doctrine of providence that is to be adequate must take into account the ambiguities of historical existence, while at the same time not giving in to those ambiguities and reifying them as

---

1. I am thus conceding a *methodological* point to Karl Barth. Content, however, is another matter.

2. Thus, the continual assigning of the quality of "mystery" to the Trinity, more so than to any other doctrine.

3. Whitehead says something similar: "The power of God is the worship he [sic] inspires." Whitehead, *Science and the Modern World*, 192.

ultimate reality. A combination of some kind of radically empirical orientation, oriented not only to the historical record but also to the experience of value and the discrimination between and among experiences that such an orientation leads to, is necessary for a contemporary doctrine of providence.

Such a view can be found in the more comprehensive views of Whitehead and Hodgson, as well as with the developments of the various feminist and liberation theologians spoken about in chapter six. All such views point toward the concrete social and political and personal contexts and activities that make up much of the theological discussion. Taking into account the doctrine of God as outlined by Whitehead and Hodgson in chapters four and five, and continuing the discussion of the shapes of freedom from chapter six, let us continue trying to answer the question of what living a life in the Spirit-filled world could look like. Naturally, any such discussion will be informed by the processive orientation of Whitehead, the concentration upon praxis and freedom in Hodgson, and a discussion of the shapes of freedom in chapter six. My contention is that a doctrine of persons and communities living in a Spirit-filled world is the best way to understand and participate in the providential divine activity in the world.

While the doctrine of the Spirit in the world can (and, indeed, has) taken a variety of forms and expressions, three areas are the natural outgrowth of our earlier discussions. The first of these is that the Spirit is the primary way in which we experience and name the action of God in the world. It must be, if the answer to the question "Where is God's providence seen?" is to be an authentic answer. The second is that the Spirit is incarnate in the world, not just once in Jesus, but again and again, in new and multi-faceted ways. This must be so if we are to avoid the deepest pitfall of pneumatological orientations—a denigration of this world, so that the other "spiritual" realm can flourish in the imaginations (and societies) of those who champion it. And the third is that the work of the Spirit is transfigurative, liberating praxis, issuing in hope. I hold that this is so because I, as a Christian and observer, judge it to be so, from my own observation and from the persuasion of my theological forebears and colleagues. It is a theologically-informed judgment on the situation. In one sense, it is a statement of faith. So, these three aspects of the life in and of and through and to the Spirit remain in our discussion: its primacy in experience and therefore in discourse, its incarnation in the world, and its orientation to transfigurative, liberating praxis leading to hope. Let us examine the first of

The Spirit in and through the World

these contentions, that the Spirit is primary, on our way to seeing what the action of God in history looks like.

THE PRIMACY OF THE SPIRIT

It is my contention, continuing the above discussion, that any convincing account or persuasive essay about the action of God in the world will have the expression of God as described by the experience of the Spirit as primary. In so doing, I take my cue from perspicuous statements John Cobb has made in his essay on the relativization of the Trinity. In this work, Cobb points out that his primary difficulty with the Augustinian formulation of the Trinity is that it is not authentic—"it does not respond to any real problem in Christianity."[4] Cobb holds that any trinitarian formulation, if it is to both be worthy of spending our time on and contribute to an actual problem in Christianity, must be authentic. It must answer a real question or problem, as the Cappadocian metaphysical doctrine of the Trinity contributed to answering the problem "How is it that the same God experienced by the early church as the Spirit and addressed by Jesus as Father is incarnate in a special way in Jesus?" This is an authentic question, as is the question that I have discussed throughout the course of this essay—how does God act in history?[5] My response is that the best answer to this question lies in an exploration of the doctrine of the Spirit, precisely because it is an authentic answer to this authentic question.

Why return to a perhaps antiquated category for an (or the) appropriate answer to the question of God's action in history? Why, for example, do we not talk about God "The Father," or "The Lord" or "She Who Is"[6] or any of the other circumlocutions that have been traditionally associated with the so-called "first person" of the Trinity? Or why not, as has been the case in much discussion of God and history, talk about Jesus, the incarnation of God, who changed history, is the "midpoint of history"[7] or the inaugura-

---

4. Cobb, "The Relativization of the Trinity," 6.

5. With, of course, its important corollary questions: "Does God act in history?"; and, "How do we know that God acts in history?"

6. This phrase is, of course, Elizabeth A. Johnson's and does not, in her work, refer to the First Person of the Trinity, but to the whole of the divine mystery. Nonetheless, in so far as it is a counterpart to the "I AM" and the "HE WHO IS" of the Hebrew Scriptures and patriarchal reflection on the mystery of divinity, it is an appropriate feminist counterpart to the terms "Father" and the first person of the Trinity.

7. See Tillich, *Systematic Theology*, vol. 2, 100.

tion of the eschatological consciousness which is the viewpoint "outside of history?" Or, if not the traditionally first or second persons of the Trinity, why not discuss the mystery of the Trinity as a whole as the most appropriate answer, the best clue to the subject? Why is concentrating on the Spirit alone better than these more traditional answers, and why is it better, more authentic, than just talk about an undifferentiated "God"?

The first reason that talk about the Spirit best answers the question of the interaction with God in history is that it is in the life of the Spirit that we experience God's action specifically in the human realm. This is an almost entirely empirical orientation of the discussion. The fact that we do not live 2000 years ago and walk and talk with Jesus is crucial to this point. While those who wrote the foundational documents of the Christian faith may have had such contact with Jesus (this is not clear), and he may have been confessed as the incarnation of God, or the Son of God, or some such person/relation/thing (the tertuim quid), those of us living in the twentieth century have not had such an opportunity. It is not through Jesus, as a person, that we experience God's action in history. While such may have been the way in which the first Christians experienced the action of God in history, those of us who come after them experience (even in the specifically Christian sense) God's action in and through the community and its ongoing life, and also in and through our own personal moral and religious lives (but these, too, are often/always mediated through communities). Even the Christians at the time of the New Testament realized this, as they wrote extensively about the life of the Spirit in the Church, to the extent that Jesus is said by the author of the Fourth Gospel to have said that he had to go so that the Advocate/Helper could come.[8] The universal had to succeed the particular, the Spirit replace the Logos. Jesus being gone, and seemingly not returning any time soon, led to the importance of the life of the Spirit.[9] In this sense, in emphasizing the category of the Spirit and its role and function, we are in agreement with the earliest Christian documents and witness.

---

8. John 16:7. And see v. 8—"he (the Advocate/Spirit) will prove the world wrong about sin and righteousness and judgment"—the Spirit will be active in the world.

9. Rudolf Bultmann points to the neutralization of the eschatological consciousness in sacramentalism and the hope of immortality, and probably a greater emphasis on Spirit would fit here as well. He sees the trajectory leading away from eschatology already in the Gospel of John, which is where the above-mentioned vignette takes place. See *The Presence of Eternity*, chap. 4, especially 51–54.

The Spirit in and through the World

Why not the Mother or the Father, or the S/HE WHO IS, or the first person of the Trinity, or something like a non-trinitarian "God" (which is, of course, a return to a more classic monotheism)? Why can we not affirm something like God's rule in history, in the manner of Karl Barth?[10] The most compelling answer to this point is like the answer to the point about Jesus: this is not the way in which contemporary people experience God. The notions of Mother or Father, or King or Lord or Ruler or S/HE WHO IS, all harkening back to a more undifferentiated[11] and (sometimes) personal monotheism, have too much about them of the control of God over history over against our experience of evil in history. In addition, the traditional notion of God as Father has been convincingly shown by contemporary feminists to be too exclusivistic to be useful for a majority of the human population of the world. As Mary Daly and others compellingly point out, God as cosmic "Father" has more to do with the attempt by the leaders of a patriarchal culture to maintain control over women, lower class men, and the natural world than it does with experiences of the divine in history. "As long as God is male, the Male is God,"[12] (especially the upper-class males in power), and the same can be applied to God the Father. Such a conception is not the way in which the liberative, emancipatory, hope-filled, love-oriented presence of God is best expressed or the divine effect upon history maintained.[13]

Even if one holds that the language of a divine "Father" or "Mother" is not simply a reification of an existing social structure, designed with the idea (conscious or otherwise) of maintaining that structure, divine parental language is still problematic. Such language encourages a "spiritual infantilism," hoping (and counting on) Mommy or Daddy coming and "making everything all right." It encourages us to think of ourselves as children in a world that desperately needs committed, principled adults to address its

---

10. Barth, of course, is Christological to the point of Christo-monism (Harnack's comment about "Marcion all over again!" comes to mind) in much of his systematic reflection. However, insofar as his doctrine of providence is "The Christian Under the Universal Lordship of God the Father," he can be thought of as having a more strictly monotheistic conception of God.

11. By trinitarian speculation or reflection, that is.

12. Daly, *Beyond God the Father*, 19.

13. As, for example, Keller, *Apocalypse Now and Then*, 298: "Patriarchal Christianity has been unveiled as such. It can no longer exist except as antifeminism, shamed into defining itself publicly in terms of women: what better example of successful symbolic deligitimation?"

problems. It encourages passivity and submission to authorities. It does not point us to think of ourselves as "humanity come of age," in Bonhoeffer's memorable phrase, but as still in our spiritual (and therefore also moral and political) minority.[14] In so far as such language expresses either relations of origin or the kind of closeness and importance that we find in familial relations, there are other ways to express these concepts. For example, language expressing the relation of origin could be addressed by words like the divine source, breath, or spirit, and language expressing closeness and importance could be exemplified by Ruether's "Divine Matrix" or Tillich's "Ground of Being." In any case, language about God as an important person in our lives is too problematic to be useful as we attempt to find a way to talk about the divine action in history. We do not experience God primarily as Jesus, by virtue of our distance from the events and history, or as Mother/Father/Lord/King/Monarch, by virtue of the difficulty of these categories in contemporary life.[15]

It remains to be seen if the Trinity as a whole will fall prey to the same objections as the characterization of the first two divine persons. In many senses the doctrine of the Trinity has been the answer of the mainstream tradition to many of the problems raised in the above discussions of the so-called first and second persons of the divine reality. It is not anthropomorphic, it is not exclusively identified with one problematic group, and is inherently relational and dynamic. Nevertheless, while the Trinity may offer resources that Mother/Father/God and Jesus/Son/Logos do not in isolation, it is my contention that the Trinity as a whole is still too problematic to be retrieved for a contemporary doctrine of providence. In its traditional form, it still has more about it of the relation between and among the members of an aristocratic family over against a world of peasants. And such an aristocratic family has, in the traditional formulations, very little to do with those whom they rule. The traditional immanent Trinity has no necessary relation with the world. And insofar as revisionist Trinitarian formulations

---

14. Many theologians make this point, including Johnson in *She Who Is*, 178: "Speaking about God as mother, as is obvious from the tradition of God as father, could be used to perpetuate psychological immaturity, maintaining childish dependence on a comforting authority figure rather than encouraging adult responsibility for the world."

15. For example, democratic forms of societal organization hold that all monarchs are illegitimate—how can one believe that one should obey a "king"—either on earth *or* in heaven—in any authentic way? It may be in linguistic continuity with the tradition, but the meaning has changed around the word to the extent that it no longer can mean the same thing.

The Spirit in and through the World

such as Hodgson's posit a necessary connection with the world, following the model of an economic Trinity, there is no need for them to come in groups of three. Even if the trinity is the best symbol the tradition offers for God, it is certainly metaphorical, pointing to "a vast multiplicity barely symbolized by 'trinity.'"[16] Spirit, with its manifold and multiform and less differentiated connotations, can offer the same advantages, while not having the same difficulties. Thus, while further exploration of the Trinity and the wealth of Trinitarian reflection in the twentieth century might offer new directions for a contemporary doctrine of providence, we will leave such work for another paper and continue with the discussion.

It remains to be seen if the traditionally subordinated third member of the Trinity, the Spirit, will fall prey to the same or other insurmountable difficulties that will render it similarly unhelpful. There are many objections to it as well, which will be explored later in the chapter, in the section on the incarnation of the Spirit. Let us turn, however, from this discussion to a continuance of our consideration of the reasons that the Spirit is the primary way in which it is appropriate to speak about the action of God in history.

Moving beyond personal or monarchical metaphors for God can have a greatly clarifying effect on our understanding of God's action in the world. Emphasizing the distance between the divine and the human can emphatically remind us of the fact that God is *not* some kind of over-sized human being, and we cannot expect the divine reality to act as if it were. Jürgen Moltmann calls attention to this fact in his discussion of the Personhood of the Spirit, where most of his metaphors are distinctly non-personal. By introducing "space, tempest, Fire, and Love" into the "Personhood" of the Spirit, Moltmann effectively shows the limits of personal language and the necessity of moving beyond it if the totality of experience of the Spirit is to be adequately addressed.[17]

One reason that the Spirit can be a useful way in which to talk about the action of God in history is precisely because of the non-human character of spirit-oriented language. Humans are defined by our bodies, even in the body-soul dualism of traditional Christian thought, and much more so in the body-only monism of more contemporary Western materialism. Insofar as spirit enters into the discussion at all, it is as something that is somewhat mercurial, vivifying, but not exclusively human. Spirit is a part

---

16. Suchocki, "Spirit in and through the World," 188.
17. Moltmann, *The Spirit of Life*, 275ff.

(maybe the most important part) of being human, but other things share in the spirit's life. Indeed, "life" is perhaps the best analogue for "spirit"—and life is shared by many creatures in many forms. The meanings of the Greek, Hebrew, German, and English words for Spirit all bear this out in various ways—*ruach, pneuma, Geist*, and spirit all have connotations or alternate meanings of wind, breath, or ghost—images of unconstrainedness and freedom, but not exclusively humanistic ways of talking and thinking about existence and action.[18] This distance from the anthropomorphic tendencies of much theological talk emphasizes, in a positive fashion, the distance between human modes of being, thinking, and acting, and the divine ones. As long as we think analogically with regard to God as a "big human in the sky," it is easier to commit the fallacy of misplaced concreteness and, at times unconsciously, try to make "our ways God's ways." Language of God as Spirit reminds us that God does not act in the same manner and fashion that we act, and that God's action will look different from human actions. Protecting us from the rampant anthropomorphism[19] of much current God-language is one positive reason to use Spirit-language as we continue to speak about God's providential action in history.

Some might, as has been the case through much of the history of theological discourse, maintain that it is appropriate to continue to use personal language about divinity and its effects, as long as the language is held to be analogical.[20] That is, as our personal relations, especially ones with primary family members are often the most important, intense, and influential in our lives; so it is perfectly natural and even correct to continue to use personal language about family members in an analogical fashion for our religious lives, and the Mother/Father God will continue to have a place. This is an influential stream of thought. In addition, there is the argument that the years of traditional language about God as a divine parent have deeply rooted spiritual presence in the lives of religious people (probably the more

---

18. See Peter Hodgson's discussions of the meaning(s) of spirit in *God in History*, 110–11; and in *Spirit in the World*, 276–82.

19. This coinage is Marjorie Suchocki's. She used it in a Feminist Theology of God course at the Claremont Graduate University in 1996. It is in reference to the Trinity, but such usage applies equally well to Spirit-language.

20. See, for example, Johnson, *She Who Is*, 44. "God is not less than personal, and many of the most prized characteristics of God's relationship to the world, such as fidelity, compassion, and liberating love, belong to the human rather than the nonhuman world. Thus it is also appropriate, at times even preferable, to speak about God in human symbols."

The Spirit in and through the World

compelling argument, in light of my previous contentions about authenticity). These, as well as other considerations, make it clear that personal language about the divine reality persists, and I realize that any objection here will not necessarily stem the tide. I would, however, like to make a point regarding its unsuitability.

Although all language is analogical, some analogies are better than others. If the analogies are misleading, as personal ones about divinity often are, then if other language can be found that better expresses the realities behind the language, it should be used.[21] If, for example, the point is that personal God-language often leads to misguided ideas about divine power and its function and role in the world, then perhaps language that makes us think about God as a person should be avoided. Such a view is rooted in the nature of the theological enterprise. We put forth proposals, hoping that they will provide more stable ground to stand on. We argue a point, hoping that such argumentation will help us traverse to new concept. We clarify, hoping the light will make the journey more sane. Revolutions do not take place overnight, but the orientation of theological language does in fact change. Movement from concentration on the power of God to the love of God, although taking centuries, seems to have won the day. Perhaps non-personal God language will have a similar trajectory.

Thus we see that, in pointing to the distance between God and humans and the different types of realities and power that are the divine and human realities, the language of the Spirit provides significant advantages. Precisely because it points to a different realm of existence, it holds before our attention the fact that our ways of being and action and existence in the world are significantly different from the divine modes of being and action. It preserves us from the difficulties of a too-literal anthropomorphism. In pointing out the distinctiveness of the divine and human modes of existence, Spirit-language helps us on our way to finding the proper way to speak about God and the divine activity in the world.

In addition to its greater authenticity than language about Jesus or about a Lord or Parent, and in addition to providing us the necessary distance to cut down on some of the more egregious and harmful forms of

---

21. This point of view implies a commitment to the sort of theological and philosophical realism argued for by John B. Cobb in his essay, "In Defense of Realism," 179–99, and assumed (I would maintain) by any who seriously enter into theological discourse, as opposed to any sort of language-based theology. I agree with Cobb's belief "in gaining as much correspondence as possible between our thought about God and the way reality is," 198.

The Purposes of God

anthropomorphism, the usefulness of the primacy of theological language related to the Divine Spirit can be seen in its universality. From "the Spirit of God moving over the face of the waters" in the creation account in Genesis to the "Spirit renewing all creation" of the contemporary hymn, Spirit language is more oriented to the universality of God's love and action than many other kinds of theological language.

A quick comparison with some of the other forms of theological language will make this abundantly clear. First, although the question of the relation of Jesus to God is one of the central ones in Christianity, too-close identification of the "Son" with the "Father" is too particularistic to be of much use. First, such language is hopelessly masculine-centered, excluding women from full personhood by splitting humanity into a dualistic opposition, with women on the losing side. This effect has been documented and discussed from at least the middle of the nineteenth century on, from Elizabeth Cady Stanton to Mary Daly to Elizabeth A. Johnson. I consider the point settled. Second, even using anthropomorphizing language performs the same kind of dualistic splitting between human beings and the rest of nature, leading to thinking about our relation to God as one of a special class related to its founder, while the rest of the creation gets subordinated and takes on the character of things which are to be used by the "special" people. The danger of particularism, and its harmful results can also be illustrated by the continuous use of theological language to legitimate and justify the interests of one group of humans opposed to or over another group. The movement from God as progenitor of some sort to the progenitor of my group of people, and to the concomitant legitimation of my group's norms, values and practices over against another group's is clearly historically traceable. From God as the God of the Jews, and not of the Gentiles, to God as the Christian God and not the Jewish or Muslim one, to God as the God of white people and not of people with more skin pigmentation, and more examples too numerous too mention, all call attention to the fact that personal God-language, by emphasizing the close (often familial) relation between the God and the persons claiming such a God merely serves as a legitimating device for their values and practices, over against the values and practices of others.[22] My contention is that by

---

22. See, for example, Jaffee, "One God, One Revelation, One People." A quick summary from 774: "Elective monotheism is driven by the assumption that the God who loves does not do so indiscriminately; rather, the divine love is a scarce commodity . . . The means of obtaining it are carefully preserved for those within the communal boundary . . . The possession of divine love . . . is itself the warrant for ontological hatred of the

The Spirit in and through the World

concentrating on the differences between divine and human modes and methods of action, the language about God as Spirit can transcend these particularist differences and reflect the cosmic scope and universality of God and the divine action and influence on the world.

Jürgen Moltmann makes an important move in this direction as he points out that the Spirit cannot be only the Spirit of Christ, or of redemption, that is primarily or solely the Spirit of the Church, that is, the exclusive province of Christianity. It must also be the Spirit of the "Father [sic]," which is the Spirit of creation, the Spirit of Life. In so doing, he has laid the groundwork for a theology of the Spirit, questioning the Filioque clause in the Nicene creed, citing both its "untrinitarianess" and its pernicious effects in *de facto* limiting the Spirit's role to identity with the Church, as the Spirit of Christ, rather than as the *ruach* of YHWH, the breath of the Creator. So, in Christian circles and reflection, spirituality is only to be found within the church, often in opposition to the movement of the Spirit found in the cycles, experiences, and ongoing revelation of the created order, not to mention personal relations either outside of or contrary to the doctrines of the established church.[23]

In these points, I am completely in agreement with Moltmann. He rightly lauds the "discovery of the cosmic breadth of the Divine Spirit"[24] wherein there is more discussion of the Spirit of God as opposed to merely the Spirit of Christ. However, even in his terms he does not acknowledge or realize the *truly* cosmic breadth or the priority of the Spirit in religion or otherwise. In place of the "Spirit of Christ" or the "Spirit of God," we must instead postulate the Spirit as revealed in God/dess, or the Spirit revealed in Christ, as the primary loci of our contemporary reflection on the interaction of the divine with the world. If we are to participate in "the community of creation" and "have the fellowship of the Holy Spirit"[25] with all that exists outside ourselves, the Spirit, unconstrained by the more and more seemingly arbitrary and abstract Trinitarian categories beloved by Moltmann,[26] will be more and more the context, object, and subject or our

---

very existence of the Other."

23. I think here of relations of love between two persons of the same sex/gender, or friendships with persons who practice religions other than Christianity.

24. Moltmann, *Spirit of Life*, 8–10.

25. Ibid., 10.

26. Although Moltmann is less and less fettered by the traditional categories, as he concentrates more and more on the Spirit. Perhaps he is being opened up by his reflection on (and the action of?) the Spirit.

divine/human reality and reflection. The Spirit is the reality in which the Creator and Incarnation have sense, rather than the other way around.

Elizabeth A. Johnson is more in consonance with the expression I am aiming for as she places her own theological effort as beginning "not with the unity of the divine nature nor even with the "first person" of the Trinity, but with the Spirit, God's livingness subtly and powerfully abroad in the world."[27] While she will move on to "a theology of the triune God that sets out from the experience of the Spirit,"[28] my contention is that even forcing the action of the Spirit into some kind of "tri-unity" can be and indeed has been so often an arbitrary, inauthentic attempt to placate orthodoxy or prove one's own credentials that it has become more and more illegitimate. Concentration on the Spirit is the correct way to God, and the Spirit resists categorization. The Spirit's freedom inspires and calls us to that same freedom. If the Trinity liberates, well and good. If it does not, let it be left behind, the empty husk that cannot contain the vibrant growth within. Rather than *procedit ex patri et filioque*, we now by our lives affirm that *pater et filius procedit ex spiritu*.

We thus enter the pneumatic age. Indeed, my contention is that we are already in it, and have been forever.[29] The task that remains for us is to show how and why this pneumatic age will not be like others, ending in unconstrained chaos or in "spiritualizing" tendencies that never allow mention of the real world. Also, can the Spirit better address the needs of a material world, that has often been opposed to it and denigrated at its hands? How and why can we affirm flesh in terms of the Spirit? And what does the Spirit do in the world? We turn to these questions in the following sections.

THE SPIRIT INCARNATE

Yet another objection to the use of language about the Spirit as the best understanding of the action of God in the world remains, and this objection must be taken seriously. It has been the source of much difficulty and division in reflection and practice regarding the Spirit, and is so serious as

---

27. Johnson, *She Who Is*, 122.
28. Ibid.
29. In many senses, this is in continuity with a great part of the tradition, that points to the Spirit as the most appropriate name for the divine reality as a whole, including Augustine, Hegel, Tillich, and others. See the discussion by Peter Hodgson, *God in History*, 96–97.

to almost persuade me that the Spirit is irretrievable as a means for expressing the interaction of God with the world, a contemporary, credible, useful doctrine of providence. I speak, of course, of the lethal mix of the exclusivism of the Spirit spoken of earlier, where the work of the Spirit was identified exclusively with the work of the church, combined with a radical spirit/flesh or spirit/matter dichotomy, that denigrates the material world at the expense of the rarefied spiritual one. This combination leads to a material-and-body-denigrating spirituality in which goodness is located solely in the church. Of course, as Keller, Daly and others point out, the bodies being denigrated were always those of women and lower-status men, who were denied a terrestrial paradise while the church hierarchies were intent upon ruling both the earthly and heavenly realms. Such a rarefied, un-grounded spirituality has been the subject of much well-grounded critique.[30]

Is then, the "Spirit" likely to go the way of the "Father" and "Son"—categories and pictures of God that have been so tainted by their use as tools of oppression that they can no longer be picked up without doing more harm than good? Are they then the "radioactive names of God"—appearing beautiful, lovely to look at and hear and use, deeply embedded in the traditions of the church, yet so insidious in their effects that they cannot even be touched, lest cancers grow and choke out the very life towards which they purport to point? This may be true of the "Father" and the "Son," but my contention is that it is not for the Spirit. We can take the Spirit out of the quotation marks. An important part of rehabilitating the Spirit will come from reframing the concept in such a way as to reground it in the matter, material, flesh of the world, to show why it is not necessarily or even best expressed as the kind of rarefied, world-denigrating concept that has occupied so much of the discourse about the Spirit. In truth, we need a doctrine of the Spirit incarnate in order to show that language about Spirit can continue to be useful in formulating a coherent doctrine of God's action in the world.

One strategy that can be adopted in the struggle to reclaim language about the Spirit from its deadening rarefiers, who use it for their own ends, is to make the case that Spirit does not work in such a fashion; that it *always*, if we are to discern it properly and understand it correctly, takes a shape and form in the matter and flesh of the world. Indeed, it is the Spirit/Wind that vivifies, that brings life to the earth, that is the Divine Spirit,

---

30. See Keller, *Apocalypse*, 195, on the Diggers in early Puritan England, and Daly, *Beyond God the Father*, 132–54.

rather than just the wind itself. This is the contention of both Mary Daly and Rosemary Radford Ruether, in that they hold and demonstrate that it is historically the case that the "spiritualizing" tendencies of patriarchal religion, especially in its Christian forms, has been at the cost of women's bodies and the other bodies of the earth. Nevertheless, the implicit claim they make is that in the face of destruction of women's spirits and bodies, there is a resistance, a core, a vivifying force that reveals the perversity and wrongness of the ideology of other-worldliness, and holds instead to an orientation towards life and fullness and beauty and love, understood and incarnated precisely in women's bodies and other earthly bodies. Ruether calls, at the end of *Gaia and God*, for new spiritual practices that reflect and express the alternative (and implicitly, more true) activity of the Spirit in the lives of women and men.[31] Mary Daly, with her continuous and radical critique of the "spiritualized" practices of patriarchy and their consequences on and for women, makes much the same point—that the "spirit" of patriarchal religion is the very antithesis of the Verb, of Be-ing, of Female Elemental Presence, which is very concretely found in and through the liberation of women's' bodies and minds.[32] Both radically affirm that true spirituality takes place and has a bodily, ecological, contextual component that is not to be found in some other-worldly paradise. Indeed, Ruether's theology, with her insistence on acceptance of death as a natural part of life, calls attention to the fact that this life is the only context in which the work of the Spirit *can* take place; ignoring or hoping away this fact will not change it, and indeed is itself a cause of many evils.[33]

Any discussion of spirit and spirituality that hopes to be taken seriously in our discussion of providence will thus have to be one that does not fall into the trap of the dichotomizing of reality into the old dualism of spirit/matter, or spirit/flesh. As Ruether, Daly and countless others have amply demonstrated, this practice of "spirituality"—whether in patriarchal or other manifestations—and its concentration upon a supposedly spiritual world as opposed to the "material" one where we live and breathe serves the insidious purpose of crushing down the material bodies of women (and men), polluting the material of the earth, sky, and seas, and sucking true spiritual life away from those who seek to practice it.[34] Any form of spiritu-

---

31. Ruether, *Gaia and God*, 268–74.
32. See for example, Daly, *Beyond God the Father*, 155ff.; *Quintessence*, 164–78.
33. Ruether, *Gaia and God*, 53, 139–41.
34. See the discussions of patriarchal spirituality in *Gyn/Ecology*, esp. 27–29, 37–42,

The Spirit in and through the World

ality, of living in and with the Spirit, must have at its core an understanding that, as Peter Hodgson, following Hegel, points out, there is never *Geist* without *Gestalt*—there is never Spirit without a Shape. And this shape takes material form, occupies space, is concretized in the actual world. Spirituality must be actualized, carnal, material, in order to not be perverted from its life-giving function. Of course, the shapes and forms the divine spirit takes point beyond themselves, are oriented to the future, to works and forms and ideas that have an ongoing life. But without concrete shape, they are not actualized and remain mere puffs of wind.

Another aspect of this orientation towards an incarnate, rather than an other-worldly, understanding of the Spirit leads us to the question and condition of the context in which this spirituality takes place. If we understand Spirit only as Spirit precisely in the incarnate sense, then it must have a concrete context in which it takes place, and also contexts that hinder its expression. Jürgen Moltmann points us towards this consideration of contexts in his discussion of the "formative metaphors" of the Spirit, and especially in his discussion of the space necessary for living things (including and especially people) to grow and thrive. He maintains that it is not enough to affirm liberty for persons without considering and attempting to provide contexts in which they will be able to exercise their freedom: "If it is to develop, every life needs its corresponding *living space*. Vital power and energy are not enough by themselves."[35] He goes on to make the point that destroying the spaces in which beings express themselves is to destroy the beings themselves, destroying their chances for living. He also relates this notion of "living space" to the Christian tradition and especially to the realities of human liberation, pointing to the paradigmatic Exodus experience: "There is no liberation without the land of liberty. There is no liberation without the day of liberty which is the sabbath."[36] Without places, both in space and in time, in which to experience the work of the Spirit, the very notion loses its meaning, and becomes a pale shadow and reflection of itself—indeed, it becomes a mockery and a perversion, and becomes a temptation to engage in the very "spiritualizing" warned against at the beginning of this section.

---

or, as Daly herself prefers, 1 *passim* (see index); and *Quintessence*, 166–86.

35. Moltmann, *The Spirit of Life*, 276. This is also, it seems to me, an attempt to reinterpret the Nazi claim for "living space" as a justification for conquest into something less harmful, to give the words a new meaning.

36. Ibid., 277.

The Purposes of God

In addition, it is not enough simply to insist on the necessity of spaces for living. It is sometimes necessary actively to resist the forces that want to take them for profit or despoiling. And much of this involves the process of redefining them so that they are considered the spaces for living and thriving that they were meant to be, under the guidance of the Spirit. A compelling revelation of an actual case of the perversion that takes place when spirituality is abstracted from its context can be found in Catherine Keller's outstanding critique of the colonial and spiritual aims of Columbus (Colón, in Spanish) in the chapter "De/Colon/izing Spaces" in her marvelous *Apocalypse Now and Then*.[37] In this outstanding work, Keller traces and dis/closes the potent combination of greed, lust, and self-deception, all fueled by Columbus' highly de-localized spirituality (location: heaven), and his paradigmatic and actual role in the commodification and appropriation of the spaces, peoples, and resources of the "new world" for the old world order. After deconstructing the modern and colonizing conception of space, with its abstract spirituality, she points to a new possibility: "A spiritualization of place consciousness, an attention to the spirit of place, may prove a critical power for sustaining struggle beyond its apocalyptic moments of mere revolution."[38] Indeed, she points out the practical and efficacious project of refusing to separate the suffering souls of human beings from their location in human (and, one hopes, animal) bodies:

> More than any theoretical nondualism, the spacetime of the social movements has begun to provide a massive if vulnerable force for the deconstruction of two millennia of mind-body dissociation: the topicality of its utopias grounds them in the suffering of present bodies, bodies whose pain cannot be deferred, pain which in a dissociative society exceeds the vicissitudes of mortality.[39]

It is in the non-dualistic, non-abstracted movements for peace and justice, rooted in their own experience of pain and suffering, that true spirituality takes place. And, such a spirituality must have a locality—both in a human body or bodies, and in a particular place. The true Spirit—as opposed to the false and/or lying ones—will take a form, will in fact become truly incarnate in the world.[40] Spirit will take place only within a particular context,

37. Keller, *Apocalypse Now and Then*, 140–80.
38. Ibid., 176.
39. Ibid.
40. Yet another reason to consider the Spirit as primary and the incarnation as derivative.

The Spirit in and through the World

and amongst particular people. The Spirit may "blow where it will," but it will rustle actual leaves, ruffle actual feathers, and may even blow down actual towers.

This understanding of the incarnation of the Spirit can be further affirmed by looking not only at the paradigmatic liberation experience of the Exodus, but also at the paradigmatic (for Christians) experience of Jesus and his life, death, and resurrection in the world. Once again following Peter Hodgson, this is a way in which to begin to understand Jesus as the Spirit incarnate, "not in the physical nature of Jesus as such, but with the *gestalt* that coalesced both in and around his person—with which his person did in some sense become identical, and by which, after his death, he took on a new, communal, identity."[41] Hodgson's elaboration of the (as he sees them) three phases of the *gestalt* of Jesus can further serve to illustrate what incarnate Spirit looks like from a Christian perspective.

The first phase of the shape of Jesus in the world is the *basileia*, the kingdom or reign of God in the world. Hodgson recognizes that this is a problematic metaphor, by virtue of both its monarchical and patriarchal overtones, but hopes that by leaving the word untranslated it can "be filled with a new meaning."[42] This new meaning is that the *basileia* is "above all an image of freedom, a realm of freedom, a place or structure or world where freedom, communion, and truth prevail as the defining relationships among human beings instead of bondage, alienation, illusion."[43] This is one way, and for Christians the paradigmatic way, in which the Spirit can be incarnated in the world.

It is this very incarnation in the world that leads to the second phase of the gestalt of Jesus in the world—an outgrowth and new incarnate form of the Divine Spirit, found paradigmatically in the cross of Jesus. This is the "image of love, of anguished, suffering, broken love."[44] The *basileia* is contrary to the economies of domination in the world. They will not let it alone to be what it is, but realize that it threatens their very existence. Thus, Jesus, and many other incarnate forms of Spirit in the world, are crucified. The cross reminds people of what they are liberated from, even as it takes it away.[45] And, also importantly, it allows them to feel the loss of that

41. Hodgson, *God in History*, 209.
42. Ibid., 210.
43. Ibid.
44. Ibid., 211.
45. This is similar to Whitehead's contention that "Each tragedy is the disclosure of

which came to be dear to them—the *basileia*. The freedom of the *basileia* "is infused with a compassionate, suffering, anguished love."[46] This fusion of the two shapes of incarnated love, incarnated Spirit, leads to the third, resurrection.

It is important, historically, that the Christian community did not become "Christian" until after the resurrection experience—all our literature is written from the perspective of the experience of a community in which the *basileia* and the cross had been superseded by the resurrection. The resurrection, following Hodgson's Hegelian understanding, is a synthesis of the *basileia* and cross. It is the "fused, superimposed images of *basileia* and cross, of freedom and love [that] acquire the resiliency and realism necessary to endure in the midst of human tragedy, as well as the power to generate a continually transformative vision of a liberated communion of free subjects."[47] Thus the incarnate Divine Spirit infuses its dynamic qualities into the historical shapes and forms that it acquires, here as elsewhere, and shows its vivifying power.

Hodgson's analysis of the paradigmatic shapes of freedom has several important emphases for a Christian trying to understand the way(s) in which the Spirit becomes incarnate in the world. The first is that the incarnate Spirit is oriented towards determinate goals. This orientation to the *telos* of the universe, to love, freedom, and their continuous actualization gives us a hint as we continue to attempt to find the Spirit in its activity in the world. The next is that the Spirit is dynamic, not static. Hodgson's analysis points us to the continuous action of the Spirit—the *basileia*, cross, and resurrection are continually being re-enacted throughout Christian (and from a certain perspective all) history, in intertwining strands of existence. The Spirit, the divine wind, is always moving, in a direction and a pattern. As it becomes incarnate in the world, the incarnations will look a certain way—they will be dynamic patterns, with movement and purpose, and will continually be developing and coming to be into new patterns of being.

In many senses, then, to have seen and felt the action of the Spirit is to realize what the Spirit does in the world—what it is, is what it does, and vice versa. The manner and activity of the Spirit's action cannot be separated.

---

an ideal:—What might have been, and was not: What can be." *Adventures of Ideas* 286. It even, in a fashion analogous to Hegel, holds the idea of its own transcendence within itself.

46. Hodgson, *God in History*, 213.
47. Ibid.

However, the direction and orientation of the work of the Spirit can be outlined more completely and effectively. The work of the Spirit flows naturally from its incarnation.

THE WORK OF THE SPIRIT

It remains to be seen and explored, after insisting on the primacy of the Spirit and examining the Spirit incarnate, to see what the work of the Spirit incarnate in the world looks and feels like. We need to see what it *does* in the various and sundry places that it blows. To a certain extent, the work flows naturally from the incarnation of the Spirit, and indeed, the two cannot be separated. The work of the Spirit is in and through its incarnation, and the incarnation is in a very important sense its work. However, that the spirit is incarnate and the manner and necessity for place in its incarnation can be viewed as somewhat distinct from the orientation and direction and specific shapes the incarnation takes, and it is the latter we will attend to in this final section.

In attempting to discern the work of the incarnate Spirit in the world, once again we turn to the insight of Peter Hodgson in his above-mentioned insistence, borrowed from Hegel, that there is never *Geist* without *Gestalt*, there is never Spirit without a Shape. This continues our discussion of the incarnate Spirit, and points us in the concretizing way in which the Spirit operates; it is not an ethereal, "other-worldly" presence, accessed only by the few or, through special practices, for those with the affluence and leisure to practice them. Instead, the Spirit is in and through, in one sense (God as the Creative Spirit) through every determinate shape there is, specifically (for our discussion) through every social shape there is.[48] It is difficult to hold, however, that in the case of social existence, there is not some difference in the level at which various forms of being approach the divine aims more closely than others. The old but tried example of the Nazis springs to mind, as does the difference between slave-holding and free societies. Thus, we are called to make a distinction between various social groups and practices as we attempt to see where the Spirit is incarnated more fully, and where less fully, in the world.

---

48. This has consonance with the point of Augustine and Aquinas, and indeed much of the classical tradition, that everything that has being at all participates in the divine nature in and through its participation in determinate existence itself.

The Purposes of God

At this point, we orient ourselves to the twin insights of Whitehead and Hodgson, in their respective theological portraits, of the aims of the Spirit as we attempt to delineate more fully the work of the Spirit in the world. In the first place, we consider Whitehead's sketching of the aims and goals of civilization.[49] His outline of the aims of civilization as Truth, Beauty, Art, Adventure, and Peace (with Justice added as well, as argued in chapter four), provides in itself a clue for the direction of our gaze as we attempt to seek out the providential action of God, the work of the Spirit in the world. The work of the Spirit is to incarnate forms of Truth, Beauty, Art, Adventure, Justice, and Peace in the world, thus shaping and molding human cultural endeavors into ever-changing and ever-renewing institutions that flesh out and further these aims.

Coupled with Whitehead's insight, in outlining fully the work of the Spirit we will also pay attention to Peter Hodgson's contention, also born of a judgment of faith, but pointing to the world for justification, that the action of God as Spirit in the world, the shapes of God's activity, the providence of God, is found in the liberative, emancipatory praxis of communities. Again, as mentioned in chapter five, this provides a somewhat greater "fleshing out" of Whitehead's ideal insights, and can narrow our focus somewhat. In addition, the emphasis on praxis—on intentional, positive, enfleshed activity; on work for communicative freedom—provides an emphasis that, while certainly present in Whitehead (for example: the subjective aim, the insistence upon freedom and therefore choice and engagement at all levels of actuality), shifts the discussion back from a somewhat less grounded emphasis on the ideal aims of society back to the level of conscious, individual, existential engagement. While reading Whitehead, one sometimes receives the impression (justified or not) that somehow the ideal aims get worked out by "civilization" with or without the conscious individual action of separate human beings. He describes processes, often cosmic, that often do not seem individually-oriented. Hodgson can provide a necessary counterpoint to this somewhat detached view, and point us back to the necessity for decision itself to provide the starting point and initial participation in the ongoing process.[50] This also reemphasizes the dynamism found in Whitehead, and underlines again the ongoing and

---

49. Itself a judgment of faith, as are all religio-aesthetic judgments. Whitehead himself obviously saw his own work as grounded in Peace, orienting itself to the adventure of furthering Civilization.

50. See Hodgson, *God in History*, 186–89.

The Spirit in and through the World

partial character of any activity of the Spirit in the world: it *is* the process, although a particular kind of process, where divine activity occurs. It will be partially actualized, partially fail, and will always be the new ground of the future and further activity of the Spirit in the world.

The work of the Spirit, then, is found in a particular kind of praxis, characterized by participation in emancipatory, liberative activity, working for the founding and maintenance of communities where love, freedom, and hope are the operative and organizing principles. But, more specifically, what sorts of activities are ongoing in the work of the Spirit—in the praxis of liberation? Once again, we turn to the Hodgsonian/Whiteheadian synthesis, with influence from John Cobb and Marjorie Suchocki, to outline and detail such work in and of and by the Spirit. The Spirit in such understandings is "the creative transformation realized in the world that is offered by "Christ"—the initial aim and Logos of God and "insofar as we instantiate that aim, the Spirit is born in us, becoming one with us in the creation of community."[51] This supports our previous point regarding the incarnation of the Spirit—Spirit is only Spirit when it ceases to be merely wind, and when it finds a home in the flesh and actions of a worldly community. The Spirit can only work if it is incarnate, and can only become incarnate in its work. With Suchocki we affirm that "the Spirit combines God and the world. . .in human history. Taking the event of Jesus to be the paradigm instance of such a revelation, those of us in the Christian tradition recognize God's incarnate Spirit wherever the Spirit may emerge."[52] Such a characterization fleshes out the discussion of the work of the incarnate Spirit in the world: in liberating praxis, in concern for making the world a better place in line with the ideal aims of God—Truth, Beauty, Art, Adventure, Justice, Peace—the Spirit works in each and every concrete act that contributes to these goals. The Spirit is in economic and ecological work, in education, in religious dialogue and pluralism, and in political and ethical work. The work of the Spirit is to fill the world with the Spirit, to incarnate itself, not to control or govern, but to work in incarnation for the salvation of the world.[53]

---

51. Suchocki, "Spirit in and through the World," 184.

52. Ibid., 186. Once again, note the similarity with Hodgson's notion of incarnation.

53. This is in striking consonance with the first of Peter Hodgson's divisions of the work of the Spirit in his later work *Spirit in the World*. Hodgson divides the work of the Spirit into two categories—the salvation of the world and the perfection of God. While detailing the second is beyond the scope of this essay, Hodgson's conception of the work of the Spirit in religious communities, interreligious dialogue, and ecologically-oriented

Spirit is therefore seen as necessarily related, incarnated, moving (and also moved) in and by and through the times and places through which it blows. Spirit is also therefore necessarily Spirituality, the relatedness to and in that Spirit to the world, in attempts—feeble or otherwise—to be in tune with that reality of realities, that relation of relations, the Spirit in and through the world. This work is grounded in the past, not simply satisfied with the transformation and transfiguration of the present, and is oriented to the future. The work of the Spirit is grounding and promoting the incarnate relations in and of the Spirit; it is a Spirituality that issues in hope.

HOPE AS LAST (BUT NOT FINAL) WORD

In a certain sense, in keeping with the content of this work, it should not be ended with anything like a conceptual period—it should be more like an ellipsis, as the work of the Spirit goes on and on, and will certainly transcend even the best attempts to formulate it. But everything comes to a termination, and in this termination, the telos (the end of the end) that best expresses what I see the Spirit pointing toward is hope. The work of the Spirit, incarnating itself in communicative, liberative, life-affirming praxis, through its orientation to aims and ideals in the world, will be visible and experienced in the world as the source and ground of hope. It might seem odd to think of hope, rather than love (a notion more traditionally associated with incarnation) as the final word on the subject, but I believe that hope will be the most fruitful category of reflection as we look for and participate in the work of the incarnate Spirit in the world.

We turn first, once again, to Cobb, in and through Suchocki's presentation of his Christology and pneumatology (they are combined, as Suchoki notes and Cobb admits).[54] In Cobb's view, mediated through Suchocki's language, the transformative aspect of God's activity is seen most clearly in Christ, in which "the abstract technical notion of God is clothed with the historical form of love, leading to hope."[55] The peace of God, the grounding of the aims to Truth, Beauty, Freedom, and Justice orients the Christian (or Spirit-filled person) toward the future and also towards the possibility that

---

action, with an eye toward increasing freedom and life across all levels of the creation provides an alternative conception that realizes many of the same goals as Cobb's. See *Spirit in the World*, 293–323.

54. Suchocki, "Spirit in and through the World," 180.

55. Ibid., 178.

The Spirit in and through the World

such aims for the future *can* become actualized; in short, it allows the hope that such transformative, liberating, life-affirming praxis is in fact possible in the world. Thus, the Spirit is not only the love of God incarnate in the world, but also the ground of the possibility of change itself. And, of course, the incarnation (generally, not specifically speaking), is in a very real way the ground of the possibility of the future, in that the concrete realities of the present are that upon which the future rests. Hope, the issue of the Spirit incarnate, is perhaps the last word that we can speak of in this present time pointing at the ongoing processes of the divine activity in the world.

Catherine Keller calls attention to this function of incarnate Spirit as the actualized ground of hope in the in/conclusive[56] final chapter of her study of apocalypse, *Apocalypse Now and Then*. In pointing to her own acquiescence to the realities that there has been progress with regard to feminism and that she would not prefer to live in any other age, she holds that such views imply a necessary concession that "the spirit has made evolutionary leaps . . . that at times our species has organized enough spatial and temporal and social vitality to labor in 'its own transformation,'"[57] as Hegel calls such an endeavor. This makes essentially the same incarnational point stressed earlier, that Spirit is not Spirit unless it takes shape in the world. Keller, however, points to the reality (also stressed by Hegel, Hodgson, and others) that such forms/shapes/incarnations are not static, but in fact have orientations, directions, trajectories. She asks the rhetorical question about where the communities where the aforementioned "leaps of faith" take place: "In this zone of zones, which the Nazarene had signified as the realm of God, do the transfiguring configurations of Spirit not accumulate as potential for 'the next step?'"[58] What can this "potential for 'the next step'" be, but a premonition of and orientation towards some new form of incarnate Spirit in the world, some new possibility for change for the better that carries within its conception the impetus for its own actualization? What can it be, but *hope*, grounded in the incarnate Spirit's work, moving into the future? Indeed, she points to the link between lack of spirit (the "dispirited," with her characteristic word play) and the turn from engagement to "apocalypse," where violence and destruction rule: "the complex demands of the present flee before the simple, deafening word; smoke and fire fill the

---

56. This is Keller's usage, calling attention to the ongoing, un-closed nature of her discussion.
57. Keller, *Apocalypse*, 307.
58. Ibid.

screen, and beasts strip the great whore."[59] Such is the dis-spiriting vision of a dis/spirited future. A Spirit-filled, Spirit-incarnated community, on the other hand, will have and exhibit in action a hope for and labor toward a new and better future. Thus, eschatology is sublated into pneumatology, "into the dis/closive play of hope as a shifting pneumatology at the edge of the present."[60] Keller holds that this hope is named and worked for/toward/in. It is "hope for mutual respect in proximate and in political relations, for justice and mercy upon the land and within the city, for transnational, trans-species healing and renewal . . . This hope can only be verified, however, by being *made true*: spirit practiced, materialized, spun, performed."[61]

This vision, shared by Cobb, Daly, Hodgson, Keller, Moltmann, Ruether, and others, of a primal, incarnate, active Spirit, living in people and communities, taking the form of love-in-praxis and issuing in hope, is what I have come to believe the action of God in history is. This is where, by my judgment of faith, by virtue of my own partial and fragmentary and at times conflicted life in and of the Spirit, I point to as the activity of God in the world, as God's providence. It is very different from the classical providences of control presented in the introductory chapter, and also very different from the Bultmannian vision of a-historical decision. It has, in an odd sense, more in common with the notion of Barth's Christian under the Universal Lordship of God the Father. Both Barth and Bultmann hold that it is in the Christian life that providence is seen, and Barth explicitly expands this to the Christian history of Scripture and the church. My understanding of Spirit in the World is (at the end of the day, and surprisingly even to me) somewhat similar, holding that it is in individual and communal lives that the life-giving work of the Spirit is seen, heard, felt, and furthered. Such a view is deeply informed by and transformed through the work of both Whitehead and Hodgson, as they point to the reality of the ongoing processes of the world, and the orientation towards Peace and Adventure, Justice, and Freedom, and call for individual and social engagement in trying to actualize such a view. The difference would be in the content of such a religious life, oriented not to the lordship of God the Father, but instead toward the life in and by and through the incarnate Spirit in the world, leading towards the ideal aims of history, including freedom, and providing both the inspiration and the ground for such aims to have the possibility of

---

59. Ibid., 308.
60. Ibid., 276.
61. Ibid., 308.

succeeding. It takes place in the lives and communities of those committed to live in the Spirit, which is in fact their ground and activity and the hope that life can and will continue in the world.

Bibliography

Anderson, Ray S. *On Being Human: Essays in Theological Anthropology*. 1982. Reprinted, Eugene, OR: Wipf & Stock, 2010.
Aquino, María Pilar. *Our Cry for Life: Feminist Theology from Latin America*. Translated by Dinah Livingstone. 1993. Reprinted, Eugene, OR: Wipf & Stock, 2002.
Augustine, Saint, of Hippo. *Concerning the City of God Against the Pagans*. Translated by Henry Bettenson. London: Penguin, 1984.
Barbour, Ian G. *Religion in an Age of Science*. San Francisco: Harper & Row, 1990.
Barth, Karl. *Church Dogmatics*. III/3: *The Doctrine of Creation*. Edited by G. W. Bromiley and T. F. Torrance. Translated by G. W. Bromiley and R. J. Ehrlich. Edinburgh: T. & T. Clark, 1960.
Bernstein, Richard J. *Beyond Objectivism and Relativism: Science, Hermeneutics, and Praxis*. Philadelphia: University of Pennsylvania Press, 1983.
Bonhoeffer, Dietrich. *Creation and Fall: A Theological Interpretation of Genesis 1–3, Temptation*. New York: Macmillan, 1966.
Brown, Peter. *Augustine of Hippo: A Biography*. Berkeley: University of California Press, 1969.
Bull, Malcolm, and Keith Lockhart. *Seeking a Sanctuary: Seventh-day Adventism and the American Dream*. New York: Harper & Row, 1989.
Bultmann, Rudolf. *Essays: Philosophical and Theological*. Library of Philosophy and Theology. New York: Macmillan, 1955.
———. *Faith and Understanding*. Edited with an introduction by Robert W. Funk. Translated by Louise Pettibone Smith. Fortress Texts in Modern Theology. Philadelphia: Fortress, 1987.
———. *Jesus and the Word*. Translated by Louise Pettibone Smith and Erminie Huntress Lantero. New York: Scribner, 1958.
———. "The Meaning of God as Acting." In *Jesus Christ and Mythology*, 60–85. New York: Scribner, 1958.
———. *The Presence of Eternity: History and Eschatology*. Gifford Lectures 1954–55. New York: Harper, 1957.
———. "The Significance of the Jewish Old Testament Tradition for the Christian West." In *Essays: Philosophical and Theological*, 262–72. Library of Philosophy and Theology. New York: Macmillan, 1955.
———. "What Does It Mean to Speak of God?" In *Faith and Understanding*, edited by Robert W. Funk, 53–65. Translated by Louise Pettibone Smith. Fortress Texts in Modern Theology. Philadelphia: Fortress, 1987.

Bibliography

Calvin, John. *Institutes of the Christian Religion.* Vol. 1. Library of Christian Classics 20. Edited by John T. McNeill. Translated by Ford Lewis Battles. Philadelphia: Westminster, 1960.

Chopp, Rebecca. *The Praxis of Suffering: An Interpretation of Liberation and Political Theologies.* Maryknoll, NY: Orbis, 1986.

Cobb, John B. Jr. *A Christian Natural Theology, Based on the Thought of Alfred North Whitehead.* Philadelphia: Westminster, 1965.

———. "In Defense of Realism." In *Theology at the End of Modernity*, edited by Sheila Greeve Davaney, 179–99. Philadelphia: Trinity, 1991.

———. *Is It Too Late? A Theology of Ecology.* Beverly Hills, CA: Bruce, 1971.

———. "Natural Causality and Divine Action." *Idealistic Studies* 3 (1973) 207–22.

———. *Process Theology as Political Theology.* Philadelphia: Westminster, 1982.

———. "The Relativization of the Trinity." In *Trinity in Process: A Relational Theology of God*, edited by Marjorie Hewitt Suchocki and Joseph A. Bracken, 1–22. New York: Continuum, 1997.

Cobb, John B. Jr., and Charles Birch. *The Liberation of Life: From the Cell to the Community.* New York: Cambridge University Press, 1981.

Cobb, John B. Jr., and Herman Daly. *For the Common Good : Redirecting the Economy Toward Community, the Environment, and a Sustainable Future.* 2nd ed. Boston: Beacon, 1992.

Crenshaw, James L. *A Whirlpool of Torment: Israelite Traditions of God as an Oppressive Presence.* Philadelphia: Fortress, 1984.

Crossan, John Dominic. *Jesus: A Revolutionary Biography.* San Francisco: HarperSanFrancisco, 1994.

Daly, Mary. *Beyond God the Father: Toward a Philosophy of Women's Liberation.* Boston: Beacon, 1973.

———. *Gyn/Ecology: The Metaethics of Radical Feminism.* Boston: Beacon, 1978.

———. *Quintessence: Realizing the Archaic Future.* Boston: Beacon, 1998.

Dean, William. *The American Spiritual Culture: And the Invention of Jazz, Football, and the Movies.* New York: Continuum, 2002.

———. "Dean Replies to Zbaraschuk." *American Journal of Theology and Philosophy* 31 (2010) 259–63.

———. *History Making History: The New Historicism in American Religious Thought.* Albany: SUNY Press, 1988.

———. "Pragmatism's Pallid Piety: For a More Effective God." Paper presented at the American Academy of Religion Annual Meeting, Boston, MA., November 21, 1999.

———. *The Religious Critic in American Culture.* Albany: SUNY Press, 1994.

———. "Sheltering Skies: A Response." *American Journal of Theology and Philosophy* 16 98–104.

Dewey, John. *A Common Faith.* New Haven: Yale University Press, 1934.

Dostoevsky, Fyodor. *The Brothers Karamazov.* Translated by Richard Pevear and Larissa Volokhonsky. New York: Vintage Classics, 1991.

Duncan, David James. *My Story as Told by Water: Confessions, Druidic Rants, Reflections, Bird-watchings, Fish-stalkings, Visions, Songs and Prayers Refracting Light, from Living Rivers, in the Age of the Industrial Dark.* San Francisco: Sierra Club, 2001.

Dunfee, Susan Nelson. *Beyond Servanthood: Christianity and the Liberation of Women.* Lanham, MD: University Press of America, 1989.

Bibliography

Foucault, Michel. "Nietzsche, Geneaology, History." In *Language, Counter-Memory, Prac-tice: Selected Essays and Interviews by Michele Foucault*, edited by Donald F. Bouchard. Translated by Donald F. Bouchard and Sherry Simon. Ithaca, NY: Cornell University Press, 1977.

Frankl, Viktor E. *Man's Search for Meaning*. New York: Simon & Schuster, 1959.

Funk, Robert W. "Introduction to Rudolf Bultmann." In *Faith and Understanding*. Edited with an Introduction by Robert W. Funk. Translated by Louise Pettibone Smith. Fortress Texts in Modern Theology. Philadelphia: Fortress, 1987.

Gilkey, Langdon. "Cosmology, Ontology, and the Travail of Biblical Language." *Journal of Religion* 41 (1961) 194–205.

Gillespie, Michael Allen. *Hegel, Heidegger, and the Ground of History*. Chicago: University of Chicago Press, 1984.

Gonzalez, Justo. *The Story of Christianity*. Vol. 2. New York: HarperCollins, 1985.

Griffin, David Ray. *God, Power, and Evil: A Process Theodicy*. Philadelphia: Westminster, 1976.

Gutiérrez, Gustavo. *A Theology of Liberation: History, Politics, and Salvation*. Translated and edited by Sister Caridad Inda and John Eagleson. Rev. ed. Maryknoll, NY: Orbis, 1988.

Harris, Judith Rich. *The Nurture Assumption: Why Children Turn Out the Way They Do*. New York: Simon & Schuster, 1998.

Harvey, Van Austin. *The Historian and the Believer: The Morality of Historical Knowledge and Christian Belief*. New York: Macmillan, 1966.

"Hegel." In *The Encyclopedia of Philosophy*. Vol. 3. New York: Macmillan, 1967.

Hegel, G. W. F. *The Philosophy of History*. Translated by J. Sibree. New York: Dover, 1956.

Hick, John. *An Interpretation of Religion: Human Responses to the Transcendent*. Gifford Lectures 1986–1987. London: Macmillan, 1989.

Hodgson, Peter C. *God in History: Shapes of Freedom*. Nashville: Abingdon, 1989.

———. *Spirit in the World: A Constructive Christian Theology*. Louisville: Westminster John Knox, 1994.

Jaffee, Martin S. "One God, One Revelation, One People: On the Symbolic Structure of Elective Monotheism." *Journal of the American Academy of Religion* 69 (2001) 753–75.

James, William. "The Moral Equivalent of War." In *Pragmatism and Other Essays*, 289–301. 1910. Reprinted, New York: Washington Square, 1963.

———. *The Varieties of Religious Experience*. 1901–1902. Reprinted, New York: Collier-Macmillan, 1961.

Johnson, Elizabeth A. *She Who Is: The Mystery of God in Feminist Theological Discourse*. New York: Crossroad, 1994.

Keller, Catherine. *Apocalypse Now and Then: A Feminist Guide to the End of the World*. Boston: Beacon, 1996.

Langer, Susanne K. "The Cultural Importance of Art." In *Philosophical Sketches*, 75–84. New York: Mentor, 1964.

Lucas, George R. *Two Views of Freedom in Process Thought: A Study of Whitehead and Hegel*. American Academy of Religion Dissertation Series 28. Missoula, MT: Scholars, 1979.

Manes, Christopher. *Green Rage: Radical Environmentalism and the Unmaking of Civilization*. Boston: Little, Brown, 1990.

Bibliography

Metz, Johann Baptist. *Faith in History and Society: Toward a Practical Fundamental Theology*. Translated by David Smith. New York: Seabury, 1980.

Min, Anselm Kyongsuk. *Dialectic of Salvation: Issues in Theology of Liberation*. Albany: SUNY Press, 1989.

Mitchell, Stephen A., and Margaret J. Black. *Freud and Beyond: A History of Modern Psychoanalytic Thought*. New York: Basic, 1995.

Moltmann, Jürgen. *The Spirit of Life: A Universal Affirmation*. Translated by Margaret Kohl. Minneapolis: Fortress, 1992.

Morrison, Toni. *Beloved: A Novel*. New York: Plume, 1988.

———. "Trouble in Paradise." Plenary address, American Academy of Religion Annual Meeting, 1995.

Nietzsche, Friedrich. *The Dawn of Day*. Translated by J. M. Kennedy. 1881. Reprinted, New York: Gordon, 1974.

Oakman, Douglas E. *The Political Aims of Jesus*. Minneapolis: Fortress, 2012.

Oates, Joyce Carol. "The Cruelest Sport." *The New York Review of Books* 34 (Feb. 3, 1992) 3–4, 17.

———. *On Boxing*. Garden City, NY: Dolphin/Doubleday, 1987.

O'Conner, Flannery. *Mystery and Manners: Occasional Prose*. Selected and edited by Sally and Robert Fitzgerald. New York: Farrar, Straus & Giroux, 1975.

Ogden, Schubert M. *The Reality of God and Other Essays*. New York: Harper & Row, 1966.

Parentelli, Gladys. "Latin America's Poor Women: Inherent Guardians of Life." In *Women Healing Earth: Third World Women on Ecology, Feminism, and Religion*, edited by Rosemary Radford Ruether, 29–38. Maryknoll, NY: Orbis, 1996.

Pinnock, Clark, Richard Rice, John Sanders, William Hasker, and David Basinger. *The Openness of God*. Downers Grove, IL: InterVarsity, 1994.

Phillips, D. Z. "The Problem of Evil: A Critique of Swinburne." In *Philosophy of Religion: An Anthology*, edited by Louis P. Pojman, 185–94. Belmont, CA: Wadsworth, 1987.

Plaskow, Judith. "Facing the Ambiguity of God." *Tikkun* 6 (Sept–Oct 1991) 70–78.

Roth, John K. "A Theodicy of Protest." In *Encountering Evil*, edited by Stephen T. Davis, 7–22. Atlanta: John Knox, 1981.

Ruether, Rosemary Radford. *Disputed Questions: On Being a Christian*. Maryknoll, NY: Orbis, 1989.

———. *Gaia and God: An Ecofeminist Theology of Earth Healing*. San Francisco: HarperSanFrancisco, 1992.

Segundo, Juan Luis. "Capitalism-Socialism." In *Signs of the Times: Theological Reflections*. Translated by Robert R. Barr. Maryknoll, NY: Orbis, 1993.

———. "The Option for the Poor: Hermeneutic Key for Understanding the Gospel." In *Signs of the Times: Theological Reflections*. Maryknoll, NY: Orbis, 1993.

Shorter, Edward. *A History of Psychiatry: From the Age of the Asylum to the Age of Prozac*. New York: Wiley, 1997.

Sobrino, Jon. *Resurrección de la verdadera Iglesia: Los Pobres, Lugar teológico de la eclesiología*. Santander, Spain: Sal Terrae, 1981.

Suchocki, Marjorie Hewitt. "Spirit in and through the World." In *Trinity in Process: A Relational Theology of God*, edited by Joseph A. Bracken and Marjorie Hewitt Suchocki, 173–90. New York: Continuum, 1997.

Taylor, Charles. *A Secular Age*. Cambridge, MA: Belknap, 2007.

Thomas Aquinas. *Summa Theologica*. Translated by English Dominican Fathers. Rev. ed. 1920. Reprinted, Westminster, MD: Christian Classics, 1981.

Bibliography

Thomas, Owen C., ed. *God's Activity in the World: The Contemporary Problem.* American Academy of Religion Studies in Religion 31. Chico, CA: Scholars, 1983.

Tillich, Paul. *Systematic Theology.* Vol. 2, *Existence and the Christ.* Chicago: University of Chicago Press, 1957.

Tracy, David. *Plurality and Ambiguity: Hermeneutics, Religion, Hope.* San Francisco: Harper & Row, 1987.

Whitehead, Alfred North. *Adventures of Ideas.* 1933. Reprinted, New York: Macmillan/Free Press, 1967.

———. *The Function of Reason.* 1929. Reprinted, Boston: Beacon, 1959.

———. *Modes of Thought.* 1938. Reprinted, New York: Macmillan/Free, 1968.

———. *Process and Reality.* Corrected ed. Edited by David Ray Griffin and Donald W. Sherburne. New York: Macmillan/Free Press, 1978.

———. *Science and the Modern World.* 1925. Reprinted, New York: Macmillan/Free Press, 1967.

———. *Symbolism: Its Meaning and Effect.* 1927. Reprinted, New York: Fordham University Press, 1985.

Wiesel, Elie. *Night.* Translated by Stella Rodway. New York: Bantam, 1960.

Wiles, Maurice. *God's Action in the World: The Bampton Lectures for 1986.* London: SCM, 1986.

Zbaraschuk, G. Michael. "Not Radical Enough: William Dean's Pragmatic Problems in Dealing with God and History." *American Journal of Theology and Philosophy* 31 (2010) 33–52.

Subject Index

Abbey, Edward, 144
actual entities, 79–84, 119
adventure (as ideal aim) 17–18, 85–86, 88–94, 98–102, 116, 118–19, 122–23, 143–44, 168–72
aesthetics, 7–8, 70–71, 77, 143–44
aim of God, 9, 17, 20, 88, 125, 138
anthropology, theological, 43
Aquinas, Thomas, *see* Thomas Aquinas
Aquino, María Pilar, 20, 135–37
Arendt, Hannah, 110–11, 119
arminianism, 95
art, 17, 89–92, 98–100, 118, 143–46, 168–69,
Augustine, 3–5, 36, 47, 105, 160, 167

basileia, 21, 107, 112, 165–66
Barth, Karl, 4, 11–14, 32–53, 77, 94–96, 105, 149, 153, 172
beauty (as ideal aim), 17, 19, 89–93, 95, 98, 118, 142–47, 168–70
Bible, interpretation of, 25
Bonhoeffer, Dietrich, 30, 125–26, 128
Bultmann, Rudolf, 10–13, 23–32, 52, 92–94, 152, 172

Calvin, John, 6–7, 33, 105,
Calvinism, 95
category of the ultimate, 16, 78–80
Chicago School, 55
Chopp, Rebecca, 100, 109
church, 4, 10, 29, 43, 47, 140, 151–52, 159, 161, 172
civilization, 17–18, 78, 85, 88–93, 99, 105–6, 120, 144, 168

Cobb, John B., 18, 60, 81, 84, 88, 105, 115–20, 151, 157, 169–72
common good, 70–71
community, 12, 25, 28, 41–43, 59, 107, 112, 117, 127, 131–33, 152, 166, 169, 172
concrescence, 80–84
concrete totality, 110, 142
Cone, James H., 113
confession of faith, 13, 45, 50
consequent nature of God, 84
contrasts, 16, 82, 89–90
conventions about God, 15, 56–60, 74, 76
conversion to the other, 140
creature, 5, 12–14, 20, 26, 32–47, 51–52, 95, 121, 129, 156
Crenshaw, James L., 61
cross, 21, 107, 112, 165–66
Crossan, John Dominic, 30

Daly, Mary, 22, 153, 158, 161–63, 172
Dean, William, 14–16, 55–76, 93, 128
decision, 11, 17, 24, 26–32, 81, 168, 172
deconstruction, 56–57, 71, 106
determinism, 80
Dewey, John, 15, 55, 61–63, 72, 75
dialectic, 18, 33, 50–54, 105, 110–11, 115, 120, 143, 147
divine Accompanying, 40–41
divine Preserving, 39–40
divine Ruling, 41–43
dualism, 134, 155, 162, 164
Duncan, David James, 100–101
Dunfee, Susan Nelson, 19, 127

Subject Index

elect, 40,
election, 6, 33, 38–40
empirical theology, 55
empiricism, radical, 15, 55–56, 61–62, 71, 75, 77
eschatology, 4, 13, 28–29, 152, 172
eternal objects, 16, 78–84
ethics, Christian, 27
existentialism, 13, 24, 30, 32, 147

feminism, 126, 135–36, 146, 150–53, 156, 171
finitude, 129
Foucault, Michel, 8, 105, 108–9
freedom, 18, 102–23, 124–47, 170
    for beauty, 142–47
    for the future 163, 167, 170
    for the self and other, 125–28
    natural context of, 128–34
    social–political context of, 134–42
    see also shapes of freedom

Gadamer, Hans-Georg, 110,
Geist, 21, 112, 156, 163, 167
Gestalt, 21, 112, 163, 167
Gifford Lectures, 27
God, as convention, 67, 71
    as creator, 12, 26, 32–46, 159, 160
    as king, 2, 154
    as love, 2
    as morally ambiguous, 56, 62–63, 66–72, 75
    as Tri-Unity, 105, 160
    as Trinitarian Spirit, 106
    call of, 10–11, 24, 26. 28, 137–38
    doctrine of, 3, 16–17, 20, 33, 57–58, 68, 71, 77, 84, 96, 105, 115, 150, 161
    in history, 2–3, 7, 9–10, 19, 22, 32, 35, 38, 48–49, 68, 72–75, 78, 94, 104–6, 111–14, 122, 124–25, 131, 134, 137, 141–43, 147–49, 151–52, 155–56, 172
    reality of, 59
God the Father, 12, 14, 20. 26, 32–34, 39–51, 53, 151, 153–54, 156, 158–59, 161, 172
grace, 29, 35–40, 42–43, 46, 64–65

Griffin, David Ray, 97
Gutiérrez, Gustavo, 19, 110, 125–28, 133, 136–37

Habermas, Jürgen, 110–12
Hegel, G. W. F., 9, 18–19, 28–29, 50, 104, 106, 108–15, 118–20, 127, 130, 146–47, 163, 166–67, 171
historicism, 7, 10, 15–16, 28–29, 55–58, 60, 64, 66, 74–76, 149
history, see God in history
history of the covenant, 4, 14, 17, 23, 33–38, 42–43, 46, 50, 54, 114
Hodgson, Peter, 3, 7, 9, 18–22, 73, 94, 104–28, 137, 140–41, 143–44, 150, 155–56, 160, 163, 165–69, 171–72
holocaust, 1, 44
hope, 22, 28, 44, 76, 92, 110, 145, 150, 152–53, 169–73

ideals, 7–8, 16, 28, 51, 62, 65, 80, 84, 87–94, 112, 122, 170
identity and difference, 126
idolatry, 38, 50, 65
incarnation of the Spirit, 21, 124, 155, 165–67, 169
James, William, 15, 55, 58, 61, 63, 72, 74, 97, 130
Jesus Christ, 12–14, 24, 33–36, 38–41, 44, 50–51
Johnson, Elizabeth A., 151, 154, 156, 158, 160
justice, 17–18, 65, 67, 71, 75, 98–103, 112–13, 118, 122, 131–32, 137, 140, 142, 147, 164, 168–70, 172

Kant, Immanuel, 28, 47, 120
Keller, Catherine, 22, 153, 161, 164, 171–72
kerygma, 29–30
king of Israel, 14, 42–43
knowledge, as provisional, 39, 49

laws, 28, 98, 121, 136
liberation, 21–22, 113, 117–18, 125, 137, 140, 142, 148, 162–63, 165, 169

Subject Index

liberation theology, 109, 113, 136–37, 140142, 147
logos, 117, 152, 154, 169
love, 2, 17, 22, 27, 29–30, 37–38, 48, 60, 64–65, 67, 74, 84–85, 95, 100, 102, 105–7, 112, 123, 125–27, 131, 142–45, 153, 155–58, 159, 162, 165–66, 169–71
Lucas, George R., 119
lure for feeling, 81
Luther, Martin, 26, 47, 61, 64–65

Marx, Karl, 11, 19, 28–29
meaning in history, 29, 52
meaninglessness, 8, 29, 96, 123
methodolotry, 10, 56
Metz, Johann Baptist, 110, 120
Moltmann, Jürgen, 22, 155, 159, 163, 172
monism, 153, 155
morality, 7–8, 59, 63, 70–71, 77, 143
Morrison, Toni, 19–20, 127–28, 144–45
multiplicities, 16, 82, 117

natural law, 40
nature, 14, 17, 23, 26, 35–36, 51, 86, 89, 93, 101, 114, 120–23, 130–33, 138, 143–44, 158
Neibuhr, Reinhold, 55, 76, 127
neo-Platonism, 4–5, 36
"Nevertheless," concept of, 48, 51, 95
New Testament, 10, 29, 32, 42, 61, 73, 152
nexus, 16, 82
Nietzsche, Friedrich, 15, 108
novelty, 15, 59, 79, 81, 85, 87–88, 91, 93, 97
nothingness, 32, 40, 107

Oakman, Douglas E., 30
Oates, Joyce Carol, 66
O'Connor, Flannery, 73
Ogden, Schubert M., 55, 115–16
Old Testament, 25–26, 29
One, Many, Creativity, 16, 63, 78–83
order, 84–88, 92–93, 97, 159

Page, Ruth, 109

Parentelli, Gladys, 20, 146
Paul, 13, 28, 47, 125
peace, 7, 17–18, 89, 92–94, 98–102, 118, 121–23, 131, 140, 164, 168–72
phenomenology, 23
philosophy of history, 8, 35,
Plaskow, Judith, 61
platonic forms, 80
platonic realism, 104
political theology, 104, 114, 120
poor, the, 19, 125, 127, 130, 132–33. 136, 139–41, 146–47
poststructuralism, 69, 108
pragmatism, 60, 72–73
praxis, 18–19, 21–22, 91, 100, 102, 104–6, 108–26, 131, 137, 150, 168–72
prayer, 44
preferential option for the poor, 140
prehension, 9, 80–82,
primordial nature of God, 84, 86
process, 7, 16, 18, 77–85, 91, 104–6, 108–23, 131, 133, 142, 147, 150, 168–72
propositions, 81–82, 84
Providence, 1 *passim*
psychoanalysis, 134

quietism, 30–31

reductionism, 55, 72, 75–76
religious critic, 15, 58–59, 61–71, 75
resurrection, 21, 111–12, 165–66
revelation, 2, 6, 10, 12–14, 24, 26, 35–36, 38–39, 41, 45–51, 53, 117, 159, 164, 169
Ricoeur, Paul, 108–9
Rorty, Richard, 72, 74, 93, 102, 110
Ruether, Rosemary Radford, 22, 31, 113, 121, 130–34, 139, 154, 162, 172

salvation history, 3, 7–8, 43, 105, 113
Scripture, 4, 6, 12–14, 26, 37, 41–46, 50–51, 64, 105, 172
Segundo, Juan Luis, 19, 139–41
sense experience, 63, 81

Subject Index

shapes of freedom, 18–20, 104, 107, 110–11, 114, 123–25, 132, 142, 150, 166
signs of the times, 19, 141–42
Spengler, Otto, 50
spirit, 14, 20–22, 41, 106–7, 112, 117–18, 123–26, 148–72
  in the world, 20–21, 118, 126, 147, 150, 156, 165, 167–72
  work of, 21–22, 117–18, 150, 161–63, 169–72
spiritual practices, 162
Stanton, Elizabeth Cady, 158
subjective aim (of God), 83, 88, 119, 168
subjective form, 81–84
Suchocki, Marjorie Hewitt, 22, 117–18, 155–56, 169–70

Taylor, Charles, 2, 33, 46
Taylor, Mark C., 55, 57, 105–6, 108
teleology, 3, 7–8, 108, 113, 118–19, 140, 143–44, 146
telos, 7, 122, 166, 170
Thomas Aquinas, 5–7, 33, 36, 41, 47, 105, 167
Tillich, Paul, 55, 109, 118, 151, 154, 160
Tracy, David, 109

Trinity, 21, 106–7, 149, 151–56, 160
tradition, 9, 15, 25–26, 36, 39, 41, 44, 47–48, 50–51, 53–54, 56, 60–62, 64–65, 68, 71, 74–76, 93, 96, 106–7, 117, 147–49, 154–55, 160, 163, 167, 169
Troeltsch, Ernst, 19, 108, 118
truth, 15, 17, 57, 67, 73, 80, 89–93, 95, 97–99, 108–9, 113, 118, 128, 130, 161, 165, 168–70

unelect, 40
universals, 16, 79–80

war, 1, 7, 102, 138
war against nature, 130
Weiman, Henry Nelson, 61, 76
Whitehead, Alfred North, 9, 16–18, 20, 22, 61, 63, 76–106, 114–23, 126–28, 130–31, 140–41, 143–44, 146, 148–50, 165, 168–69, 172
Wiesel, Elie, 99–100
whole, the, 15, 61–64, 68–71
word of God, 34–36, 38, 40, 43–44
World War I, 44
World War II, 44

www.ingramcontent.com/pod-product-compliance
Lightning Source LLC
Chambersburg PA
CBHW051744230426
43670CB00012B/2155